WHY IRISH?

for Thomas J. and Kathleen O'Donnell

Brian Ó Conchubhair
EDITOR

WHY IRISH?
Irish Language and Literature in Academia

ARLEN
HOUSE

Published in 2008 by
ARLEN HOUSE
an imprint of Arlen Publications Ltd
PO Box 222
Galway, Ireland
Phone/Fax: 00 353 86 8207617
Email: arlenhouse@gmail.com

Distributed in North America by
SYRACUSE UNIVERSITY PRESS
621 Skytop Road, Suite 110
Syracuse, NY 13244–5290
Phone: 315–443–5534/Fax: 315–443–5545
Email: supress@syr.edu

ISBN
978–1–903631–59–1, paperback

Cover Art ¦ Seán Ó Flaithearta
Typesetting ¦ Arlen House
Printing ¦ Betaprint

Bord na
Leabhar
Gaeilge

Clár | Contents

Gabhann an t-eagarthóir buíochas leis na daoine seo a leanas a chabhraigh le heagrú na comhdhála agus le foilsiú an leabhair: Cartlann na hOllscoile/The Archives of the University of Notre Dame; Institute for Scholarship in the Liberal Arts, University of Notre Dame; Roinn Theanga agus Litríocht na Gaeilge, Ollscoil Notre Dame/Department of Irish Language and Literature, University of Notre Dame; Institiúid Mhic Eochaidh-Uí Neachtain um an Léann Éireannach/Keough-Naughton Institute for Irish Studies, University of Notre Dame.

Táthar an-bhuíoch do na daoine seo a leanas leis: Shelly Barber; Beth Bland; Clare Carroll; Seán Clancy; Jamie Cripe; Sorcha de Brúch; Seamus Deane; Erik Dix; Dave Dosmann; Hugh Fogarty; Christopher Fox; Ted Fox; Daniela Furthenova; John Gibney; Susan Guibert; Tom Hachey; James W. Hamrick; David Horn; Godard Ives; Brendan Kane; Charles Lamb; Enda Leaney; Tim Lindgren; Jean Ann Linney; Tara MacLeod; Jim McCloskey; Sarah McKibben; Peter McQuillan; Sarah McKinne; Aedín Ní Bhroithe-Clements; Máire Áine Ní Fhlatharta; Dairearca Ní Néill; Deaglán Ó Briain; Breandán Ó Buachalla; Sean O'Brien; Tomás Ó Cathasaigh; Micheál Ó Conghaile; Éamon Ó Cuív; Thomas J. agus Kathleen O'Donnell; Seán Ó Flaithearta; Peadar Ó Muircheartaigh; Caitríona Ó Torna; Robert O'Neill; Mary Ann Pride; Gretchen Reydams-Schils; Mark Roche; Charles Sheehan; Irv Sikorski; Sharon Sumpter; John Tully; Sherri J. Turbinis; Calvert Watkins; Linda Whyte.

Ag deireadh gabhaim fíorbhuíochas le Micheal agus le Kristin Murphy as an tacaíocht agus as an spreagadh a thugann siad do Roinn Theanga agus Litríocht na Gaeilge.

LÉARÁIDÍ ¦ ILLUSTRATIONS

Why Irish?

Profs James McCloskey, Tomás Ó Cathasaigh and Seamus Deane

CAD CHUIGE AN GHAEILGE SAN OLLSCOLAÍOCHT?

Brian Ó Conchubhair

Ollsccoil Notre Dame

In aiste dá chuid sa bhliain 1937 d'fhiafraigh an scoláire Ceiltise Myles Dillon de féin cén cuspóir ba chóir a bheith ag Léann na Gaeilge. D'fhreagair sé á rá gur samhlaíodh do roinnt daoine gurb é dualgas na scoileanna cainteoirí líofa Gaeilge a dhéanamh de na daltaí agus an Ghaeilge a úsáid mar theanga teagaisc laistigh agus lasmuigh den Ghaeltacht. Dar le daoine eile gur cheart an Ghaeilge a mhúineadh ar nós gach aon ábhar eile sna scoileanna agus go mbainfeadh an mac léinn oideachas faoi leith aisti.[1] Níor samhlaíodh do leithéid Dillon go mbeadh saol domhandaithe againn riamh agus go mbeadh Éire, faoi réim an Tíogair Cheiltigh, ag cruthú 90,000 post nua in aghaidh na bliana, ag mealladh 200,000 oibrí eachtrannach, a bhformhór ó stáit aontachais nua an AE.[2] Ach an cheist a chuir sé, agus an tír ag teacht chuici féin tar éis ghéarchéim eacnacmaíochta na 1930í, is ceist í ba chóir a chur arís. Má bhí Stát na hÉireann, a bhí ar an dé deiridh go heacnamúil, buartha an tráth sin faoi imeachtaí cultúrtha agus intleachtacha, an amhlaidh nach féidir le hÉire an Tíogair Cheiltigh am a chaitheamh ar an gceist seo? D'fhreagair Dillon a cheist féin mar seo:

> If an Irish book is silly or dull or badly written, there is no use in pretending that it is not so, although one has to beware of discouraging where only encouragement is needed. In other spheres of activity standards are high, and they are likely to be higher. The standard in regard to Irish should be the highest of all.[3]

Laistigh de dhioscúrsa cúng oileánda agus faoi thionchar an náisiúnachais chultúrtha amháin a phléitear cás agus scéal na Gaeilge – mar theanga, mar áis chultúrtha nó mar ábhar léinn. Ó thráth go chéile le linn na haoise seo caite, dhéantaí iarracht argóint loighciúil a tharraingt le chéile ar mhaithe leis an teanga a chaomhnú, a athnuachan agus a fhorbairt. Is annamh, áfach, sna díospóireachtaí úd a shamhlaítí an Ghaeilge mar ábhar spéise do dhaoine lasmuigh den tír. Is é atá in *Why Irish?* ná sraith aistí a dhéanann iniúchadh ar an nGaeilge mar ábhar léinn idirnáisiúnta agus is é an fócas seo a idirdhealaíonn é ó iarrachtaí eile dá shórt.[4] Buntéis an leabhair seo ná gur fiú do scoláirí agus do mhic léinn ar fud na cruinne staidéar a dhéanamh ar theanga agus ar litríocht na Gaeilge. Tá fiúntas ag baint leis an nGaeilge thar a lárionad i gcultúr náisiúnta na hÉireann agus seachas meas a bheith ag gnáth-Éireanneach uirthi. Fiosraíonn na haistí seo fiúntas, luach agus saibhreas na Gaeilge mar ábhar léinn seachas ról na teanga sa pholaitíocht, sa tsochaí nó sa chultúr mar tuigtear gur fearr an toradh a bheidh ar anailís ghéarchúiseach seachas ar thionscnamh ollmhór.

Is tráthúil é foilsiú na n-aistí seo nuair a chuimhnítear ar a bhfuil ag titim amach in ollscoileanna, ní hamháin in Éirinn ach ar fud na cruinne, agus iad faoi thionchar, dar le Seamus Deane ag an 'current demented belief in the market as the object of our common idolatry'.[5] Is é cás na Sean-Ghaeilge sa Choláiste Ollscoile, Baile Átha Cliath an sampla is soiléire den mheon seo i gcás na Gaeilge. Is fada meas ag pobal na hÉireann ar an gColáiste úd. Tá cáil ar fud na cruinne ar na mic léinn agus ar na scoláirí a oileadh ansin agus chualathas an t-olagón a spreag cinneadh na hOllscoile fáil réidh leis an gCathaoir sa tSean-Ghaeilge i gcéin agus i gcóngar.

Tuigtear an tábhacht a bhaineann le staidéar a dhéanamh ar theanga, ar litríocht agus ar chultúr i gcóras oideachais ar bith a chuireann béim ar an léann daonna. Is léir tábhacht na Gaeilge don acadamh in Éirinn ach go háirithe. D'fhógair Ian G. Roberts, Ollamh le Teangeolaíocht in Ollscoil Cambridge, san *Irish Times*, mí an Mhárta 2007, an tábhacht a bhaineann leis an tSean-Ghaeilge go háirithe dóibh siúd a dteastaíonn tuiscint uathu ar stair agus ar chultúr na hÉireann.[6] Is gné bhunúsach eiliminteach de stair agus de chultúr na tíre í a leithéid de léann. Ní foláir scileanna áirithe – an Ghaeilge ach go háirithe – a bheith ag an té a thugann faoi staidéar léannta a dhéanamh ar Éirinn. Dar le George Huxley, Scoil na gClasaiceach, Coláiste na Tríonóide, Baile Átha Cliath, ní hamháin go bhfuil an tSean-Ghaeilge riachtanach chun stair na hÉireann a thuiscint ach tá sí riachtanach chun féintuiscint a fháil ar ár linn féin freisin.[7] Má theipeann ar léann na Sean-Ghaeilge, beidh impleachtaí tromchúiseacha aige do léann na staire, do léann na Laidine in Éirinn agus don fhileolaíocht chomparáideach. D'áitigh scoláirí Ceiltise i litir san *Irish Times* gurb í an tSean-Ghaeilge, i dteannta na Laidine, bunsraith na teangeolaíochta ar a dtógtar na foinsí do luathstair agus litríocht na hÉireann.[8] Cháin Seamus Deane ar tharla maidir leis an tSean-Ghaeilge sa Choláiste Ollscoile, Baile Átha Cliath:

> But this sort of decision seems to be entirely innocent of its ramifications beyond UCD; for this is a loss that will eventually have economic as well as cultural repercussions. To throw away the prestige of long-accumulated scholarly achievement in an anchor discipline like Old Irish at this moment in a general renovation, to which Old Irish will contribute and from which it will benefit – although not at UCD – is so wanton that one would prefer not to believe that it is the product of calculation.[9]

Is laistigh den ollscoil, laistigh den chomhthionól acadúil amháin is féidir an t-eolas agus na scileanna seo a chothú agus a fhorbairt. Níl sé éasca gan dabht. Ach ní haon slat tomhais é líon na mac léinn do stádas ná d'fhiúntas ábhair léinn ar bith.[10] Mar a deir George Huxley, ní hionann líon na mac léinn atá i mbun ábhair agus stádas an ábhair féin. B'amhlaidh moladh David Agger, Ollamh le Teangeolaíocht in Ollscoil Londan, nuair a chomhairligh sé nárbh ionann brabús gearrthéarmach nó buntáiste áitiúil d'ollscoil amháin dá ndéanfaí dochar don chultúr ar bhonn náisiúnta nó do stádas na Gaeilge.[11]

Tá dualgas ar ollscoileanna na hÉireann a ghlacann le maoiniú an Stáit cuspóirí, cultúr agus oidhreacht an Stáit a chaomhnú, a chothú agus a spreagadh.[12] Tá dualgas orthu, leis, an léann daonna a fhiosrú mar aircív d'fhorbairt agus de shamhlaíocht an chine dhaonna, díreach mar atá dualgas ar scoláirí toradh a gcuid taighde a fhoilsiú agus a chur os comhair an phobail i bhfoirm shothuigthe lena spreagfar spéis an phobail. Tá dualgas ar an dá ghrúpa seo oideachas a chur ar an bpobal, taighde a chur chun cinn agus meas a chothú ar an léann. Is annamh, dar le Fintan O'Toole, a thuigeann polaiteoirí an tionchar cultúrtha a bhíonn ag cinntí lena gcúngaítear gníomhaíocht intleachtach ollscoile:

> Even judging what universities do by strictly economic criteria, the current narrowing of the national mind is counter-productive. In the 21st century, companies are looking increasingly for what they call 'soft skills': analytic intelligence, the capacity to communicate, problem-solving, creativity, intellectual flexibility. The bizarre paradox is that FÁS, which is in the business of meeting the training needs of the economy, seems to know this better than our universities do. While the universities are belatedly adapting to a 1980s understanding of the nature of business, successful businesses have already moved on. They have grasped that what matters is not what you learn but how you learn. And how a student learns is ultimately dependent on the quality of the intellectual environment in a university.[13]

Tá dualgas faoi leith ar ollscoileanna na hÉireann mic léinn atá cáilithe agus oilte i dteangacha agus litríochtaí na hÉireann a sholáthar. Chun filleadh ar a ndúirt O'Toole:

> Universities do need to reflect and serve the societies in which they work, but they also need to protect the intellectual ecology. If that means having a few nature preserves where hardly anyone goes and exotic scholarly beats root around in quiet obscurity, so be it.[14]

Ach fiú anseo agus argóint ar son na Sean-Ghaeilge á déanamh aige, tá dul amú air maidir le nádúr teanga. Tuigtear dó gur gné shochar bhuan í teanga seachas gné atá de shíor ag athrú agus ag forbairt de réir mar a fhásann agus mar a thránn cultúr, smaointeoireacht agus samhlaíocht.

Feictear tuiscint níos ciallmhaire in alt Phóil Uí Mhuirí áit a léiríonn sé gurb éasca meas agus urraim a bheith ar ráthanna, ar chaisleáin agus ar a leithéid mar ní chuireann a leithéid aon stró orainn:

> Yet what they forget is that, unlike dolmens, Irish is a language, a medium of the living and breathing, a voice of long established communities, of drunks and drop-outs, of professors and pimps, of somebodies and nobodies. Language is all about people, and a language is only as good as the opportunities that people have to use it. That's why making Irish an official and working language in the European Union is so important. Language is not a heritage like a tin whistle or a *bodhrán*; it is not a traditional art or a craft. It is more than a tool; it is more than basket-weaving. … Language is not like a session in the pub or an afternoon in Croke Park – though it can be as much fun when, suddenly, it all clicks and aspiration and eclipses and tenses knot together and move like Christy Ring. More often than not, however, it is akin to a life-time commitment to a diet – an intellectual diet.[15]

Ní féidir le hinstitiúidí Stáit cuíchóiriú a dhéanamh de réir a dtola féin beag beann ar an Stát agus an fhreagracht i leith chothú an léinn a fhágáil faoi chúram coláistí beaga gan na hacmhainní ná an maoiniú céanna.[16] Más gá cuíchóiriú a dhéanamh ar acmhainní, is gá díospóireacht phoiblí seachas cinneadh faoi rún. Más gá athdháileadh freagrachta, is gá athdháileadh acmhainní agus é a bheith ciallmhar, straitéiseach agus beartaithe go fadtéarmach.

Léiríonn na cathaoireacha maoinithe agus na hollúnachtaí a bunaíodh timpeall na cruinne a fiúntas idirnáisiúnta. Is teistiméireacht í sin dá fiúntas léinn. Múintear an Ghaeilge go hidirnáisiúnta – Harvard, Berkeley, Chapel Hill, Bonn, Berlin, Cambridge, Hamburg, Lublin (An Pholainn), Moscó, Oxford, Páras, Utrecht, Marburg, Murdoch (Iarthar na hAstráile), Joensuu (An Fhionlainn), Ollscoil Adam Mickiewicz, Poznań (An Pholainn) – rud a dhearbhaíonn a stádas idirnáisiúnta. Bhláthaigh Léann na Gaeilge nuair a tháinig borradh ar an Léann Ceilteach ó lár an naoú haois déag ar aghaidh. Cé go bhfuil an Léann Ceilteach ag teip le tamall de bhlianta anuas, tá borradh anois faoi Léann na hÉireann, sna Stáit Aontaithe ach go háirithe, ach ar fud na cruinne, leis, áit ar bith ar chuir na hÉireannaigh fúthu. Ach mar a deir Ruairí Ó hUiginn:

> Given the exigencies of the present in higher education, courses in Celtic Civilisation and Irish Studies are likely to be very much part of the future in Celtic Studies. While they may offer the security of larger student numbers, it is essential that the core areas of language are protected, and indeed that students are always given the opportunity to familiarize themselves with the languages, to confront the primary sources, and to equip themselves in whatever ways are necessary to deal with them.[17]

Ábhar réasúnta nua is ea an Léann Éireannach agus in ainneoin go bhfuil ag éirí go maith leis, ní fios cén todhchaí atá roimhe san ollscoil ná go deimhin cén réimse taighde a bhaineann leis. Ba ghné lárnach iad na teangacha sa Léann Ceilteach, ach is minic a dhéantar neamhshuim den teanga laistigh den Léann Éireannach. Ba bheag spéis a léiríodh sa Ghaeilge sna leabhair éagsúla a foilsíodh faoi thodhchaí Léann na hÉireann le tamall de bhlianta anuas. D'fhógair an *Forum on the Future of Irish Studies*, a eagríodh i Florence na hIodáile chun todhchaí an Léinn Éireannaigh a fhiosrú, gur '*sine qua non* for the full and proper development of Irish Studies as a whole' ab ea an teanga agus go raibh an teanga riachtanach 'to realise the full potential of Irish Studies, the intrinsic role of Irish-language studies has to be acknowledged more widely and promoted more vigorously than heretofore'.[18]

Beidh le feiscint cén éisteacht a thabharfar don Florence Forum mar is beag aird a thugtar ar an nGaeilge i bhformhór na gcúrsaí sa Léann Éireannach. Cuirtear béim ar ghnéithe áirithe i bhfoirm an aistriúcháin ach déantar neamhshuim iomlán de ghnéithe eile. Is deacair neamhshuim na n-iarrthóirí dochtúireachta sna Stáit a thuiscint nuair a bhíonn orthu go minic an dara nó an tríú teanga a bheith acu chun an chéim a bhaint amach. Is í an tuairim atá ag Hazard Adams 'the linguistic incapacity of America Ph.D.s has always been a joke' ach, a deir sé, 'in the present intellectual situation it has become a scandal'.[19] Ar nós aon teanga eile, is gá dua agus dúthracht chun an Ghaeilge a fhoghlaim. Níl sna ranganna agus sna cúrsaí ollscoile ach tús na hoibre; is gá leanúint ar aghaidh go dícheallach bliain i ndiaidh bliana agus is minic nach bhfeictear toradh go ceann i bhfad. Mar a deir Doug Steward:

> Learning foreign languages and their literatures and cultures is difficult and slow work, but this is not a reason to excuse Ph.D. candidates from doing it. English monolingualism inevitably leads to national isolationism and intellectual segregation.[20]

D'oirfeadh an Ghaeilge mar an dara teanga do mhic léinn an Bhéarla a thugann faoi litríocht na hÉireann. Chabhródh sé leo ní hamháin chun na riachtanais dochtúireachta a bhaint amach, ach thabharfadh sé tuiscint níos doimhne agus níos ilghnéithí dóibh ar mheon agus ar dhearcadh na sochaí as ar tháinig na húdair is spéis leo. Má fhilltear ar Steward arís:

> If this is a problem in the United States English-language population at large, I can think of no good reason to condone such isolationism among the most educated Americans – those with research degrees – or among those who specialize in research on literatures written in English, which is after all a world language and as such, in the best cases, bumps elbows and noggins with all manner of other languages and literatures and, in the worst cases, unilaterally tramples them underfoot. In terms of intellectual work, English monolingualism means ignorance of context and of one's limits.[21]

Admhaíonn Deane gur beag an líon daoine a bhfuil an Ghaeilge acu, ach maíonn sé leis nach aon leithscéal é sin, do staraithe ach go háirithe, neamhshuim a dhéanamh di:

> The fact that we don't speak, read or write it, or that only a minority of us do – a very special minority since it contains an inordinately large number of highly motivated and gifted people whose tenacity should not be under-rated –

emphasizes what a curious attitude we have towards our history.[22]

Leanann sé air: 'It surely is risky to speak of, say, eighteenth-century Irish history without knowledge of the Irish language. But many historians do'. Cúis bhróin don staraí Éamonn Ó Ciardha an easpa leasa a bhaintear as foinsí Gaeilge agus stair na hÉireann á scríobh go háirithe sna tréimhsí nuair ab í an Ghaeilge príomhtheanga na ndaoine.[23] Dar le Francis John Byrne i dtaobh an staraí: '[he] must at least pay the subject of his study the elementary courtesy of learning their language'. Chuir James Lydon, 'doyen of medieval Ireland', dar le Ó Ciardha, an-bhéim ar bhuneolas na teanga a bheith ag an té a raibh spéis aige nó aici sa nua-ré.[25] Is ionann an port ag Kevin Whelan a dúirt go bhfuil staraithe ann nach raibh '[a] conception that an understanding of the majority language of the island until the nineteenth century might be a necessary qualification for an Irish historian'.[26] Chuir Ó Ciardha críoch lena chur síos ar an tábhacht a bhaineann le foghlaim teangacha i gcomhthéacs staraithe a oiliúint le tagairt do Ghearóid Ó Tuathaigh a thug le fios:

> ... it is difficult to see how a discussion of cultural or 'national' consciousness in Ireland in the early modern period can be conducted very sensibly by those who cannot comfortably handle sources.[27]

Is deacair don mhac léinn an Ghaeilge a fhoghlaim, idir Shean- agus Nua-Ghaeilge, ach mar dhúshlán is fiú agus is féidir é a dhéanamh. Agus imní ag fás faoi chaighdeáin a bheith ag titim agus faoi bhoilsciú grád is cúis eile é sin ábhar 'deacair' ar nós na Gaeilge a chur chun cinn.[28]

I gcomhthéacs na díospóireachta seo faoi ról na Gaeilge sna hollscoileanna agus faoi thodhchaí Léann na Gaeilge, is onóir é cuid de na léachtaí a tugadh ag an gcomhdháil dar theideal *Why Irish?* sa bhliain 2005 a chur in eagar. Comóradh ab ea é ní hamháin ar bhunú Roinn Theanga agus Litríocht na Gaeilge in Ollscoil Notre Dame, an t-aon roinn dá sórt sna

Stáit Aontaithe, ach ceiliúradh ab ea é freisin ar Ollúnacht de chuid Thomas J. agus Kathleen O'Donnell i dTeanga agus i Litríocht na Gaeilge. Seo í an chéad chathaoir mhaoinithe sa Ghaeilge a bunaíodh ó ceapadh an tAthair Risteárd de Henebry san Ollscoil Chaitliceach i Washington DC sa bhliain 1896. Is é an tOllamh Breandán Ó Buachalla, MRIA, an chéad ollamh sa chathaoir úd. Ba cheiliúradh cuí ar an gceapachán é an siompóisiam seo ina ndearnadh plé agus iniúchadh ar fhiúntas agus ar acmhainneacht na Gaeilge mar ábhar léinn san acadamh. Eagraíodh an siompóisiam in Ollscoil Notre Dame ar an 29–30 Meán Fómhair 2005 agus is éard atá sa leabhar seo cuid de na páipéir a cuireadh i láthair ag an ócáid. Le linn na comhdhála, dhírigh gach cainteoir ar ghné amháin a bhain le téama na hócáide – is é sin, cén fiúntas a bhaineann le staidéar a dhéanamh ar an nGaeilge in ollscoileanna agus i gcoláistí idirnáisiúnta? Tugadh dúshlán do na cainteoirí an cheist sin a fhreagairt ina gcuid páipéar. Roghnaíodh na cainteoirí ar an mbonn gur saineolaithe iad a bhaineann leas as an nGaeilge ina gcuid taighde agus ina gcuid foilseachán. Spreag na páipéir agus na tuairimí a nochtadh iontu díospóireacht bhríomhar i measc na n-éisteoirí maidir le todhchaí Léann na Gaeilge. Is eol dúinn cheana féin gur ábhar ríspéisiúil agus ríluachmhar í an Ghaeilge, ach léiríonn formhór na n-aistí anseo an tairbhe agus an buntáiste atá le baint as teanga, as litríocht agus as cultúr na Gaeilge agus iad idir lámha ag scoláirí den scoth.

Soláthraíonn Calvert Watkins clár oibre taighde do mhic léinn iarchéime agus do scoláirí i réimsí na filíochta, na meadarachtaí, na teangeolaíochta agus an Léinn Ind-Eorpaigh. Tosaíonn an aiste seo le seanchas faoi scoláirí a thug faoin disciplín, scoláirí a bhfuil a dtionchar fós le sonrú. Is é freagra Watkins don dúshlán a tugadh dó ná dúshláin eile a thabhairt don chéad ghlúin eile; músclaíonn sé ceisteanna maidir le comhréir ghiniúnach nua-aoiseach agus teoiric chomhréireach, teoiric dhúchasach na gramadaí Gaeilge agus filíocht na mbard sa Ghaeilge Chlasaiceach.

Léirítear cumhacht na samhlaíochta agus cumas na litríochta chun athruithe agus teannas cultúrtha a shamhlú agus go deimhin a bhrath sa léamh a dhéanann Tomás Ó Cathasaigh ar *Tochmharc Étaíne*, ar ceann de mhórscéalta na Gaeilge é. Ní hamháin go bhfuil sé ar cheann de na scéalta is gleoite agus is casta dá bhfuil againn ó thréimhse na Sean-Ghaeilge ach tá sé ar cheann de na téacsanna is casta agus is dúcheistí dá bhfuil ann. Taispeántar fiúntas na litríochta luaithe seo in aiste Uí Chathasaigh, litríocht arbh fhéidir léi a bheith láidir, bríomhar, caolchúiseach, an teanga á húsáid ar bhealach glic inti agus téamaí á bhforbairt go hionnúsach. Tugann an litríocht seo guth in insint chomhleanúnach do thuiscint ar an saol agus ionad an duine sa saol sin. Léirítear cumas na litríochta labhairt leis an léitheoir thar am agus thar spás agus thar chultúr.

Meabhraíonn sé don léitheoir na buntáistí iomadúla a bhaineann le taighde a dhéanamh ar an tSean-Ghaeilge (600–900) agus ar an Meán-Ghaeilge (900–1200) agus léiríonn a mhionléamh ar *Tochmharc Étaíne* an argóint seo. Scéal é seo a eascraíonn ó aos cumhachtach meabhrach lena dtugtar fuinneamh agus acmhainn na cléire, na n-údar agus scríbhneoirí na tréimhse seo le chéile i dteannta le filí dúchasacha na Gaeilge. Scríobhadh an aiste chun léitheoirí a spreagadh chun tabhairt faoi na lámhscríbhinní agus faoi na scéalta eile a tháinig aníos chugainn. Tuigtear d'aon duine a léann an aiste seo an tábhacht a bhaineann le hanailís a dhéanamh ar am, ar thalamh agus ar fhéiniúlacht sa tsochaí seo agus arís eile feictear go síolraíonn tuiscint chultúrtha ó mhionléamh ar an litríocht.

Tá cáil ar James McCloskey as a leabhar dátheangach *Guthanna in Éag/Silenced Voices*. Ina aiste anseo bheartaigh sé léargas a thabhairt ar an leas is féidir le sochtheangeolaí a bhaint as staidéar a dhéanamh ar chás na teanga in Éirinn. Is ábhar spéise í an Ghaeilge agus na hiarrachtaí éagsúla chun í a chothú ní hamháin don sochtheangeolaí ach do scoláirí idirnáisiúnta ag obair ar athbheochan teanga agus ar chaomhnú teanga. Dar le McCloskey is minic cúiseanna mothúcháin agus siceolaíochta laistiar de dhíospóireachtaí faoin nGaeilge seachas díospóireachtaí macánta. Rómhinic baineann na díospóireachtaí teanga in Éirinn le múineadh na teanga sna scoileanna agus leis an macnamh oibiachtúil a mbaintí leas astu. Tugann McClosley faoin nGaeilge mar a phléitear in Éirinn agus go hidirnáisiúnta í le chéile san alt seo agus mar aidhm aige:

> to try and think about the situation in Ireland and Irish in a way that is shaped by knowledge of the larger context, and then reciprocally to bring back to that larger debate whatever is to be learned from the Irish experience.

Ag deireadh na haiste, freagraíonn sé an cheist a cuireadh air – cad chuige an Ghaeilge san ollscoil – leis an bhfreagra, mar is teanga í ar nós gach teanga eile.

Feictear cumas na litríochta chun sinn a oiliúint agus a stiúradh in aiste bhreá Philip T. O'Leary ar úrscéalta Alan Titley. Taispeánann O'Leary go soiléir buanna litríocht comhaimseartha na Gaeilge trí mhionchur síos a dhéanamh ar shaothar próis Titley. Ní hamháin go scaiptear cáil Titley mar údar san aiste seo ach rianaítear dea-thréithe na litríochta comhaimsire Gaeilge, litríocht a ndéantar dearmad uirthi go minic ar mhaithe leis an bhfilíocht Ghaeilge, go háirithe na haistriúcháin Bhéarla ar an bhfilíocht chéanna. Cé go n-aithnítear Titley go forleathan i saol an Bhéarla mar cholúnaí Gaeilge de chuid an *Irish Times* – post a bhí ag Brian Ó Nualláin/Myles na Gopaleen tráth den saol – cuirtear i láthair anseo é mar údar mór Gaeilge a scríobh *Méirscrí na Treibhe*, úrscéal ar 'intellectual and stylistic *tour de force*' é dar le O' Leary ar féidir é a phlé ón iliomad taobhanna. Cuirtear síos anseo air mar a leanas: 'among the most provocative explorations in Irish literature, regardless of language, of the personal and cultural wounds of colonialism and unrealized liberation'. Cad is fiú ceapadóireacht Ghaeilge i dtír ilteangach, ceist a fhiafraíonn O'Leary de féin agus maíonn sé: 'No contemporary writer of Irish has, in my opinion, provided a better literary answer to that question than has Alan Titley'. Is minic a cheaptar go dtagann friotal Titley idir a scéal agus a léitheoir ach spreagfaidh a bhfuil le rá anseo ag an gcriticeoir léitheoirí na Gaeilge chun tabhairt faoi agus spreagfaidh sé spéis i measc léirmheastóirí an Bhéarla chomh maith. Dar le O'Leary tá Titley, atá anois ina Ollamh le Gaeilge i gColáiste na hOllscoile Corcaigh, tar éis ceannródaíocht a dhéanamh ar úrscéal na Gaeilge agus mar a deir sé 'has taken the Irish novel places no one would have expected it to go, in the process providing an irrefutable artistic response to the question at the heart of this book'.

Is beag taighde a deineadh ar stair na Gaeilge i Meiriceá go dtí seo. Sa séú haiste, tugtar léargas ar staid na Gaeilge mar ábhar sna hollscoileanna agus sna coláistí sna Stáit Aontaithe agus rianaítear stair na teanga mar ábhar léinn in Harvard, Catholic University, University of California, Berkeley, Boston College agus Notre Dame. Stair í seo atá briotach go maith ach is cuid lárnach í de stair na nGael thar lear agus cruthúnas ar an meas agus ar an stádas a bronnadh ar an teanga thar lear.

Má d'fhéach an chéad aiste ar staid na teanga in Éirinn, caitheann an aiste dheireanach ón Aire Éamon Ó Cuív, Teachta Dála, súil ar thodhchaí na teanga ar fud na cruinne. Cuirtear síos san aiste seo ar iarrachtaí agus ar bheartais Rialtas na hÉireann chun Léann na Gaeilge a chur chun cinn go hidirnáisiúnta. Shir an tAire go Notre Dame chun *Why Irish?* a oscailt go hoifigiúil agus le linn a chuid cainte d'fhógair sé dhá scéim nua – Ciste na Gaeilge agus scéim Fulbright chun oidí óga a chur go Meiriceá chun an teanga a mhúineadh in ollscoileanna agus chun oiliúint agus taithí múinteoireachta a fháil sna Stáit. Is cinnte go mbeidh dea-thoradh ar an dá fhiontar seo sna blianta amach romhainn. Thagair an tAire le linn na cainte d'iarrachtaí an Stáit chun an Ghaeilge a chur chun cinn i dtúsbhlianta an Stáit, iarrachtaí ar mhinic nár éirigh leo agus a raibh drochthoradh orthu uaireanta. Is minic go mbítear ag déileáil le toradh na n-iarrachtaí sin sna díospóireachtaí ar an nGaeilge inniu. Mhínigh an tAire na difríochtaí atá idir cur chuige an Rialtais inniu agus an lá úd agus tuiscint an Stáit anois ar an nGaeilge mar léargas bríomhar ar 'ár bhféiniúlacht náisiúnta, ar ár gcultúr Gaelach agus ar ár gcuid cluichí, ar gcuid damhsaí, ár gcuid ceoil, srl'.

Tarraingíonn sé codarsnacht idir a chuairt féin agus cuairt a sheanathar, Éamon de Valera, sa bhliain 1919 ag bailiú airgid don Stát nua-fhógartha. Tháinig an tAire Ó Cuív go Notre Dame chun na comhdhála seo, mar a dúirt sé féin, ina Aire Rialtais ó Stát neamhspleách atá ag iarraidh an Ghaeilge a chur chun cinn ar fud an domhain agus san aon ollscoil is caoga ina múintear í. Luaigh an tAire gurb é cás na Gaeilge mar ghnáth-theanga labhartha an chloch is mó ar a phaidrín agus is cinnte gur thaitin caint Uí Laoire ar an litríocht chomhaimseartha leis ar an mbonn sin. Cuirtear críoch leis an leabhar seo le haiste an Aire ní hamháin mar tugann sé deis d'ollscoileanna ar fud na cruinne teacht ar fhoinse maoinithe ach ina theannta sin cuireann an fógra faoi scéim Fulbright dóchas i gcroí aon duine ar spéis leis nó léi an Ghaeilge agus sinn ag tús na haoise nua seo.

Mar a dúradh roimhe seo, tugadh dúshlán do gach cainteoir fiúntas na Gaeilge dá dhisciplín nó a disciplín féin mar a chonacthas dó nó di é a léiriú i bhfoirm aiste. Níl spás do gach aiste ná do gach díospóireacht a lean, ach má thógtar le chéile iad in ainneoin na ndifríochtaí stíle agus ábhair, is é atá anseo ná forógra a léiríonn cumas, fiúntas agus acmhainn foráis na Gaeilge mar ábhar léinn don acadamh, bíodh sé in Éirinn nó thar lear. Don speisialtóir acadúil tá ábhar anseo a chuirfidh lena thuiscint nó lena tuiscint ar théas canna nó ar údar faoi leith. Tá anailís anseo ar *Tochmarc Étaíne*, ar *Méirscrí na Treibhe*, ar *Stiall Fhial Feola* agus ar *An Fear Dána*. Anuas air sin, tá suirbhé anseo ar athbheochan na Gaeilge san fhichiú haois agus léargas agus bonnmhíniú ar bheartas Rialtas na hÉireann i leith na Gaeilge agus ar chur chun cinn na Gaeilge go hidirnáisiúnta. Foilsítear na haistí seo ionas go spreagfar díospóireacht agus machnamh in Éirinn agus thar lear agus go gcuirfear daoine ag caint faoi ról agus faoi fhiúntas Léann na Gaeilge sa chóras ollscoile.

Nótaí

1   Myles Dillon, 'Irish in the Schools', *Ireland To-Day*, Feabhra 1937, Iml. II, Uimhir 2, lth. 19.

2   http://www.state.gov/r/pa/ei/bgn/3180.htm

3   Dillon, lth. 24.

4   Íte Ní Chionnaith, *Tábhacht na Gaeilge don Náisiún* (BÁC: Conradh na Gaeilge, 1989). Féach leis *Why Irish? Irish Identity and the Irish Language*, eag. Tovey *et al.* (Dublin: Bord na Gaeilge, 1989) agus *Who Needs Irish? Reflections on the Importance of the Irish Language Today*, eag. Ciarán Mac Murchaidh (Dublin: Veritas, 2004).

5   Seamus Deane, *Irish Times*, 16 Bealtaine 2007.

6   Ian G. Roberts, *Irish Times*, 23 Márta 2007.

7   George Huxley, *Irish Times*, 29 Márta 2007.

8   *Irish Times*, 13 Márta 2007.

9   Seamus Deane, *Irish Times*, 16 Bealtaine 2007.

10 Féach Brian Mooney, '"Purist" maths course is a dismal failure', *Irish Times*, 9 Meitheamh 2005.

11 David Agger, *Irish Times*, 22 Márta 2007.

12 Dar leis an *Forum on the Future of Irish Studies* '... Celtic Studies on the continent of Europe have gone into a very worrying decline, with key universities, which had long-established Celtic Studies programmes, now closing them down – a factor which adds further to Ireland's responsibilities to provide advanced training in this field, for both native and non-native scholars'. *The Future of Irish Studies: Report of the Forum*, eag. Christina Hunt Mahoney *et al*, http://www.irishforumflorence2005.com/ proceedings. html Féach lth. 18.

13 Fintan O'Toole, *Irish Times*, 14 Aibreán 2007.

14 *ibid.*

15 Pól Ó Muirí, 'What is a country without its language?', *Irish Times*, 20 Meán Fómhair 2005.

16 *Irish Times*, 13 Márta 2007.

17 Ruairí Ó hUiginn, 'Future Directions for the Study of Irish', in *Retrospect and Prospect in Celtic Studies*, eag. Máire Herbert and Kevin Murray (Dublin; Four Courts Press, 2003), p. 96.

18 'Irish-language Teaching and Irish-language Literature', *The Future of Irish Studies: Report of the Forum*, eag. Christina Hunt Mahoney *et al*, lth. 16.

19 Hazard Adams, 'Definition and/as Survival', *ADE Bulletin*, Uimhir 80, 1985, lth. 5, luaite ag Doug Steward, 'The Foreign

Language Requirements in English Doctoral Programs', *Profession 2006*, lgh. 214–5.

20 Doug Steward, 'The Foreign Language Requirements in English Doctoral Programs', *Profession 2006*, lgh. 214–5.

21 Doug Stewart, lgh. 214–5.

22 Seamus Deane, 'Remembering the Irish Future', *Ireland: Dependence and Independence, The Crane Bag*, Iml. 8, Uimhir 1, lth. 87.

23 Éamonn Ó Ciardha, *Ireland and the Jacobite cause, 1685–1766* (Dublin: Four Courts Press, 2002), lth. 41.

24 Francis John Byrne, luaite ag Éamonn Ó Ciardha, lth. 41.

25 James Lydon, luaite ag Éamonn Ó Ciardha, lth. 41.

26 Kevin Whelan, luiate ag Éamonn Ó Ciardha, lth. 41.

27 Gearóid Ó Tuathaigh, luaite ag Éamonn Ó Ciardha, lth. 42.

28 George Huxley, *Irish Times*, 29 Márta 2007. Féach *Network for Irish Educational Standards*.

http://www.stopgradeinflation.ie/papers.html

Professor Breandán Ó Buachalla and Mr. Michael Murphy

WHY IRISH IN ACADEMIA?

Brian Ó Conchubhair
University of Notre Dame

In a 1937 article, Celtic Studies and Irish-language scholar Myles Dillon posed a rhetorical question regarding what should constitute the object of Irish-language studies in Irish schools. It is the duty of the schools to make fluent Irish-speakers at all costs, and even to use Irish as a medium of instruction outside as well as within the *Gaeltacht*, he suggested as one answer. Others, he responded, hold that Irish should be taught in the schools as an educational subject like any other, and that to an Irish boy its educational value may be very great.[1] For Dillon the idea of a globalized world and a Celtic Tiger Ireland that since 2004 'has generated roughly 90,000 new jobs annually, attracting over 200,000 foreign workers, mostly from the new EU accession states, in an unprecedented immigration influx'[2] was unimaginable. Yet his question, posed in the aftermath of the economic depression, is as relevant now in times of economic boom, as it was then. In answering his self-posed question, he rationalised that:

> If an Irish book is silly or dull or badly written, there is no use in pretending that it is not so, although one has to beware of discouraging where only encouragement is needed. In other spheres of activity standards are high, and they are likely to be higher. The standard in regard to Irish should be the highest of all.[3]

Debates on the intrinsic merits and demerits of Irish – as a language, as a cultural resource, as a national inheritance, or as an object of intellectual pursuit – are governed almost exclusively by the insular context of Irish politics and cultural nationalism. In such debates, Irish is, however, rarely conceived of as a topic of importance, relevance or interest outside of Ireland. *Why Irish?* is a collection of essays that considers the study of Irish as an academic endeavour in an international context. Various efforts to provide a coherent rationale for reviving, fostering and promoting Irish have occasionally appeared in print throughout the twentieth century.[4] This volume argues that the Irish language and its concomitant culture and literature is worthy of study in universities and by scholars whose motivation derives from intellectual curiosity rather than cultural nationalism or a sense of national pietas. It is this focus that distinguishes *Why Irish?* These essays consider the roles, values and potentials of Irish in international academia rather than in Irish society, politics, media and culture in the belief that a singular focus produces a more coherent and purposeful discussion.

Such a discussion is both timely and apt, given the current rationalisation of the humanities and arts not alone in Ireland, but throughout the world where educational philosophy is governed by what Seamus Deane terms the 'current demented belief in the market as the object of our common idolatry'.[5] The clearest manifestation of such lamentable and short-term thought is the abolition of the Chair of Old Irish at University College Dublin, an institution long respected not only for the calibre of its students and scholars, but its contribution to the intellectual and cultural life of Ireland. The public outcry at the announcement spawned a correspondence that provides an assessment of the role of the language in Irish and international academia. The loud chorus of objection and dismay that greeted this announcement resonates with many of the themes and opinions expressed at the *Why Irish?* conference organised at the University of Notre Dame.

The importance of language, literary and cultural studies as fields of study in any educational system that values the humanities is incontestable. Writing in the *Irish Times* newspaper in March 2007, Ian G. Roberts, Professor of Linguistics, University of Cambridge, asserts the importance of the study of Old Irish, especially for those wishing to understand the history and culture of Ireland. Such scholarship and teaching, he cogently argues, is a fundamental aspect of Ireland's history and culture.[6] Accessing this central facet of Ireland's, and indeed Europe's, rich cultural heritage and origins demands a particular set of skills combining linguistic and cultural knowledge. George Huxley, School of Classics, Trinity College Dublin, also contends that Old Irish language and literature are vital not only to the understanding of Irish origins but also for modern Ireland's perception of itself. Failure to support and cultivate the study of Old Irish would lead to damaging consequences for the serious study of Irish history, Irish Latinity, and comparative philology.[7] A distinguished group of Celtic scholars argued in a similar letter to the *Irish Times* that 'Together with Latin, Old Irish is the linguistic bedrock on which all study of the sources for the early history and literature of Ireland is founded'.[8] Seamus Deane, while fully supporting 'properly financed and administered education', also laments the demotion of Old Irish 'to what is in effect the point of extinction' at UCD:

> But this sort of decision seems to be entirely innocent of its ramifications beyond UCD; for this is a loss that will eventually have economic as well as cultural repercussions. To throw away the prestige of long-accumulated scholarly achievement in an anchor discipline like Old Irish at this moment in a general renovation, to which Old Irish will contribute and from which it will benefit – although not at UCD – is so wanton that one would prefer not to believe that it is the product of calculation.[9]

This knowledge and skill set, and its future cultivation, can only be fostered and promoted in an academic setting. The skills in question are not easily attained, but low student enrolment, or a dip in student up-take, is hardly a barometer for any subject's cultural importance and scholarly status.[10]

The worth of a scholarly or scientific subject cannot be estimated by counting heads alone as Huxley succinctly stated. David Agger, Professor of Linguistics, University of

London, also echoes this sentiment and warns that immediate financial gain at a local level or at individual universities cannot be estimated to be more important than maintaining the cultural importance of Irish over the long term and in a global context.[11] State funded Irish universities have a responsibility to the state and its citizens to maintain, preserve, cultivate and popularize national heritages and cultures.[12]

Universities are obliged to explore and develop the humanities as the archive of human achievement and imagination just as scholars are obliged to publish and popularise their research. Both are charged with educating the public, promoting research and popularising scholarship. Failure to do so amounts to withdrawal into an even more removed ivory tower or further capitulation to the corporate world that views universities as low-cost research and design units that exist to service corporate profit alone. Cultural commentator Fintan O'Toole opines that governments barely consider the cultural consequences of the rash and imprudent narrowing of intellectual and scholarly diversity in third-level institutions.

> Even judging what universities do by strictly economic criteria, the current narrowing of the national mind is counter-productive. In the 21st century, companies are looking increasingly for what they call 'soft skills: analytic intelligence, the capacity to communicate, problem-solving, creativity, intellectual flexibility. The bizarre paradox is that FÁS, which is in the business of meeting the training needs of the economy, seems to know this better than our universities do. While the universities are belatedly adapting to a 1980s understanding of the nature of business, successful businesses have already moved on. They have grasped that what matters is not what you learn but how you learn. And how a student learns is ultimately dependent on the quality of the intellectual environment in a university.[13]

Irish universities have a special obligation to foster and develop competent and trained students in the vernacular languages and literatures of early, medieval and modern Ireland. To quote O'Toole again:

> Universities do need to reflect and serve the societies in which they work, but they also need to protect the intellectual ecology. If that means having a few nature preserves where hardly anyone goes and exotic scholarly beats root around in quiet obscurity, so be it.[14]

Yet even this sympathetic argument is flawed. It mistakenly perceives language as some static, fixed and moribund object rather than a dynamic, creative and evolving entity combining culture, literature and thought. A more enlightened and savvy perception of the role of language in culture and society and its potential for scholarship is contained in Pól Ó Muirí's perspicacious assessment. The physical manifestations of heritage – standing stones, dolmens, castles – are easily cherished, or in the case of Tara, abused, but this, he argues, is a lazy, effortless type of engagement:

> Yet what they forget is that, unlike dolmens, Irish is a language, a medium of the living and breathing, a voice of long established communities, of drunks and drop-outs, of professors and pimps, of some-bodies and nobodies. Language is all about people, and a language is only as good as the opportunities that people have to use it. That's why making Irish an official and working language in the European Union is so important. Language is not a heritage like a tin whistle or a *bodhrán*; it is not a traditional art or a craft. It is more than a tool; it is more than basket-weaving. … Language is not like a session in the pub or an afternoon in Croke Park – though it can be as much fun when, suddenly, it all clicks and aspiration and eclipse and tenses knot together and move like Christy Ring. More often than not, however, it is akin to a life-time commitment to a diet – an intellectual diet.[15]

Individual state institutions cannot be allowed to rationalize at will and transfer the onus for maintaining literary and linguistic knowledge to lesser universities with fewer resources, fewer faculty and weaker libraries.[16] If rationalization of resources is necessary, public debate, not the frivolous fiat of the few, is required. Reallocation of resources, if necessary, must be structured, planned and judicious.

While the significance of Irish-language studies in Ireland is patent, this volume interrogates its international value, and in particular in the United States. The establishment of chairs and positions throughout Europe in the nineteenth-century attests to its international scholarly significance. The current teaching of Irish in universities across the globe – Harvard, Berkeley, Chapel Hill, Bonn, Berlin, Cambridge, Hamburg, Lublin (Poland), Moscow, Oxford, Paris, Utrecht, Marburg, Murdoch (Western Australia), Joensuu (Finland) Adam Mickiewicz University, Poznań (Poland), etc – substantiates its continuing international scholarly and educational merit. Irish-language studies flowered under the rise of Celtic Studies in the mid-nineteenth century, itself a benefactor of comparative linguistics. The decline in Celtic Studies has to some degree been off-set by a rise in Irish Studies, particularly in the United States, but also on other continents. But as Ruairí Ó hUiginn warns:

> Given the exigencies of the present in higher education, courses in Celtic Civilisation and Irish Studies are likely to be very much part of the future in Celtic Studies. While they may offer the security of larger student numbers, it is essential that the core areas of language are protected, and indeed that students are always given the opportunity to familiarize themselves with the languages, to confront the primary sources, and to equip themselves in whatever ways are necessary to deal with them.[17]

Irish Studies is a relatively new discipline and despite its popularity and appeal, its long term future remains unclear as does the precise scope of its field of study. While languages and philology were central to scholarship in Celtic Studies, Irish Studies often tends to treat the language with disdain and tokenism. Of the several publications on the future of Irish Studies to appear at the turn of the millennium, hardly any considered the role or potential contribution of language studies. The Florence *Forum on the Future of Irish Studies*, organised to debate the discipline's future, agreed that Irish-language studies are 'a *sine qua non* for the full and proper development of Irish Studies as a whole', and stated that in order 'to realise the full potential of Irish Studies, the intrinsic role of Irish-language studies has to be acknowledged more widely and promoted more vigorously than heretofore'.[18] The future will reveal whether the various universities and programs involved adopt these recommendations or if they remain pious aspirations.

The disinterest exhibited by Ph.D. candidates in English literature/Irish Studies programs is particularly bizarre given the language requirements of many doctoral programs in the United States. Hazard Adams controversially comments that 'the linguistic incapacity of American Ph.D.s has always been a joke' but, he continues, 'in the present intellectual situation it has become a scandal'.[19] Irish-language study, like any foreign language study, is time-consuming and labour-intensive. In truth, the language study undertaken in graduate schools is only the beginning with the results only visible in later years and after persistent effort. 'Learning foreign languages and their literatures and cultures is difficult and slow work, but this is not a reason to excuse Ph.D. candidates from doing it',[20] writes Doug Steward. English monolingualism inevitably leads to national isolationism and intellectual segregation. For students of Irish literature in English, especially doctoral candidates in the Unites States and Canada, Irish seems a perfect language to study in order to satisfy their second or third language requirements. It compliments their academic interest and bolsters their study of the societies and intellectual thought that produced the authors and works they research. To quote Steward again:

> If this is a problem in the United States English-language population at large, I can think of no good reason to condone such isolationism among the most educated Americans – those with research degrees – or among those who specialize in

research on literatures written in English, which is after all a world language and as such, in the best cases, bumps elbows and noggins with all manner of other languages and literatures and, in the worst cases, unilaterally tramples them underfoot. In terms of intellectual work, English monolingualism means ignorance of context and of one's limits.[21]

Turning attention to history, Seamus Deane, acknowledging the relatively low number of Irish-speakers, comments:

> The fact that we don't speak, read or write it, or that only a minority of us do – a very special minority since it contains an inordinately large number of highly motivated and gifted people whose tenacity should not be under-rated – emphasizes what a curious attitude we have towards our history.[22]

Yet he notes 'It surely is risky to speak of, say, eighteenth-century Irish history without knowledge of the Irish language. But many historians do'. Historian Éamonn Ó Ciardha laments the poor use of Irish-language material by historians and in his extensive study of eighteenth-century Irish-language verse as a historical source acknowledged the need of linguistically competent historians of Ireland when Irish was the language of the vast majority of the population. To paraphrase Ó Ciardha, the neglect of Irish poetry as a source for eighteenth-century Irish history typifies the general treatment of Irish-language sources by historians.[23] Francis John Byrne commented that the sympathetic historian 'must at least pay the subject of his study the elementary courtesy of learning their language'.[24] James Lydon, described by Ó Ciardha as the 'doyen of medieval Ireland', stressed the importance of a grounding in the language for any Irish historian focusing on history of the modern period,[25] and in a similar vein Kevin Whelan remarked that there is 'no conception that an understanding of the majority language of the island until the nineteenth century might be a necessary qualification for an Irish historian'.[26] Ó Ciardha concludes his overview of the role of language in the training of historians with reference to Gearóid Ó Tuathaigh who claims:

> ... it is difficult to see how a discussion of cultural or 'national' consciousness in Ireland in the early modern period can be conducted very sensibly by those who cannot comfortably handle sources.[27]

To master Irish, both Old and Modern, is admittedly a challenge; yet in and of itself is rewarding and worthy of the effort. The perceived impenetrability of Irish is an excellent reason for promoting its study at a time of growing concern over falling standards and soaring grade inflation in both Ireland and the United States.[28]

In the context of such a public debate over the roles of Irish in universities and the future of Irish-language studies, it is a great pleasure to introduce these lectures delivered at the *Why Irish?* symposium at the University of Notre Dame, United States of America in 2005. This symposium not only commemorated the founding of the Department of Irish Language and Literature, the first such department in a North American university, but celebrated the Thomas J. and Kathleen O'Donnell Professorship of Irish Language and Literature at the University of Notre Dame. This chair is the first endowed professorship of Irish in the United States since the Reverend Richard Henebry occupied his position at the Catholic University, Washington D.C. in 1896. The first holder of the O'Donnell Chair at the University of Notre Dame is Professor Breandán Ó Buachalla, MRIA and this symposium, dedicated to exploring the roles and potentials of Irish in the academy, is a fitting and appropriate manner to celebrate his appointment. *Why Irish?* was organised at the University of Notre Dame, 29–30 September, 2005 and this volume represents a selection of the papers delivered there. During the symposium each speaker addressed a specific topic related to the central theme: what is the value of studying Irish in international universities? *Why Irish?* challenged these scholars to suggest why Irish matters in international academia. The speakers, selected on the basis of the use they make of Irish in their research projects, prompted the audience to reflect on the roles of Irish in academia and the challenges facing future Irish scholars. Rather than simply assert the obvious – Irish is a rewarding and fascinating topic of study – these essays and striking case studies illustrate instructively how this language and its concomitant culture and literature are worthy of study in top tier universities by leading scholars. These essays represent a selection of the symposium participants' responses.

Calvert Watkins suggests a research agenda for graduate students and scholars in the fields of poetry, metrics, linguistics and Indo-European studies. This contribution includes some wonderful reminiscences of Irish scholars who not only defined the field of study, but whose legacy lingers still. Watkins, in response to the volume's challenge, lays down his own challenges for future scholars to solve including problems in modern generative syntax and syntactic theory, native Irish grammatical theory and Classical Modern Irish bardic poetry.

The power of imagination and ability of literature to see, perceive and indeed anticipate cultural change and turmoil is evident in Tomás Ó Cathasaigh's revealing study of *Tochmharc Étaíne*. It is, according to Ó Cathasaigh, not only one of the most beautiful and intricate tales of Early Irish literature but arguably the most complex and puzzling of Irish tales. It vividly reveals the value of Early Irish literature which at its best, he argues, is robust, vibrant and exuberant; subtle and ingenious in its use of language and very rich in its thematic content. This literature gives expression in narrative form to a view of the world and of mankind's place in it and he exposes its ability to speak directly and edifyingly to audiences across time and space. He reminds readers that Early Irish, the period comprising Old (600–900) and Middle Irish (900–1200) offers numerous gains for students, and his close textual reading of *Tochmharc Étaíne* illustrates this potential for elucidation. This narrative, produced by a member of a powerful intellectual and artistic elite, combines the energy and resources of ecclesiastical scholars, authors, and artists with those of traditional Irish-language poets, jurists, and storytellers. It is his hope that it will inspire readers to look at it for themselves, and also to seek out some of the other tales the Irish manuscripts bequeath to us. As a case-study in the value of early Irish literature and an examination of time, land and identity as depicted in the tale, it demonstrates the truism that literature is the bedrock of cultural understanding.

James McCloskey, known in Ireland for his highly acclaimed bilingual book *Guthanna in Éag/Silenced Voices*, chooses a broad canvas and examines the value of Irish for socio-linguistics. He reveals why Irish is not alone of interest to the field of socio-linguistics, but of value for international scholars engaged in language revival and preservation studies. McCloskey shrewdly observes that exchanges about the roles and positions of Irish in public life are less debates than frenzied altercations fuelled by emotive and psychological factors. Considering Irish as debated and discussed in Ireland and in international socio-linguistic discourse, he attempts a synthesis of both discourses in order:

> to try and think about the situation in Ireland and Irish in a way that is shaped by knowledge of the larger context, and then reciprocally to bring back to that larger debate whatever is to be learned from the Irish experience.

He concludes by answering the question that dominates this volume – Why Irish? Because it is a language like any other with much to offer both student and scholar.

The value of literature to guide and enlighten is again manifest in Philip O'Leary's ground-breaking survey of Alan Titley's prose fiction. Selecting Titley's novels for his case study, O'Leary demonstrates the merits of contemporary Irish-language literature. Introducing Titley to a wider audience, O'Leary makes a strong case for the value of contemporary prose, so often overshadowed by the critical attention lavished on Irish-language poetry in translation. Titley, known to many in Anglophone circles as a weekly contributor to the *Irish Times* newspaper – a position previously held by Flann O'Brien/Myles na Gopaleen – is here revealed as a noteworthy writer whose novel *Méirscrí na Treibhe*, is, in O'Leary's opinion, an intellectual and stylistic *tour de force* that could be discussed from any number of perspectives. It deserves to be considered among the most provocative explorations in Irish literature, regardless of language, of the personal and cultural wounds of colonialism and unrealized liberation. Questioning the relevance of Irish in a country growing increasingly multilingual, O'Leary asserts that 'No contemporary writer of Irish has, in my opinion, provided a better literary answer to that question than has Alan Titley'. O'Leary's insightful and astute essay will merit for Titley the critical attention of a wider audience and encourage Irish-speakers to explore the impressive range and scope of his literary and linguistic domain. Titley has, according to O'Leary, taken the Irish novel places no one would have expected it to go, in the process providing an irrefutable artistic response to the question at the heart of this book.

The Irish language in North America has yet to receive sustained critical attention. The penultimate essay surveys the language's history in colleges and universities in the United States and chronicles the history of Irish-language teaching at key institutions, including Harvard, Catholic University, Linguistic Society of America, University of California, Berkeley, Boston College and Notre Dame. This history is often forgotten, fractured and obscured. Nevertheless, it serves as an indicator of the Irish diaspora's perception of language's centrality when seeking a higher education that acknowledged and privileged ethnicity.

If the first essay focuses on the role of the language in Ireland, the final essay takes a global view and looks to the future. Here Minister Éamon Ó Cuív, *Teachta Dála*, looks to the future and the Irish Government's practical and financial efforts to promote the study of Irish as a language and as a discipline across the world. Ó Cuív travelled to Indiana to open Why Irish? and in the course of this address announced the establishment of two new programs – *Ciste na Gaeilge* and the Fulbright FLTA program – undertakings that will contribute significantly to the promotion of Irish-language studies not only in North American institutes of higher learning but globally. The Minister, in the course of this address, also addressed the failed, unrealistic and impractical strategies adopted by the Irish Free State and early governments of the republic in the early decades of the twentieth century. The consequences of these strategies continue to have an impact on debates concerning Irish.

The Minister outlines the difference between current Government policy regarding the means of promoting Irish and earlier policies. His article acknowledges the Irish state's recognition of Irish as a vibrant expression of national identity, and of Irish culture, along with games, dance, music and stresses the wide public support in Ireland for retaining, cultivating and promoting the language. He contrasts the 1919 visit of his grandfather, Éamon de Valera to Notre Dame seeking funds for the newly declared Irish republic, with his grandson's 2005 visit as a representative of an independent government seeking to promote the Irish language worldwide and in particular in the fifty-one third-level colleges teaching Irish worldwide. The Fulbright Irish-language Teaching Assistantship program which the Minister announced would send Irish graduates and senior scholars to the United States to teach Irish language and Irish-language literature.

The positive and far-reaching impacts of such developments cannot be overestimated. Expressing his primary concern with the use of Irish as a modern vernacular in every-day life, the Minister will have found much to please him in O'Leary's contribution on contemporary vernacular literature. McCloskey's piece contends that advocates and critics of Irish rarely discuss the issues in an international context. Ó Cuív's essay is, therefore, placed close to end of the volume to indicate the importance of Government funding for

Irish-language programs and departments abroad, in North America, Russia, Poland, the Czech Republic and Australia. The announcement of such funding in tandem with the Fulbright Foreign Language Teaching Assistantships offers a potentially bright and encouraging beginning to twenty-first century Irish language studies beyond the confines of the language's traditional base.

The challenge posed to each contributor was to articulate the value of Irish-language studies to their respective disciplines. Space does not allow for every contribution, and responses varied in style and approach, but taken together they illustrate the rich benefits to be reaped by the student of Irish and argue for the value of Irish-language studies at universities in the United States and elsewhere. *Why Irish?* is a collection of papers by eminent scholars who draw on Irish-language material for their research projects. For academic specialists and general readers, this volume offers much of value and merit. It contains not only illuminating close readings of medieval tales (*Tochmarc Étaíne*/The Wooing of Étáin) and of Alan Titley's contemporary novels (*Méirscrí na Treibhe, Stiall Fhial Feola* and *An Fear Dána*), but affords important surveys of the contemporary state of Irish that critique the twentieth-century revival project and also provide a rationale for Irish Government policy and the promotion of the Irish language internationally. It is the hope that these essays will provoke and inspire thought, discussion and productive debate and will promote the future development of Irish-language studies internationally.

Notes
1   Myles Dillon, 'Irish in the Schools', *Ireland To-Day*, February 1937, Vol. II, No. 2, p. 19.
2   US Department of State, http://www.state.gov/r/pa/ei/bgn/3180.htm
3   Myles Dillon, p. 24.

4   See Íte Ní Chionnaith, *Tábhacht na Gaeilge don Náisiún* (BÁC: Conradh na Gaeilge, 1989). See also the bilingual *Why Irish? Irish Identity and the Irish Language*, ed. Tovey *et al.* (Dublin; Bord na Gaeilge, 1989) and *Who Needs Irish? Reflections on the Importance of the Irish Language Today*, ed. Ciarán Mac Murchaidh (Dublin: Veritas, 2004).

5   Seamus Deane, *Irish Times*, 16 May 2007.

6   Ian G. Roberts, *Irish Times*, 23 March 2007.

7   George Huxley, *Irish Times*, 29 March 2007.

8   *Irish Times*, 13 March 2007.

9   Seamus Deane, *Irish Times*, 16 May 2007.

10 See Brian Mooney, '"Purist" maths course is a dismal failure', *Irish Times*, 9 June 2005.

11 David Agger, *Irish Times*, 22 March 2007.

12 This onus is all the more pressing given as the *Forum on the Future of Irish Studies* noted '... Celtic Studies on the continent of Europe have gone into a very worrying decline, with key universities, which had long-established Celtic Studies programmes, now closing them down – a factor which adds further to Ireland's responsibilities to provide advanced training in this field, for both native and non-native scholars'. *The Future of Irish Studies: Report of the Forum* ed. Christina Hunt Mahoney et al, http://www.irishforumflorence2005.com/proceedings.html See p. 18.

13 Fintan O'Toole, *Irish Times*, 14 April 2007.

14 *ibid.*

15 Pól Ó Muirí, 'What is a country without its language?', *Irish Times*, 20 September 2005.

16 *Irish Times*, 13 March 2007.

17 Ruairí Ó hUiginn, 'Future Directions for the Study of Irish', *Retrospect and Prospect in Celtic Studies* ed. Máire Herbert and Kevin Murray (Dublin: Four Courts Press, 2003), p. 96.

18 'Irish-language Teaching and Irish-language Literature', *The Future of Irish Studies: Report of the Forum* http://www.irishforumflorence2005.com/proceedings.html p. 16.

19 Hazard Adams, 'Definition and/as Survival', *ADE Bulletin*, No. 80, 1985, p. 5. cited by Doug Steward, 'The Foreign Language Requirements in English Doctoral Programs', *Profession 2006*, pp. 214–5.

20 Doug Steward, 'The Foreign Language Requirements in English Doctoral Programs', *Profession 2006*, pp. 214–5.

21 Doug Stewart, pp. 214–5.

22 Seamus Deane, 'Remembering the Irish Future', *Ireland: Dependence and Independence, The Crane Bag*, Vol. 8, No. 1, p. 87.

23 Éamonn Ó Ciardha, *Ireland and the Jacobite cause, 1685–1766* (Dublin: Four Courts Press, 2002), p. 41.

24 Francis John Byrne, cited by Éamonn Ó Ciardha, p. 41.

25 James Lydon, cited by Éamonn Ó Ciardha, p. 41.

26 Kevin Whelan, cited by Éamonn Ó Ciardha, p. 41.

27 Gearóid Ó Tuathaigh, cited by Éamonn Ó Ciardha, p. 42.

28 George Huxley, *Irish Times*, 29 March 2007. See also See Network for Irish Educational Standards, http://www.stopgradeinflation.ie/papers.html

Professor Calvert Watkins

WHAT MAKES THE STUDY OF IRISH WORTHWHILE

Calvert Watkins
University of California, Los Angeles

Let me say at the outset that my title is intended as a statement, not a question. I have no intention to enumerate all the possible responses – 'Let me count the ways' – but only to offer first, by way of illustration, some not so random reminiscences and musings on coming to Ireland to do Celtic Studies fifty years ago.

I arrived in Dublin in the fall of 1957, and my first impression as one who had lived in New York and Massachusetts was that the country was minuscule. One phonebook did for the entire country. The twenty-six counties had a population of some 2,800,000, and fully a quarter of them lived in Dublin. Emigration was at its highest. I found myself a bed sitter with a kitchen – later discovering it was next to a *shebeen* – and in very un-Irish fashion settled into cooking for myself, but drinking in Irish fashion in the pub. Cooking took little time and effort – in 1957 there were two kinds of cheese in Ireland, white cheese and yellow cheese, and to buy garlic you had to go to a fledgling gourmet store on Grafton Street. So I spent most evenings in O'Neill's pub off Stephen's Green, or Davy Byrnes, depending on the company. It was there I learned that the chief indoor sport in Ireland was conversation, and that the Irish were very good at it indeed. And it was there I learned Irish history, politics and sociology, as well as the finer points of Irish grammar and Irish studies past and present, what you might call 'living philology'. Given the size of the country I also learned very quickly that everybody who is anybody in Ireland knows everybody else in Ireland who is anybody, and usually isn't speaking to them. An exaggeration perhaps, but applicable to my teachers it is one which made the study of Irish interesting as well as worthwhile. One of the special benefits of Irish studies, more than most I know, is the tradition of knowing and recounting anecdotes about scholars of the past, the elders, the teachers, their strengths and wit as well as weaknesses, foibles and prejudices. Learning this folklore we gradually become part of it ourselves while still alive and well.

Once when I was teaching a course on Early Irish Poetry one student – he's now the editor of the journal *Language* – said at the end of class, 'That's the fifth (or maybe it was the tenth) poem you said was the most beautiful in Old Irish'. Some years later I heard from the then Regius Professor of Latin at Cambridge a story about a predecessor in the chair of Greek, who used to preface each of a certain set of lectures in the classical tripos with 'This too is Pindar's finest ode'. *Nihil novi sub sole*, there's nothing new under the sun, but it's another argument for what makes the study of Irish worthwhile.

The very smallness of the field also makes the study of Irish worthwhile. Myles Dillon, Brian Ó Cuív, and David Greene once had a lengthy and inconclusive discussion of how you said 'two cows' in Old Irish. Greene reporting this to me said simply, 'If the three of us don't know, the chances are nobody knows'. Mark that down as another problem for the future: as Dillon used to say, 'Nobody knows Irish'.

The same Myles Dillon – whom in his early years another eminent Celticist once styled 'a young fogey' – said to me one day, quite rightly, 'Most of us tend to do either Old Irish or Modern Irish, but David Greene bestrides both fields like a colossus'. As another scholar on this podium knows, David's characteristic response was a laconic 'Stand underneath a colossus and look up, all you see is balls'. A field like that, with principals like that, has something unique.

'No man was ever so fortunate in his teachers', was a sentiment voiced by Dan Binchy in an acknowledgment in 1941 that I could only humbly echo in my turn. For all his veneer of *severitas* which would have done a Roman proud, my revered teacher Binchy was an incurable romantic. Read from his essay 'Irish history and Irish law II', in *Studia Hibernica* of 1976:

> Indeed one can hardly imagine a greater contrast than that between the Irish Republic of today and an essentially rural and hierarchical society, a congeries of primary units each ruled by a tribal king ... a society in which status was the determining factor and a cash economy was unknown ...

> Yet, granted all this, the fact remains that the Gaelic inheritance still lingers on; ... it has bequeathed even to the average English-speaking Irish men and women of today an *Eigenart*, an unmistakingly separate outlook on life and manners which differentiates them from other people who speak the same language. The historian, therefore, is bound to investigate the source of this impalpable but none the less powerful influence, which is only another way of saying that he must examine and describe the salient features of native Irish society before and after the coming of the Normans.[1]

A lot of water has flowed under the bridge in Ireland in the thirty-one years since Binchy wrote that; but a dose of romanticism is a good tonic for an *apologia pro vita sua*.

I pass now happily out of the autobiographical mode, to offer some observations on language and literature in Ireland, on what makes the study of Irish worthwhile. I once wrote, and somebody once quoted me, that 'Irish has the oldest vernacular literature in Western Europe'. By vernacular I, of course, meant what followed that classical tradition of late antiquity, in a non-Latin language. Latin was the language of Christianity and Christianization, the language of literature and poetic art in the West. It has often been remarked that the ideology of the Eastern Church held that the Lord was magnified by the number of languages and alphabets used to worship Him, which is why we have the gospels in Gothic, Armenian, Syriac, Georgian and Slavonic. In most of these (Gothic in the fourth century is an exception) the Bible translation was followed by a flowering of literature, historical, hagiographic, and translation. In the Western Church the spread of Christianity entailed no 'systematic' translation of the gospels which might have been associated with for example the mission of Saint Patrick, as in the case of Ulfilas, Mesrop, or Cyril and Methodius. But the pragmatic exigencies of conversion are such that a more or less 'authorized', at least conventional translation of widely scattered parts of the Bible into Irish did exist, orally perhaps but capable of being written at any time (for example for sermons). This is clear from the widely scattered citations in the glosses and texts like the Cambrai homily, where the repetition in Irish of biblical passages cited in Latin makes an extraordinarily vivid and moving impression. And as we have learned in the last quarter century, Biblical citations in Irish are widespread in the Laws and much else in Early Irish literature. Much of this can be gleaned from the pages of *Peritia* and other places; it would perhaps be useful to have a complete collection.

The intellectual ferment and florescence of literature we observed in the East associated with conversion and literacy from the fifth century on certainly took place in Ireland at about the same time and for the same reasons, though much of the development must have taken place outside our view.

Once in my student days in Dublin I tried to set down a ranked list of the styles of Irish written, in descending order of complexity, difficulty and obscuration. These ranged from 'The language of the poets' – *bérla na filed* – hermetic and quasi-mantic passages embedded in the law tracts and elsewhere to the more straightforward classical Old Irish law texts, the so-called rhetorics of the *Táin* and other sagas beside the ultra-short sentences of telescoped and telegraphic prose of early saga literature, these to the straightforward and 'comfortable' expository prose of later legal and literary texts, some extended passages in the glosses, especially as one approached Middle Irish. But the simplest and most direct prose in Early Irish, the most 'user-friendly' as we would say today, was hagiographic and pietistic, from archaic fragments like the Cambrai homily to the Life of Saint Brigit and ultimately the later Saints Lives. The styles of written Irish, prose and poetry, is an extraordinary laboratory for the student of literature. And written Irish, the range of Early Irish literature, seems to have developed and grown to this degree of complexity in the period from the beginnings of Christianization and literacy in Latin letters to the beginning of the seventh century, when we can observe it around 600 and before the earliest monuments of written Irish like the 'Amra Coluimb Chille', the poems of Colmán Mac Lénéni, and the *Book of Leinster* genealogies.

It is surely not an accident that this extraordinarily rapid development of Irish as a literary language coincides with the period of the greatest change of the language itself. For Irish probably changed more drastically and dramatically between roughly 400 and 600 than from Indo-European to 400, or from 600 to present. That is to say that in something like 200 years (think 1805 to 2005; my great-grandfather was born in 1801, in the presidency of John Adams) it went from a language like Sanskrit to a language like French. We're still not sure just how this occurred – a breakdown in communication between the generations is my personal best guess – but it is a sociolinguistic problem for the future, that is, for you.

Although by training and inclination I am a linguist, that is all I am going to say about the linguistic reasons which make the study of Irish worthwhile. Others on this podium can speak better than I of the role of Irish in modern generative syntax and syntactic theory, or native Irish grammatical theory and Classical Modern Irish bardic poetry, to name a few of the most important 'frontiers' of Irish studies today.

In 1962 while a visiting professor at the Dublin Institute I wrote two lengthy articles published the following year in *Celtica* 6; one on the historical and comparative syntax and morphosyntax of the Old Irish verbal complex – thus belonging to linguistics – and one on historical and comparative metrics and versification in Early Irish – thus belonging to poetics. Together they prefigured the twofold program of my research and writings for the next half-century or so, a program which is still ongoing. Witness the two volumes of my *Selected Writings*, one subtitled *Language and Linguistics* and the other *Culture and Poetics*. And I'm not finished yet.

In the time remaining I would like to present a couple of case studies of the comparative approach to the study of poetic literature, by way of illustrating what makes the study of Irish worthwhile. These involve purely synchronic and typological comparison, be it noted, rather than the diachronic and genetic comparison presented in my *How to Kill a Dragon*. There will be not a whiff of Indo-European, save in the affiliation of most of the languages referred to.

Now creation myths, creation tales, and creation catalogues are widespread in the literatures, religions and cultures of the world, and probably approach universality. The first sentence of the foundation text of the Judaeo-Christian tradition is 'In the beginning God created the heaven and the earth', (Berešiθ bara' Elohim 'eθ hašamayim we'eθ ha'aretz).

Just as an aside: Semitic and several Indo-European traditions begin the creation catalogue with 'heaven and earth' (or 'earth and heaven'), but the Mayan creation catalogue of the K'iche' in the pre-Columbian epic *Popol Wuj* Time was created first, and only then Heaven and Earth. Small wonder that the Mayans invented writing in order to fix time and write dates.

Now an Old Iranian creation catalogue (YH 37.1) goes in translation:

> And so we worship now the Wise Lord (Ahura Mazda)
> who created the Cow and the Truth,
> created the waters and the good plants,
> created light and the earth
> and all good things.[2]

Another is woven into Zarathustra's interrogation of Ahura Mazda on the nature of things (the Gāθā *tat(θβā pərəsā* 'this I ask you') Yasna 44.3–5:

> Who is by begetting the primal father of Truth?
> Who created the path of the sun and the stars?
> Who held the earth below and the sky
> (to keep it) from falling?
> Who (created) the waters and the plants?
> What master created light and darkness?
> What master created sleep and waking?[3]

To these two Old North-Eastern Iranian examples, probably of the second millennium BC, should be added a third creation catalogue, from Old South-Western Iranian, a blessing which recurs prominently in several Old Persian inscriptions of King Darius (DNa1, DElvend1, etc.), ca. 600 BC, but unquestionably – in view of closely parallel phraseology, word order, and metrics in the Rig Veda, as I argue elsewhere – reflecting a verbal tradition centuries older, probably also of the second millennium BC. The text reads in translation:

> A great god is Ahuramazdā
> Who created this earth
> Who created yonder heaven
> Who created man
> Who created happiness for man.

We have in these few lines a worshipful and moving prayer of thanksgiving to the Iranian Wise Lord (Ahura-mazdā) of Creation. The prayer immediately calls for comparison with an Old Irish quatrain dated by Gerard Murphy to the ninth century, and entitled by him 'The Lord of Creation'. Here is Murphy's text and translation, with slight variants (*Early Irish Lyrics* 4) of the ninth-century Irish response to the same universal challenge of the creation catalogue:

> Adram in Coimdid
> cusnaib aicdib amraib,
> nem gelmár co n-ainglib
> ler tonnbán for talmain.[4]

Let us adore the Lord
with the wondrous works,
great bright heaven with its angels,
the white-waved sea on earth.

The poem is found only in two manuscripts of the *Mittelirische Verslehren*, the Middle Irish treatises on metrics, as an example of the meter called *breccbairdne* or 'speckled bardic verse'.[6] Murphy began the 'Introduction' to his *Early Irish Lyrics* with the famous sentence, 'Irish lyric poetry is unique in the Middle Ages in freshness of spirit and perfection of form'. This poem is an ideal illustration, and another part of what makes the study of Irish worthwhile.

In terms of the native Irish tradition it is described as ($5^2 6^2 6^2 6^2$), *rinnard* 'end-high' six syllable lines with the first shortened, and disyllabic riming finals bd *amraib* : *talmain* and disyllabic consonating finals ac *Coimdid* : *ainglib*, together with alliteration in b and d, *aicdib amraib* and *tonnbán for talmain*. Notice that no less than ten of the poem's twenty-three syllables are thus wholly or partially fixed. Small wonder that I contrasted as chapter headings in *How to Kill a Dragon* 'Greece and Vedic India and the art of the word' with 'Ireland and the art of the syllable'.

But there are also non-traditional, non-canonical features here that the modern student of poetics and poetic form must take account of. Such are the phonetic figure linking the consonants of *gel-* and *ainglib* in c, and above all the semantic antithesis of the critical words *nem* 'heaven' and *ler* 'sea', marked by the phonetic virtual identity of consonant and vowel of the opposing members, which form by Irish rules a perfect riming pair: the consonants belong to the same class. (Think of '*last* but not *least*' for a similar effect in English). We may add the grammatical figure in the three sequential dative plurals in line b *cusnaib aicdib amraib* (homoeoteleuton), and the striking compound adjectives in c and d, literally:

heaven *bright-great*
sea *wave-white*

But most arresting of all is the imbalance, in the context of Biblical creation, of the syntactically focused pair *heaven* (*nem*) and *sea* (*ler*), each with parallel epithets, which produces a poetic tension which is not resolved until the very last word of the quatrain, the prepositional phrase *on earth* (*for talmain*), as in the book of Genesis, the Old Persian creation hymn of King Darius, and for that matter the K'iche' Popol Wuj of Guatemala. Universal moments like that make the study of Irish worthwhile.

I conclude very briefly with another elemental vignette of comparative literature, one of universal appeal to poets and representational artists everywhere at a certain stage of cultural development, which belongs to the economic world of women.

The Western coastal regions of Anatolia, present-day Turkey, knew in classical antiquity a goddess called Maliya in Lycia in the southwest, and Malis in Greek sources in Lydia (Hipponax sixth century BC) and Lesbos (Sappho or Alcaeus seventh century BC). Of native Anatolian origin, Malis was syncretised with Athena by the Greeks, and specifically with Athena Erganē (Delphic Wargana), Athena the 'worker'. The work in question was the quintessential work of women, namely spinning. A line of a poet of the island of Lesbos, either Sappho or Alcaeus, is cited anonymously by a Byzantine writer on metrics:

Μᾶλις μὲν ἔννη λέπτον ἔχοισ᾽ ἐπ᾽ ἀτράκτωι λίνον
Malis was spinning with a slender thread on the spindle.

An ivory statuette of a spinning woman in Lydian headdress with distaff, spindle and slender thread was found in the temple of Artemis in Ephesus, ca. 600 BC, now in the Istanbul museum. She could be an illustration of the Greek line about Malis the spinner [see fig. 1].

Figure 1.

Ivory statuette from Istanbul Museum

Now the Irish response to this same universal topos is also known; it is in a very Celtic literary genre which by itself would make the study of Irish worthwhile. *The Triads of Ireland*:

> Trí cóil ata ferr fo-longat in mbith:
> cóil srithide hi foilderb,
> cóil foichne for tuinn,
> cóil snáithe tar dorn dagmná.[7]

> [Three slender things that best support the world:
> the slender stream of milk from the cow's dug into the pail,
> the slender blade of green corn upon the ground,
> the slender thread over the hand of a skilled woman].

I beg your indulgence to conclude once again as I did in 1963, without prejudice, with the words of J.B. Bury in his *Life of St. Patrick*:

> But the absence of such civilising influences [as Rome] protected and preserved the native traditions, and the curiosity of those who study the development of the human mind may be glad that Ireland lay safe and undisturbed at the end of the world ...[8]

Notes

1 D.A. Binchy, 'Irish History and Irish Law: II', *Studia Hibernica* (1976), No. 6, pp. 9–10.

2 Yasna Haptaŋhāiti, 37, 1, *The Gāthās of Zarathushtra and the Other Old Avestan Texts*, Part 1, ed. Helmut Humbach in collaboration with Josef Elfenbein and Prods O. Skjærvø (Heidelberg: Carl Winter, 1991), p. 146.

3 Yasna Haptaŋhāiti, 44, 3–5, *Ibid.*, pp. 147–8.

4 Gerald Murphy, *Early Irish Lyrics: Eighth to Twelfth Century* (Dublin: Four Courts Press, 1998), p. 4.

5 *Mitterlirische Verslehren*, ed. R. Thurneysen, *Irish Texte*, ed. W.H. Stokes and E. Windisch (Leipzig: Verlag Von S. Hirzel, 1891), Vol. 3, Text II, p. 43, line 54 [B].

6 Gerald Murphy, *Early Irish Metrics* (Dublin: Royal Irish Academy, 1961), Section 59, p. 64.

7 Kuno Meyer, *The Triads of Ireland: Royal Irish Academy Todd Series of Lectures*, Vol. XIII (Dublin: Hodges and Figgis, 1906), p. 75.

8 J.B. Bury, *Life of St Patrick and his Place in History* (London: Macmillan, 1905), p. 58.

Professor Tomás Ó Cathasaigh

Myth and Saga:
'The Wooing of Étaín'

Tomás Ó Cathasaigh
Harvard University

Irish has a long history, stretching from the *ogam* inscriptions of the fifth century up to the present day. In a colloquium devoted to the study of Irish, Modern Irish language and literature may well be accorded pride of place. But Early Irish also offers a very rewarding field of study, as Calvert Watkins shows in his contribution to this volume. What I want to do is to say a little about the splendid heritage of myth and saga that survives in Irish, and specifically in Early Irish, which can be taken in this context to include Old and Middle Irish, the language respectively of 600–900 and 900–1200. I should point out that we also have some accomplished tales from the later period – *Tóraíocht Dhiarmada agus Ghráinne* 'The Pursuit of Diarmaid and Gráinne'[1] may be mentioned as an especially fine specimen – but for the most part it is the tales of the Early Irish period that appeal to us today. Much of what I have to say in what follows will focus on *Tochmarc Étaíne*, 'The Wooing of Étaín',[2] a trilogy of tales that tell how the god Midir sought and, after many vicissitudes, ultimately won the hand of Étaín. This is one of the most remarkable works of Irish storytelling, and it is my hope that readers will be inspired to look at it for themselves, and also seek out some of the other tales that have come down to us in the manuscripts.

Early Irish narrative literature was one of the products of a powerful intellectual and artistic elite that combined the energy and resources of ecclesiastical scholars, authors and artists with those of traditional Irish-language poets, jurists and storytellers. The accommodation of the clerical and native learned classes in Ireland was made possible by the circumstances in which the country was converted to

Christianity. Early in the fifth century – in the year 431, to be precise – Pope Celestine sent a bishop to the Irish 'who believed in Christ'. The fact that there were Christians in Ireland at that time indicates that there was some degree of Latin literacy in the country. As Ireland never became part of the Empire, the Churchmen had to come to terms with a political structure and an intellectual tradition that were very different from those of Rome. At a very early stage, the clerics began to use and write the vernacular, and it was not long before they took an active interest in the native storytelling tradition. The earliest surviving tales date from the seventh century, and they must have been written – and in some sense composed – in ecclesiastical settings. On comparative grounds, the content of many of these tales can be shown to be indebted to an oral tradition stretching back to the Common Celtic era, and even beyond it, to that of Proto-Indo-European. The manuscripts do not name the authors of these tales, but we must be thankful to them for what they have given us. The narrative literature is extensive, and inevitably somewhat variable in quality. At its best, it is robust, vibrant and exuberant. It can also be subtle and ingenious in its use of language, and very rich in its thematic content.

It has become conventional in modern times to classify the material in cycles. The so-called Mythological Cycle – which I prefer to call the Cycles of the Gods and Goddesses – recounts the adventures of the *Túatha Dé*, 'The Peoples of the God(s) / Goddess(es)', also known as *Túatha Dé Danann*, 'The Peoples of the Goddess Danu'. These adventures have to do with the relations of the *Túatha Dé* among themselves, with other divinities or quasi-divinities such as the Fomoiri or Fomoreans, and even on occasion with the human inhabitants of Ireland.

The Ulster Cycle has to do with the martial activities of a warrior aristocracy centred at the court of king Conchobor at Emain Macha (Navan Fort in County Armagh), and subsisting in a state of endemic warfare with the *Connachta*, ruled by Ailill, with more than a little help from his wife

Medb, and centred at Crúachu (Rathcroghan in County Roscommon). The great hero of this cycle is Cú Chulainn, and its centerpiece is *Táin Bó Cúailnge* ('The Cattle-Raid of Cooley')[3] in which the hero defends the province of Ulster against the invading forces of Ailill and Medb at a time when the adult warriors of Ulster are stricken with a debility that puts them out of action for three months. The army mustered by Ailill and Medb is described as 'the men of Ireland': it includes battalions from Munster and Leinster beside those from Connacht, and for good measure includes a number of formidable Ulstermen who have gone into exile following an unforgivable violation of their personal honour by king Conchobor.

The Ossianic or Fenian Cycle also celebrates the heroic deeds of fighting men, but they are quite different from the warriors of the Ulster Cycle. In the Ossianic Cycle, Finn mac Cumaill presides over a *fían* or band of warriors that is available for hire and lies outside the bounds of society. In early tales of the cycle, Finn confronts and defeats an otherworld adversary. He acquires wisdom, and becomes a poet. He is a warrior, a hunter and a seer, and comprehends within himself the competencies required for the functioning of society. Cú Chulainn and the other Ulster warriors are 'heroes of the tribe'; the *fían*-warriors are outside the tribe, and frequently at odds with it.

The Cycles of the Kings recount the adventures of various Irish kings. There are some very fine short sagas among them, but the greatest of them is *Togail Bruidne Da Derga* ('The Destruction of Da Derga's Hostel')[4] which tells the tragic tale of Conaire the Great, whose reign as king of Tara ushered in a Golden Age of peace and prosperity in Ireland, but who was ultimately hounded to an ignominious death in the 'hostel' or *bruiden* of the red god called Da Derga.

An older system of classification was based on the titles of the tales. Some of them have to do with major events in the life of an individual, such as *comperta* ('conceptions'), *aitheda* ('elopements'), *tochmarca* ('wooings'), *echtrai* ('expeditions [to the Otherworld]'), *immrama* 'sea-voyages', and *aitte/aideda* ('violent deaths'). Others relate momentous or cataclysmic events in the social and political history of population groups, such as *catha* ('battles'), *tomadmann* ('eruptions [of lakes or rivers]'), *tochomlada* ('migrations'), *oircne* ('slaughters, destructions'), *togla* ('destructions'), and *tána bó* ('cattle raids').

These tales give us access to imagined worlds that are full of danger and of opportunity, and where wonderful things can and do happen. One characteristic of the material that I should like to mention here, however, is that very often the tales give expression in narrative form to a view of the world, and of humankind's place in it, that also informs the laws and the wisdom texts. One of the great tales in the Cycles of the Gods is *Cath Maige Tuired*[5] ('The Battle of Mag Tuired'), which depicts the epic defence of Ireland by the god Lug against an invading army led by Bres son of Elatha, who had been king of Ireland but was deposed by the Túatha Dé Danann when he proved himself unworthy to hold the office. The tale lingers at length on the ill-fated rule of Bres, and in its depiction of Lug and Bres provides us respectively with positive and negative paradigms of kingship. Its description of early Irish kingship as a contract between king and people is wholly consistent with what we find in the early Irish laws. Its exploration of various aspects of the relationship between a man and his kindred is similarly on all fours with what we find in other Early Irish sources.

Cath Maige Tuired is in many respects our most important mythological text. Yet, as Gerard Murphy has said:

the otherworld atmosphere which gives its special beauty to (the Mythological) cycle is [...] better illustrated in other tales, such as the ninth-century *Tochmarc Étaíne* or 'Wooing of Étaín', which tells how Étaín, wooed and won by Midir in the otherworld, was transformed into a brilliantly coloured fly by her rival Fúamnach, who blew her into this world, where, swallowed in a drink by an Ulster queen, she was reborn as a human. Wooed once more in human shape by the king of Tara, she was ultimately won back to the otherworld by Midir as the result of a rash stake made by the king in a game of fidchell.[6]

What I would like to do in the space that remains to me is to introduce you to Tochmarc Étaíne, which has rightly been called 'the most extraordinary of all early Irish "wooings"'.[7]

In the first of the three tales in Tochmarc Étaíne, Midir wins the hand of Étaín with the assistance of his foster-son Óengus, but his scorned earlier wife Fuamnach soon deprives Midir of his new bride. These early adventures take place in the Otherworld, which in Irish tradition mainly comprised a number of síde or hollow hills dotted around Ireland. These include the síd at Bruig na Bóinne, Newgrange in the necropolis at the bend of the River Boyne in County Meath, where Óengus presides; Midir's dwelling at Brí Léith in Tethba (west of Ardagh in County Longford); and Mag nInis in south-east County Down, around Downpatrick in Ulster, the home of Étaín's father, Ailill (and also, it would seem, of none other than Bres, son of Elatha, who plays such an inglorious part in Cath Maige Tuired). When Fuamnach blows the fly into Ireland, she lands in a house in Ulster and falls into the cup of the (unnamed) wife of a warrior named Étar. Étar's wife swallows the fly, which is then conceived in her womb and is born as Étaín, daughter of Étar. And 'it was a thousand and twelve years from the first begetting of Étaín by Ailill until her last begetting by Étar' (TE1 §21). In the second tale, Echaid Airem, king of Ireland, takes Étaín as his wife. The king's brother Ailill falls in love with Étaín, and becomes dangerously ill. In order to cure Ailill of his love sickness, she agrees to sleep with him, but the person she actually meets in Ailill's guise is Midir. When Midir reveals his true identity to her and invites her to go away with him, she declines, but says that she would willingly do so if bidden by Echaid. In the third part, Midir again presses his suit upon Étaín, and she says that she will go only if Midir obtains her from her husband. When Midir wins the game of fidchell, Echaid is obliged to allow him to embrace and kiss Étaín. Echaid refuses to sell Étaín to Midir, but he permits him to embrace her, and when Midir does so he bears her up and out through the skylight of Echaid's heavily fortified dwelling at Tara, and the couple fly in the form of two swans to an Otherworld dwelling in Munster.

Midir's great and abiding love for Étaín is the over-arching subject of *Tochmarc Étaíne*. The gods have magical powers, and enchantment is an important component in the saga. Yet Midir's wooing of Étain unfolds as a series of transactions – of promises, pledges, purchases, wagers and so on. The exercise of magical power is in great measure subject to legal or quasi-legal constraints. These considerations are established in the opening episodes of the saga, which have to do with the conception and birth of Midir's foster-son Óengus, the assumption by Óengus of the Lordship of Bruig na Bóinne, and the circumstances which led to Óengus's involvement in the initial wooing of Étaín.

Tochmarc Étaíne begins with the primeval mating of the Dagdae, king of the Túatha Dé (Danann), and Boann, eponymous goddess of the river Boyne; and the conception and birth of their son Óengus. The opening lines have to do with power:

> There was a famous king of Ireland of the race of the Túatha Dé, Eochaid Ollathair was his name. He was also named the Dagda [i.e. good god], for it was he that used to work wonders for them and control the weather and the crops. Wherefore men said he was called the Dagda (TE1 §1).

The Dagdae wants to make love to Boann, but she is married to Elcmar who is lord of Bruig na Boinne [literally, 'the land of (the river) Boann'], and although she would happily yield to the Dagdae's suit, she fears her husband's great power (*cumachtae*). The Dagdae sends Elcmar away on an errand, and works great spells (*tincheadla mora*) on him. Elcmar declares his intention of returning before nightfall (literally, 'between day and night'), but the Dagdae ensures that nine months go by in what seems to Elcmar no more than one day. In the meantime the Dagdae has slept with Boann, and she has borne him a son, Óengus. He is known also as In

Mac Óc [the Young Son] 'for his mother said: "Young is the son who was begotten at the break of day and born betwixt it and evening"' (TE1 §2). When Elcmar returns Boann is her old self, and Elcmar remains unaware of her sexual adventure with the Dagdae.

Óengus is sent into fosterage with Midir at Brí Léith. Since Midir brings him up as his own son, Óengus is completely unaware of his biological parentage until he is taunted one day on the playing field by what we would call the captain of the opposing team, and who describes Óengus as 'a hireling whose father and mother are unknown' (TE1 §4). Following this incident, Midir tells Óengus who his parents are, whereupon Óengus demands to be taken to his father to try to get him to acknowledge Óengus as his son. Midir takes the boy to Uisnech in the centre of Ireland, where the Dagdae resides and where he is holding court. Midir speaks for Óengus, saying that the boy wishes to be acknowledged by his father and for land to be given him. The Dagdae readily acknowledges his son: *Is mac dam* 'He is my son' (TE1 §5). But he says that Bruig na Bóinne, the land that he wishes to bestow upon Óengus, is not yet available, for it is in the possession of Elcmar, and the Dagdae does not wish to annoy him further. Midir presses the Dagdae to give him advice for Óengus, and the Dagdae proposes a course of action that entails taking what, on the face of it at least, seems rather an unfair advantage of a lack of vigilance on Elcmar's part. The Dagdae's advice is that Óengus should approach Elcmar in Bruig na Bóinne at *Samain* (November 1). That, we are told, 'is a day of peace and amity among the men of Ireland, on which none is at enmity with his fellow' (TE1 §6). Elcmar will therefore be unarmed, and Óengus is to threaten to kill him, promising to spare him, however, if Elcmar grants him what he demands. What Óengus is to demand is that he be king for a day and a night in Bruig na Bóinne. When Elcmar comes to reclaim the land Óengus is not to return it: he is to say that the land is now his in perpetuity, for he has been given the kingship for a day and a night, and 'it is in days and nights that the world is spent' (TE1 §6). He is to insist that the matter be submitted to the Dagdae for his adjudication.

Óengus follows the Dagdae's advice to the letter. In the face of great threats from Elcmar when he comes to reclaim the land, Óengus declines to give it up until the matter is put to the Dagdae for his adjudication in the presence of the men of Ireland. The Dagdae finds in favour of Óengus, and in addressing Elcmar he adds the detail that Elcmar gave his land for mercy shown him, for his life was dearer to him than his land. He sweetens the pill, however, by promising him land that will be no less profitable to him than Bruig na Bóinne:

> 'Where is that?' said Elcmar. 'Cleitech', said the Dagda, 'with the three lands that are round about it, thy youths playing before thee every day in the Brug, and thou shalt enjoy the fruits of the Boyne from this land' 'It is well', said Elcmar, 'so shall it be accomplished' (TE1 §8).

Elcmar goes to Cleitech and builds a stronghold there, and Óengus remains in the Bruig.

Midir comes to visit Óengus a year later, and in the course of an incident one of his eyes is knocked out. This blemish will prevent him from returning to the land of which he is king, but Óengus arranges for the god of medicine to heal the eye. Óengus then invites him to remain at Bruig na Bóinne for a year. Midir will do so only if he is paid for it. The payment (*lóg*) that he demands comprises a worthy chariot, a suitable cloak and 'the fairest maiden in Ireland' (TE1 §8). Óengus has no problem with the chariot and the cloak, but he wonders who this maiden is that according to Midir 'surpasses all the maidens in Ireland in form'. Midir lets him know:

> 'She is in Ulster', said Midir, 'Ailill's daughter Étaín Echraide, daughter of the king of the north-eastern part of Ireland. She is the dearest and gentlest and loveliest in Ireland' (TE1 §11)

And so Óengus sets out to seek her hand from Ailill at Mag nInis.

I have dwelt at some length on these episodes because they introduce certain themes that are taken up and developed in various ways in the course of the trilogy. There is the matter of magic power, which we are told both the Dagdae and Elcmar possess, though only the former is seen to exercise it here. We may note in passing the contrast between the Dagdae's opportunistic sexual desire for Boann, and Midir's overweening love for Étaín. The taking of the Bruig is cast in legal terms: the Dagdae, as the text has it, 'adjudged each man's contract in accordance with his undertaking' (*Concertasidhe cor caich amal a indell*, TE1 §8). The question of time is all-important in *Tochmarc Étaíne*: for Elcmar, nine months are spent in what seems to be one day; Óengus is conceived at the break of day, and born between the end of the day and the beginning of the night; all time (we are told) is spent in days and nights. In the second tale, the simple matter of one day following another is used by Étaín to console her husband's distraught brother. The difference between appearance and reality, which we see in Elcmar's perception of the passing of time, is at the very heart of the second tale, and has a crucial bearing on the aftermath of Midir's wooing of Étaín in the third. It is related in both of them to the question of identity, something that also arises in the case of the young Óengus. Land is a matter of great concern in this tale: the inheritance and possession of it, the ruling of it, and, most fundamentally, the very shaping of it.

Let us return now to the price that Midir has demanded for remaining as Óengus's guest at Bruig na Bóinne. Óengus offers to buy Étaín from her father Ailill, who in turn exacts a heavy price. He requires Óengus to clear twelve plains and to drain the land by making twelve rivers flow from it to the sea. It is the Dagdae who accomplishes these tasks for Óengus. Since their accomplishment is for the general good, Ailill then demands for himself Étaín's weight in gold and silver. When the price has been paid, Óengus returned to Bruig na Bóinne. Étaín sleeps with Midir that night, and on the next morning a mantle befitting him and a chariot were given to him. He is pleased with his foster-son and stays with him in the Bruig for a full year.

The mention together here of chariot, cloak and wife is not to be taken as mere zeugma. The bestowing of a chariot and a cloak upon a man is part of the ritual of making a king. We see this in the scene depicting the election of the king of Tara in *Togail Bruidne Da Derga*: the lesser kings see the young Conaire approaching them in a manner that has been prophesied, and they put upon him the clothing of a king and place him in a chariot (*do-bertatar étach ríg dó imbi 7 da-bertatar i carpat*).[8] As for the fairest maiden in Ireland, there are clear indications, as T. F. O'Rahilly noted, that Étaín is the goddess of sovereignty.[9] To be married to Étaín, therefore, is to be king. We recall that when Midir is blinded he laments that he cannot return to the land of which he is king. The allusion here is to the requirement that an Irish king must be without physical blemish: Midir has become ineligible to retain sovereignty. Óengus not only ensures that his sight is restored, but he enhances Midir's sovereignty by winning for him the hand of Étaín and presenting him with the trappings of kingship in the form of a chariot and cloak.

When his year at Bruig na Bóinne is up, Midir returns with Étaín to his own land at Brí Léith. As they set out, Óengus warns Midir to beware of the dreadful, cunning woman who awaits him. The woman in question is Midir's wife Fuamnach who had been reared by a druid, Bresal, and 'was wise and prudent and skilled in the knowledge and magic power of the Túatha Dé Danann' (TE1 §15). She is evidently free to exercise her magical power (*cumachtae*), because, as Óengus warns Midir, she has Oengus's 'word and warranty before the Túatha Dé Danann' (TE1 §15). When Midir returns home with his new wife, Fuamnach welcomes them, but it is not long before she strikes Étaín with a wand, so that she turns into a pool of water. Fuamnach returns to her foster-father, Bresal, and Midir leaves the house to the water into which Étaín has turned. Midir is now without a wife. But then another transformation occurs:

The heat of the fire and the air and the seething of the ground aided the water so that the pool that was in the middle of the house turned into a worm, and after that the worm became a purple fly. It was as big as a man's head, the comeliest in the land. Sweeter than the pipes and harps and horns was the sound of her voice and the hum of her wings. Her eyes would shine like precious stones in the dark. The fragrance and the bloom of her would turn away hunger and thirst from any one around whom she would go. The spray of the drops she shed from her wings would cure all sickness and disease and plague in any one round whom she would go. She used to attend Midir and go round about his land with him, as he went. To listen to her and gaze upon her would nourish hosts in gatherings and assemblies in camps. Midir knew that it was Étaín that was in that shape, and so long as that fly was attending upon him, he never took to himself a wife, and the sight of her would nourish him. He would fall asleep with her humming, and whenever any one approached who did not love him, she would awaken him (TE1 § 17).

Here the cosmic forces that transform the pool of water into a magic fly trump the malevolent power wielded by Fuamnach. The cosmos, as traditionally envisaged by the Irish, is tripartite, its three components being *nem, talam, muir* 'heaven, ground and sea', or more precisely the heavens, the surface of the earth, and the underneath (whether marine or subsurface).[10] These three components, in the shape of the heat of the fire and the air, and the seething of the earth and the water, combine to liberate Étaín from her inanimate entrapment. Her beneficent effect as she accompanies Midir around his territory, dispelling hunger and thirst and curing the sick, reminds us of the doctrine that is expounded in the wisdom literature and reflected in both the Laws and the sagas, that the king who was wise and just brought about the physical well being of his people.

The love and contentment that Étaín, in the shape of a fly, has brought to Midir and his people are not destined to last. Fuamnach visits Midir, bringing with her as sureties Lug, the Dagdae and Ogmae, here described as the three Gods of

Danu (Dé Danann). They now have the right and duty to protect Fuamnach, a role that had earlier been assumed by Óengus. Fuamnach has brought powerful incantations from Bresal and she uses her power to stir up a magical wind that drives the fly into the air where she moves around for seven years until she alights on the breast of Óengus at Bruig na Bóinne. Óengus cares for her so that her good spirits return to her. But Fuamnach uses a ruse to have Óengus removed from the scene and she once more used her powers to blow Étaín away, this time sending her to the house of Étar in Ulster.

Fuamnach oversteps the mark on this occasion. At Bruig na Bóinne, Étaín is under Óengus's protection, and in assailing her there, Fuamnach violates Óengus's honour. Her powerful sureties will be of no avail to her now. Óengus follows her traces to Bresal's house, and he cuts off her head and brings it with him to Bruig na Bóinne.

Myles Dillon said of *Tochmarc Étaíne* that 'there is a strange beauty there which perhaps no other Irish story shares'.[11] We can see something of that in the first story; it is amplified in the other two, which I cannot discuss in detail here. Dillon went on the say: 'The temper of love is there and the power of magic – this is a pure fairytale – and a happy ending'.[12] To say that *Tochmarc Étaíne* is a pure fairytale, however, is to do less than justice to the thematic content of the tale. And it has a happy ending only in a limited sense. It is true that Midir is reunited with Étaín at the end, but there is trouble in store for the people of Ireland. For Echaid is not content to let matters rest when Midir has taken Étaín away from him. He sets out with his men to recover Étaín, and they are determined to dig up every *síd* in Ireland until they find her. When they assail the *síd* of Brí Léith, Midir appears before them. He rebukes Echaid, but promises to return Étaín. The next morning fifty women appear at Tara all like Étaín in form and dress. Echaid chooses one of them and the rest depart. The men of Ireland are well satisfied with what Echaid has done to rescue the woman from the beings of the *síde*. Some time later, however, Midir appears to Echaid and tells him that his wife was pregnant when Midir took her from him, and that she bore a daughter, and it is the daughter that Echaid now has as his wife. To make matters worse, Echaid's daughter is pregnant by him, and she bears him a daughter. Echaid decrees that his incestuous child be thrown into a pit of wild beasts. But his men leave her instead in a kennel at the house of the herdsman of Tara. The herdsman and his wife rescue the girl and bring her up in secret. Eterscél – the king of Tara – hears about her, and he takes her away by force; she remains with him thereafter as his wife. She was the mother of Conaire, son of Eterscél, also known as Conaire Mór: the story of his tragic downfall is told, as we have seen, in *Togail Bruidne Da Derga*. In that text Conaire is described as 'the king whom phantoms banished'.[13] Elsewhere it is said that because Conaire was descended (through his mother) from Echaid 'he was killed for Echaid's crimes, for it is the beings from the *síd* of Brí Léith who mustered (for) the slaying (of Conaire) because their *síd* had been broken up by Echaid as he sought Étaín'.[14] Conaire, and the people of Ireland, were to pay a heavy price for Echaid's harrowing of Midir's Otherworld abode.

Of the two great works in the Cycles of the Gods and Goddesses, *Cath Maige Tuired* has to do with the relations of the gods among themselves and with other divine or quasi-divine personages, whereas *Tochmarc Étaíne* concerns itself with both the relations of the gods among themselves and their dealings with the human inhabitants of Ireland. The relationship between god and man, between the denizens of the *síde* and the men and women living on the surface of Ireland, is a central and abiding feature of Irish saga, and it is explored in a variety of ways in each of the cycles. The major tale-types are also shared among the cycles. I have noted above that some of the tale-types have to do with major events in the life of an individual, and that others relate momentous or cataclysmic events in the social and political history of population groups. *Tochmarc Étaíne* fits both descriptions. Midir's wooing of Étaín is clearly the most significant event – or rather sequence of events – in his life, and in hers. But we are also presented here with cosmogonic myth: the tasks laid upon Óengus in the first tale, and performed by the Dagdae, entail the clearing of the plains and the drawing out of the rivers of Ulster; those laid directly upon Midir in the third tale have to do with the formation of the midlands of Ireland.

Notes

1   Nessa Ní Shéaghdha, ed. *Tóruigheacht Dhiarmada agus Ghráinne: The Pursuit of Diarmaid and Gráinne*, Irish Texts Society, Vol. 48 (Dublin: Educational Company, 1967).

2   Osborn Bergin and R. I. Best, eds. 'Tochmarc Étaíne', *Ériu* 12 (1934–38), pp. 137–96. See also Jeffrey Gantz, *Early Irish Myths and Sagas* (Harmondsworth: Penguin Books, 1981), pp. 37–59. Quotations here (text and translation) are from Bergin and Best. TE1 refers to the first of the three tales, and reference is to the numbered sections in Bergin and Best.

3   Cecile O'Rahilly, ed. *Táin Bó Cúailnge: Recension 1* (Dublin: Dublin Institute for Advanced Studies, 1976); Cecile O'Rahilly, *Táin Bó Cúailnge from the Book of Leinster* (Dublin: Dublin Institute for Advanced Studies, 1967). See also Thomas Kinsella, *The Táin* (Oxford: Oxford University Press, 1969).

4   Eleanor Knott, ed. *Togail Bruidne Da Derga* (Dublin: The Stationery Office, 1936); See also Gantz, *Myths and Sagas*, pp. 60–106.

5   Elizabeth A. Grey, ed. *Cath Maige Tuired: The Second Battle of Mag Tuired* (London: Irish Texts Society, 1982).

6   Eleanor Knott and Gerard Murphy, *Early Irish Literature* (London: Routledge and Kegan Paul, 1966), pp. 112–13.

7   Alwyn Rees and Brinley Rees, *Celtic Heritage: Ancient Tradition in Ireland and Wales* (London: Thames and Hudson, 1961), p. 271.

8   Knott, *Togail Bruidne Da Derga*, lines 157–58.

9   Thomas Francis O'Rahilly, 'On the Origins of the Names *Érainn* and *Ériu*', *Ériu* XIV (1943), p. 16. See also Thomas Charles-Edwards, '*Tochmarc Étaíne*: A Literal Interpretation', in Michael Richter and Jean-Michel Picard, eds. *Ogma: Essays in Celtic*

Studies in Honour of Próinséas Ní Chatháin (Dublin: Four Courts Press, 2002), pp. 172–73.

10 William Sayers, '"Mani Maidi an New …": Ringing Changes on a Cosmic Motif', *Ériu*, Vol. 37 (1986), pp. 99–117. See also Liam Mac Mathúna, 'Irish Perceptions of the Cosmos', *Celtica* Vol. 23 (1999), pp. 174–87.

11 Myles Dillon, *Early Irish Literature* (Chicago: University of Chicago Press, 1948), p. 51.

12 Dillon, *Early Irish Literature*, p. 51.

13 Knott, *Togail Bruidne Da Derga*, line 250.

14 Tomás Ó Cathasaigh, 'On the *Cín Dromma Snechta* Version of *Togail Bruidne Uí Dergae*', *Ériu* Vol. 41 (1990), p. 107.

Professor James McCloskey

IRISH AS A WORLD LANGUAGE

James McCloskey
University of California, Santa Cruz

I would like to consider some aspects of the current situation of the Irish language and some aspects of its recent history. In particular, I would like to think about that situation, and about the history that has shaped it in recent times, in fairly broad context – that is, in the light of certain worldwide shifts and trends.

I always feel more than a slight embarrassment when embarking on this kind of discussion – an uncomfortable sense of pretending to a kind of expertise that I do not in fact have. I know something about the language situation in Ireland, but there are others who know much more. I am a linguist by profession, but the work I do is mostly in theoretical syntax (in the Chomskyan mode) and I have no particular expertise, beyond what almost any linguist would have, in the area of language-maintenance or language-loss. So what I have to say on these matters, as far as most linguists are concerned, consists in the main of banalities.

For all that, though, what I am in a position to do, and what I have been trying to do in recent years, is to bring together two streams of knowledge and observation – one from Ireland, the other from linguistics. To the extent that this is a useful thing to do it is because these two streams of thought and commentary have not much met or much influenced each other. On the one hand, a lot of what I read in the linguistics literature about the language situation in Ireland strikes me as being wrong or incomplete in important ways. On the other, debates about the language situation in Ireland seem to me to have been extraordinarily parochial and insular – conducted largely in ignorance of, or in inattention to, the larger context in which they should most naturally and usefully be framed.

My goal here, then, as it has been in a number of such discussions in recent years, will be first to try to think about the situation of Ireland and Irish in a way that is shaped by knowledge of the larger context, and then reciprocally to bring back to that larger debate whatever there is to be learned from the Irish experience. There is something to be learned, I think, in both directions.

When I speak here of a 'larger context' for the discussion of the language situation in Ireland, the framework that I have in mind, of course, is that of global language extinction. There is less need now than there would have been even five years ago to spell out here what the facts are. Within the profession, the alarm bells were first rung in an article published in 1991 in *Language*, the journal of the Linguistic Society of America.[1] In the years that have gone by since that paper appeared, there has been considerable debate within the profession about what the causes of these changes are, and about what the response (in professional and ethical terms) ought to be. About the facts themselves, however, there has been no argument, and there has been no challenge that I am aware of to the original bleak assessment made by Hale, Krauss and their colleagues in the 1991 paper. In more recent years, the facts have also become widely known, in outline at least, in the wider world beyond technical linguistics.

Nobody knows exactly how many distinct languages are spoken in the world today. That is in part because there are still corners of the world about which we in the West know little. In part it is because the term itself, the term *language,* is fundamentally obscure. Do we count all forms of Chinese as 'one language'? Do we include Haitian creole as a kind of 'French' or do we count it as a separate language? On what basis do we say that the modes of speech of working-class Glaswegians and of Shetland farmers count as kinds of 'English' (whatever that is), but that Tok Pisin (the official language of New Guinea) does not? There are no facts-of-the-matter here, no definitive answers to such questions.

This conceptual unclarity is interesting and important; difficult questions lurk within it. But there are also certain facts about which there is neither unclarity nor doubt.

The first such fact is that, no matter how you count or categorize them, there are many fewer distinct varieties of human language now than there used to be. This is true whether one counts national languages or local dialects. Recent studies in the United States and in the Netherlands, among many others, confirm that the same socio-political forces which are driving independent 'languages' to extinction are doing exactly the same to local varieties of apparently strong national languages.[2]

The second important fact is that the speed with which languages are now being lost is prodigious – the world is losing varieties of speech and writing at a rate never before seen in human history. Put another way: the web of linguistic diversity that has been a steady feature of human life for tens of thousands of years is unravelling very quickly indeed. Not everyone reacts to these facts in the same way. Some welcome them. Many are appalled by them, and there are others who think one should just look on with Zen-like calm as these processes work themselves out. Whatever view one takes, though, it is surely true that this shift represents a profound change in the way that human beings organize their lives and their interactions with each other and it is one which needs to be taken account of and understood. Taking account of it in a serious way tends to change the way that one thinks about the situation of Irish.

So let me organize what I have to say around the effort to answer a linked pair of questions, with this larger frame of reference firmly in place at every point:

1   What is there to learn from the Irish experience about global language endangerment and how one might respond to it?

2   What is there to learn in Ireland from thinking about the Irish experience and the Irish situation in this global context – the context of rapid language extinction?

The first of these questions is particularly important, for the following reason.

The effort to resist the tide of language-extinction began in Ireland in the late nineteenth century and was enshrined as official national policy at the time of partial independence in 1922. For a century or so now, that effort has been working itself out in various domains and in various efforts, official and unofficial. That means that we have in the case of Irish what is surely the oldest and most sustained attempt so far to organize consciously and systematically against the threatened extinction of a language. That being so, we would like to assess rationally and carefully what has been achieved in that effort, so that we might better assess what it is possible in principle to do if a community decides to work against the death of one of its languages – what works, what does not work, what is difficult but achievable. There now exists in Ireland a deep well of knowledge and experience about such questions. However, the idea that that well of knowledge and experience might be drawn on in other contexts and in other places – that it might be, as it were, an exportable asset – is not one that figures much in discussion of language issues in Ireland.

But that well of knowledge is all the more important today. If Irish people were among the earliest to have to face into this kind of task, or to choose to face into it, they have been joined in the intervening years by hundreds and thousands of other communities across the globe – communities in which local languages are being driven into disuse by a combination of external and internal pressures.

In discussions of these matters, the situation of Irish is often compared with that of other languages – with Hebrew, with Czech, with Lithuanian (or more recently with Catalan). All of there languages have indeed been the focus of more or less systematic efforts to re-shape them and to introduce or re-introduce them into domains of use from which they had previously been excluded. Needless to say, in the Irish context the comparisons when made are always invidious, and the tone is almost always one of self-recrimination (why can't we manage what the Israelis and the Czechs have managed?)

All of these languages have their own stories and their own lessons to teach. However, for the most perilous cases of language-loss and language-endangerment around the world at present, it is clear that Irish is a closer and more useful model than any of these other languages. By that I mean that the point to which Irish had been reduced by the second half of the nineteenth century (in the eyes and in the hearts of its own speakers) is very close indeed to the point to which Maori has now been reduced in New Zealand, or to which Ojibwe has been reduced in North America, or to which Inuit has been reduced in Labrador. The census of 1891 reveals that the number of people recorded as being able to speak Irish had been reduced at that point to about 680,000 – some 14.4% of the overall population. A far more telling statistic from the same census, however, is that Irish-speakers under the age of ten represented in that year no more than 3.5% of their age-group. That arithmetical gap, representing the decision of the vast majority of Irish-speakers not to pass the language on to their children, is the mark of a community which, by way of one mechanism or another, has been brought to feel that its language is a burden to be thrown off, rather than a tool which will serve useful purposes. And it is when large numbers of language communities are brought to that same point that we get the phenomenon of widespread language extinction.

The challenges that must be faced by communities which reach that point are chillingly similar to those that have been faced by Irish-speaking communities over the last 150 years. The urge is strong to yield to the external and internal pressures and to be free of the weary burden of seeming and feeling different. That urge often presents itself in the clothes of modernity and in the guise of rational and unsentimental self-interest. As the shift works its way through the various layers and strands of the community, the choices that have to be somehow made are difficult and painful ones – What will be the language of instruction in our schools? What will be the language of religious observance? How much pressure should we bring to bear on our young people to make sure that they learn 'our' language? Is it legitimate to apply such pressure, and do we do harm to our children in applying it? How will they respond? Is there agreement on what the first person plural pronoun refers to in the first place? These are questions that people and communities in Ireland are all too familiar with.

My own experience is that many of those around the world who are grappling with such questions and problems in their own communities are very aware of what has happened in Ireland (in broad outline if not in detail) and that they look to Ireland for guidance and for models. And that is a very natural thing, given the length and depth of the Irish experience in these matters (a century and a quarter now).

For these kinds of reasons, the question of what can be learned from the Irish experience is an important one. There should be something to learn from that experience about what can, in principle, be achieved if one decides to try to work against the tide of language-extinction. Accepting that the question is a reasonable one, the task then becomes to assess – as rationally and as realistically as possible – the history of language maintenance and revival efforts in Ireland. This should not be such a difficult thing to achieve, given the large quantity of evidence easily available. In practice, however, rational assessment is rare. Discussions of language policy in Ireland are, in the first place, insular and parochial (and therefore uninformed) and, in the second place, clouded by a corrosive mist of cynicism, apathy, and anger – a mist which seeps into just about every corner of the discussion, clouding judgement and making rational assessment difficult and rare.

This negativity emerges in at least two forms – in the almost universal consensus that the 'revival movement' is a failure and in the irrational anger that that consensus then gives rise to. One of the most curious and most revealing features of this strange consensus is the way in which it is shared and mirrored across 'both sides' of the language debate – by those who are active in the language movement (such as it is) and by those who strongly oppose it. The anger and polemic found in the writings of Máirtín Ó Cadhain often seem to me to shadow and reflect the anger and polemic found in the writings of a critic of language policies such as the newspaper columnist Kevin Myers. What the two share is a deep sense that official efforts to support Irish have been hypocritical and ineffective, the sense that those efforts have clearly failed, and a kind of fury that these obvious facts are not publicly recognized and acted on. Of course they differ (or seem to differ) in their sense of exactly how these realisations should be acted on. But for all that, it is hard to escape the sense that the one is a strange *doppelgänger* to the other.

These threads of cynicism, pessimism, and anger about the fate of Irish seem to me to be among the most pervasive themes in contemporary Irish cultural and political life. Perhaps in part because of having achieved some distance from them (by being involved in linguistics as a profession and by having moved to the United States), I am constantly now taken aback by the force with which such feelings are commonly expressed.

There is a kind of interaction which, I think, everyone who has a personal connection with Irish (as a teacher, as a speaker, as a writer, as a parent) has been involved in many times.

You meet some young person, usually a young man in his twenties, in some random social context. Conversation proceeds along more or less normal paths until it emerges that you have some connection, personal or professional, with the Irish language.

The conversation then shifts from its conventional paths, and the person you are talking to launches in to a fierce diatribe about how many years he or she spent at school studying Irish and how he or she emerged at the end of that long period knowing next to nothing, has never been capable of putting more than three words together, and has forgotten even how to do that much in the years since leaving school.

The strangest thing about this kind of conversation, in my experience, is that these announcements are almost always made with a kind of defiant pride, or with a certain fierce kind of pleasure (the kind of pleasure, I suspect, that accompanies the satisfaction of deeply felt but un-articulated desires).

A number of things are striking about these interactions: The first is that they take place so often. The second is that they concern only Irish. While I have conducted no survey, I am virtually certain that physicists, mathematicians and geographers rarely find themselves in conversations with people eager to make a fierce boast of how little physics, mathematics, or geography they know after years of schooling, or to express their anger at having been made study such things.

Here too, though, there is a strange *doppelgänger* effect, in that this anger is mirrored by that of language activists who can drive themselves into paroxysms of anger in deliberately confronting and exposing official hypocrisy about the status of Irish as the 'first official language' of the Irish republic.

It is worth asking, I think, what the source of this anger and cynicism might be. At one level the answer is obvious. At the beginning of the maintenance effort, there was a great deal of excessive optimism and a sense that large gains could be made relatively quickly and relatively easily. That this was so is not surprising, because there were few if any models to use as guides, and there was at that point therefore no well of knowledge and experience to draw from which could guide people in the setting of realistic goals. It was not known at that time how difficult the task would turn out to be, or how difficult it is in general to work against the forces which act within a community to lead to language abandonment.

But heightened expectations lead quickly and inevitably to disappointment when they are not met. And that must be part of the explanation for the fog of disillusion and cynicism that covers almost all talk of language maintenance in Ireland.

Some of this anger and sourness clearly also grows out of a distaste for the authoritarian and insular turn of mind with which language activism in Ireland has been, fairly or unfairly, associated (witness Hugo Hamilton's chilling recent memoir *The Speckled People* for instance). Put another way, Irish-language activism was co-opted by some of the narrowest and darkest forces in twentieth-century Ireland.

But it has always seemed to me that there was something darker and less rational at play here as well. When you listen to a young man or young woman speak with a kind of defiant and furious pride about how little Irish they know after years of schooling, you know that a nerve has been touched, that the language is acting as a symbolic lightning rod for feelings that will never attach to more routine subjects like geometry, chemistry or French.

My step-daughter is Chinese-American – a California girl. She spent three months attending a national school in Dublin at the age of eight or so, when my wife and I were spending a three month sabbatical in Ireland. She had, of course, not one word of Irish before she began attending school in Dublin. Her previous exposure to the language did not go much beyond a vague knowledge that I and some of my friends in Ireland spoke it, along with whatever knowledge might derive from an affection for the music of *Altan*. For that reason, she was very nervous indeed at the prospect of being required to study Irish in her new school. As it turned out, from the first week, she was doing better in her Irish homework and exams than anyone else in her class – a pattern which continued until the end of her period in the school and one which caused some surprise (and needless to say some resentment among her classmates). Towards the end of our stay in Dublin, we talked about this (to us surprising) pattern of events with her teacher and with the principal of the school – a wise and experienced woman who had neither a particular sympathy for, nor a particular antipathy towards, the language. Both confirmed that the pattern we had seen was, in their experience, a very common one – that children coming from abroad to attend the school for brief periods tended to do extremely well in Irish, to fare, in fact, much better than their Irish counterparts. The reason seemed to them completely obvious: the foreign students did not bring to the task of learning Irish the emotional and cultural baggage that Irish children are burdened with as they approach the same task.

Anecdotes are dangerous when used as evidence, but still such stories seem to me to reflect a persistent reality in contemporary Irish life. Cynicism, anger, negativity, and a barely buried guilt pervade almost all talk of the language, of its situation, and of the various efforts that have been made to change its situation. And it seems obvious that, whatever other sources such feelings have, their principal breeding ground has been within the long, long post-colonial shadow.

John Waters put it best in a perceptive piece published some years ago, in which he said that the language had become 'the repository of much of our post-colonial neurosis'.[3] But whatever the source of these feelings, there is no doubt, I think, that they have clouded, and continue to cloud, almost all discussion in Ireland of the situation of Irish and of the various efforts and policies that were designed to affect that situation. Distance and rationality have been hard to achieve.

It is also true, I think, that this dark emotional background, this central element, is the feature of the Irish scene which has been most ignored in discussions outside Ireland of the revival effort.

So say we try to detach ourselves from all this sound and fury, try to achieve some distance, and return to the first of our two questions above and ask what actually has been achieved in Ireland in the effort to resist language extinction, and what there is to be learned from that experience. Once again, we will try to frame the question at every point in the broader context of what is known about the forces that work towards the extinction of weakened languages.

Those efforts have been directed at achieving two broad goals:

1 to preserve the use of Irish in those communities in which it had continued to be the vernacular
2 to create the circumstances under which communities which had made the transition to English, at one point or another in their histories, could become, in a sense which shifted as the effort proceeded, 'Irish-using' communities.

For the first strand, no great success can be claimed.

Among those who were young adults or who were middle-aged at the time of the 1891 census – those who in large numbers had already determined not to pass on the felt burden of the language to their children – the ones who had not emigrated were dying in the 1920s, the 1930s and the 1940s. As those generations died in those decades, so we see the inevitable death with them of many varieties of Irish – the Irishes of Derry, of Monaghan, of Sligo, of Leitrim, of Tipperary and of Roscommon. Despite what was perhaps thought at the time, there was never a chance that the course of language extinction could have been turned in such places. The decision to hide the language from the younger generation had been made long before, and that magical but delicate generational link, once broken, cannot be re-forged.

For other *Gaeltacht* communities, a claim frequently made is that the use of Irish has declined in them exactly as rapidly as it would have, had there been no official effort to halt that decline. This seems not to be true. Lillis Ó Laoire, for instance, has documented how the change of government in 1922, and the consequent change in policies and attitudes towards Irish which followed, led to a significant strengthening of the position of the language in the parish of Cloich Chionnaola in

County Donegal (a community which continues to be strongly Irish-speaking to this day).[4] In his view, a view which is based on a detailed and intimate knowledge of the community in question, a generation which ought to have been fully Anglophone if established patterns had persisted ended up being bilingual in Irish and English, or else monolingual in Irish (much to their economic and social disadvantage when they had to emigrate to Scotland and to England). This is probably not an isolated case.

The harshest assessments are therefore probably wrong. For all that, the decline of the use of Irish in traditional *Gaeltacht* communities has continued and continues apace. In the 1960s, the Irish of County Clare reached the point that the Irish of County Derry had reached in the 1920s (spoken only by a relatively small number of old people) and is now no more. Similarly, the Irishes of East Galway, of East Kerry, of Clear Island, and of much of County Cork exist now only in archival form, and there is some reason to believe that the Irish of County Mayo is now close to the point that was reached by the Irish of County Clare some forty years ago. Donegal is the county with the largest Irish-speaking population, but here too, the Irish of Fanad, the Irish of Ros Goill and the graceful dialects of the southern peninsula around Killybegs seem to be largely moribund.[5]

An important additional consequence of these shifts has been that the chain of mutual intelligibility which formerly connected the continuum of dialects from North to South has been broken and the sense of linguistic unity and community correspondingly weakened (although the creation of first *Raidió na Gaeltachta* and then of *Teilifís na Gaeilge/TG4* has done much to repair this damage).

These changes too have been the focus of a great deal of angry commentary. Whether or not outcomes would have been different had different policies been pursued is of course now unknowable (although much discussion of these matters in Ireland takes for granted that it is knowable).

For what it's worth, my own suspicion is that the outcomes would have been roughly the same no matter what policies had been pursued. When a community first starts down the path ordained to it by the forces which drive language extinction, the process seems to proceed with a terrible kind of mechanistic inevitability. Colleagues who know other such situations well have often talked to me about how one can lay the various sub-communities out on a single time-line and say 'Village A is now at the point that Village B was at ten years ago, and Village B is now at the point that Village C had reached ten years ago', and so on for each of the villages in question. A given village may be placed at different points on this time-line at a given moment, but the trajectory for all is identical. This may be how language extinction works quite generally.

The conflicts and complicities that define the process work themselves out in the kitchen and in the bedroom, in the school playground rather than in the school classroom – in private, familial, and domestic spaces defined by solidarity, where official and external agencies have virtually no influence. It is one of the very few social processes in which significant power is ceded to fairly young children, children who at one level act as autonomous agents within their own communities and at another level act as proxies for, or instruments of, the larger forces beyond the immediate community – rejecting the traditional language and adopting the new, in acts of solidarity which bind them to each other and separate them from their grandparents. It is very difficult indeed (and it is probably immoral) for governments or movements to design and implement policies which will reach into such private spaces. But those private spaces, and the freedoms inherent in them, are where the conflict is worked out. It is therefore not surprising, I think, that it has proven so difficult to arrest the decline in use of Irish in *Gaeltacht* communities. Nor is this a uniquely Irish failure, although, as usual, much of the Irish commentary on the matter would have it otherwise.

With respect to the second aim, assessment has to be rather different.

Here too, initial hopes were unrealistic. It seems to have been thought that progress would be rapid, that the *Gaeltacht* communities would expand relatively quickly, covering what was previously English-speaking territory, and that they would then meet and join, ultimately creating an Irish-speaking polity. Nothing remotely like this, of course, ever happened, and it is easy now to look back with scorn on the *naïveté* of such expectations. However, it is again unsurprising that expectations should have been *naïf* and unrealistic, given that at the time of their conception there were no models to learn from, no well of experience or knowledge to draw from.

No doubt partly for that reason, and partly because of the general sourness surrounding policy towards Irish, this strand of effort too is standardly regarded in Ireland with some cynicism and often also with some resentment – a resentment bundled up into the term *Gaeilgeoir*, which has now become (in English) almost a blanket term of abuse.

A less insular and more sober assessment, however, would lead to a different conclusion. What emerges from such an assessment, I think, is that this part of the effort to maintain Irish represents one of the most notable achievements so far attained in the global struggle against language extinction. It represents, in fact, the single most successful instance of language revival, or of language maintenance, known to me (the very strange and singular case of Modern Hebrew set aside for the moment). What is un-paralleled in the Irish situation is not what has happened in *Gaeltacht* communities, but rather what has happened, almost un-noticed, outside the *Gaeltacht* – in the creation of a large and energetic second language community, a community now many times larger than the traditional *Gaeltacht*, and one which calls into question (as Angela Bourke in particular has consistently argued) traditional (geographical) notions of what a *Gaeltacht* is.

This 'second language' community is made up of those who, for one reason or another (ideological or sentimental or personal) feel some attachment to the language and to *Gaeltacht* communities, and who as a consequence have attained strong second language (L2) ability in the language. Many use Irish consistently in their daily routines, listen to Irish language broadcasts, watch Irish language TV, buy, read, and write books in Irish, send their children to Irish language play-groups (*naíonraí*) and to Irish-medium schools (*Gaelscoileanna*).

It is a large, disparate, well educated, and mostly middle class community. One of the signs of its vibrancy (pointed out to me by a friend who produces Irish-language current affairs programming on TV) is the fact that it is possible, in any town in Ireland, to produce a report on any aspect of current affairs entirely in Irish. There will always be a sufficient number of relevant people (trade union officers, political activists, journalists, teachers and the like) with sufficient command of the language that they can be interviewed and the story presented.

Out of this community have come great cultural riches in the face of enormous odds and difficulties – the poetry of Biddy Jenkinson, of Michael Davitt, of Liam Ó Muirthile, and of Gearóid Mac Lochlainn, the novels of Séamas Mac Annaidh, the criticism of Declan Kiberd, and the songs of John Spillane. Spillane's weekly program on *Raidió na Gaeltachta* proudly proclaims its use of *Gaoluinn na Galltachta* – 'the Irish of the non-Irish-speaking community' – a term which ought to be paradoxical but which isn't.

How was this community created? Clearly, it was a community (rather than an official) achievement. The crucial actors have been parents and teachers, and among the crucial institutions have been the *naíonraí* – Irish-language pre-schools established in a pioneering effort by a small group of women (Helen Ní Mhurchú, Aingeal Ó Buachalla, Helen Ó Ciosáin especially) with virtually no institutional support, the *Gaelscoileanna* (Irish-language immersion schools established outside the official *Gaeltacht*), and the *coláistí samhraidh* (summer colleges in *Gaeltacht* areas for children from non-Irish-speaking areas). More often than not, whatever was achieved was achieved in spite of, rather than thanks to, the efforts of the state (whose actions have often been shameful – as in the closing of the *Coláistí Ullmhúcháin* (teacher training colleges for students from Irish-speaking areas), the resistance to parents' groups trying to set up Irish-medium schools, or the inexplicable failure to provide public services in Irish to *Gaeltacht* communities). Maybe the most important single part of the community effort has been the epic feats of hospitality and language pedagogy performed by the people of the *Gaeltacht*, as they open their houses, schools, and communities each summer to students from non-Irish-speaking areas – efforts that were perhaps in a certain sense self-sacrificial in that the influx of thousands of English-speakers stretched already fragile linguistic communities to the limits of tolerance.

I have called this the 'Second Language Community' above, but there is a central sense in which this term is inaccurate. There are now many children who have grown up in this community with a new urban version of Irish as one of their first languages, and who have in turn passed that new language on to their own children. In the communities that have coalesced around the *Gaelscoileanna* especially, the normal processes of inter-language mixing, perhaps even of pidginization and creolization, have been at work and have produced new urban calques, new and strange mixtures of Irish and English.

There is as a consequence a great range of language-varieties called 'Irish' in use in the 'second-language' community. There are people like me who work hard at speaking some close approximation to traditional *Gaeltacht* Irish, and there are many people who speak (fluently and carelessly) new urban hybrids, heavily influenced by English in every way. For the communities of children growing up around Irish-medium schools in urban centers, it may be right to speak of pidginization and creolization (along with a lot of clever inter-language play like the recent 'cad-ever'). Many teenagers are thoroughly bi-dialectal, switching easily from the version of *Gaeltacht* Irish they have from their parents to the new urban varieties in use among their peers.

There are many who will disparage and sneer at the mixed varieties that are emerging in these complex and shifting environments, but before yielding to that easy urge, it is as well to bear two truths in mind. The first is that such language mixing is the only engine we have for creating new languages; the processes of pidginization and creolization are the only forges in which new languages are cast. A second truth worth bearing in mind is that it was of just such a mongrel mix (of Anglo-Saxon and French) that Chaucer's English was born.

It will be interesting to see what will happen to these new varieties in the sad event that traditional *Gaeltacht* Irish should become a memory. One thing, though, that is completely clear is that these new linguistic communities are not going to fade away just because the *Gaeltacht* as we now know it fades away.

I know of no parallels to this achievement anywhere else in the world.

In the face of that truth, it is important not to give in to a facile optimism. All communities of Irish-speakers face great difficulties, and it is rational to take the bleak view that the Irish experience reveals nothing except what the limits of the possible are in the area of language maintenance. Nevertheless, what has been achieved is real enough and it deserves to be celebrated – celebrated coldly and quietly, in a wide-eyed and unsentimental way. It should be celebrated in full recognition of the limits of what has been achieved, in full realization of what we thereby learn about the limits of what is in principle achievable in this domain, but with a sense of celebration which is all the larger and more expansive for that realization.

And maybe that is what a half-successful language maintenance effort has to look like. Perhaps the real lesson of the Irish experience is that this is what can be hoped for. By which I mean that it seems to be extraordinarily difficult to work against the historical processes which act within a community to undermine language loyalty and lead to language-shift, to work against the forces which bring people to feel (always irrationally) that knowledge of a language is burdensome. But perhaps what the Irish experience most teaches us is that it is far from impossible to create a new community, whose language draws on elements of the old and elements of the new, and which possesses all the usual and lively public trappings of a language community – literature, music, radio, TV, journalism, schools, drama, politics, comedy, jokes, puns and gossip. Of course what is 'maintained' or 'revived' in this process, is very different indeed from the language which was the original focus of revivalist efforts and you may very well not much like the mongrels and hybrids that you bring into being along the way.

But in this context, as in most, purism is surely misplaced. For you probably cannot 'revive' a seriously weakened language without in the very process transforming it in deep and unexpected ways, and the processes of pidginization and creolization will inevitably play a role in forging new languages and new versions of old languages. We need not be alarmed or put off by these developments, for, if current research is on the right track, creolization is a true and bare reflection of the human language faculty, and is therefore the furnace in which new languages will be formed. This is the living, breathing process of language-creation and all one can do is to keep possibilities alive for it to work on.

We should return finally to the question posed in the title of the workshop out of which this volume grows – 'Why Irish?'

Because it is a language like any other.

Because, as such, it represents one valuable strand in a rapidly thinning and unravelling network of cultural and intellectual resources available to humankind.

Because, in addition to that, it represents one of the most interesting and successful language revitalization projects so far undertaken, and there is therefore much to be learned from its recent history.

It remains to be seen where that project is going to take us, but the one thing that is very clear is that it will take us to some interesting, important and at present unexplored, place. It will be a place in which there will be a great deal to learn and a great deal to enjoy.

Notes

1   Kenneth Hale, Michael Krauss, Lucille Watahomigie, Colette Craig, and Laverne Jeanne, 'Endangered Languages', *Language* Vol. 68 (1992), pp. 1–42.

2   See Walt Wolfram and Natalie Schilling-Estes, 'Moribund dialects and the endangerment canon: The case of Ocracoke brogue', *Language* Vol. 71 (1995), pp. 696–721. See also Geert Driessen, 'In Dutch? Usage of Dutch regional languages and dialects', *Language, Culture, and Curriculum* No. 18 (2005), pp. 271–285.

3   John Waters, 'Taking the tyranny out of Irish', *Irish Times,* 12 July 2004.

4   Lillis Ó Laoire, 'Níl sí Doiligh a Iompar/No Load to Carry: A Personal Response to the Current Situation of Irish', *Who Needs Irish?: Reflections on the Importance of the Irish Language Today,* ed. Ciarán Mac Murchaidh (Dublin: Veritas, 2004), pp. 46-63.

5   'Moribund' in the technical sense that they are now spoken only by some older people and so are at the point reached by the Irish of County Derry in the 1920s and 1930s.

Alan Titley: dust jackets

TEANGA GAN TEORAINN:
THE NOVELS OF ALAN TITLEY

Philip O'Leary
Boston College

In 1898 an anonymous correspondent in *Fáinne an Lae* declared:

> Má's don tuaith amháin oireas an Ghaedhilg, ní teanga náisiúin í ar aon chor, acht canamhaint bhocht nach fiú aighneas ná díospóireacht 'n-a taoibh. Beidh sí marbh sul a mbeidh an cheist réidhtighthe (20 August 1898).

> [*If Irish is only suited for the countryside, it is not a national language at all but only a poor dialect that is not worth discussion or debate. It will be dead before the question is settled*].

His concern has resonated ever since as writers of Irish have experimented with ways of expressing urban life through a language long exiled to the countryside and sheltered from many of the events and issues of the wider world. This problem has been particularly acute given the number of city dwellers who have mastered Irish over the decades while insisting that they had the right to live the life they knew in all its complexity through their adopted language. At various points throughout the revival, Irish-language critics have welcomed works they saw in some way as proof of the language's capacity to root itself in the city – Pádraic Ó Conaire's *Deoraidheacht* (1910), W. P. Ryan's *Caoimhghin Ó Cearnaigh* (1913), Liam Ó Rinn's *Cad ba Dhóbair Dó agus Sgeulta Eile* (1920), various plays by Piaras Béaslaí, Art Ó Riain's *Lucht Ceoil* (1932), the mystery stories of Cathal Ó Sándair in the 1940s and 1950s, Séamus Ó Néill's *Tonn Tuile* (1947), Tarlach Ó hUid's *An Dá Thrá* (1952), Máiréad Ní Ghráda's play *An Triail* (1964), Diarmaid Ó Súilleabháin's *An Uain Bheo* (1968), Eoghan Ó Tuairisc's *An Lomnochtán* (1977), to name just a few that were assigned particular significance as landmarks by critics in their own time.

Yet even some of the writers who took on this challenge, no matter how good their Irish or how long they had lived in the city, found it all but impossible. Diarmaid Ó Súilleabháin was troubled by what he called 'staid scitsifréineach an úrscéalaí Ghaeilge' [*the schizophrenic state of the Irish-language novelist*] in Anglophone Ireland.[1] The novelist and essayist Pádraig Ua Maoileoin, for decades a guard in Dublin, declared: 'Dá mbeadh aon mhisneach agamsa is ag scríobh ar shaol Bhaile Átha Cliath a bheinn féin mar is é is fearr a thuigim'.[2] [*If I had any courage I myself would be writing about the life of Dublin because that is what I understand best*]. But he always turned for his inspiration to his native Corca Dhuibhne in the Kerry *Gaeltacht*. More optimistic was Máirtín Ó Cadhain, who in a 1955 piece in *The Irish Times* written before his own breakthroughs with urban fiction, stated: 'Is fada cuid againn ag rá nach bhfuil aon deacracht ná mínádúrthacht ar leith faoi chur síos a dhéanamh ar an mbaile mór'. [*Some of us have long been saying that there is no special difficulty or artificiality about depicting the town*] but he then added a significant qualification: 'Caithfidh, dar ndóigh, fonn a dhéanta a bheith ort, thú taithithe ar an áit, taithithe ar do cheird agus taithithe ar an nGaeilge'.[3] [*Of course you must want to do it and you must have command of the place, command of your craft, and command of the Irish language*].

Given that Ireland is becoming an ever more urban and suburban mainstream European society, it seems more than ever legitimate to ask 'Why Irish?' if the language is in any way inadequate to the needs of the actual Irish people living in an Ireland that is, for better or worse, an overwhelmingly Anglophone nation, indeed a nation that, despite its constitutional assertion of the primacy of Irish, is far less bilingual than, say, the United States. No contemporary writer of Irish has, in my opinion, provided a better literary answer to that question than has Alan Titley, the Cork-born novelist, story writer, fabulist, playwright, scholar, critic and general agent provocateur in Irish-language literary circles. Yet precisely because of the pyrotechnic mastery that makes it possible for him to rise to this challenge in so many genres, as well as his zestful willingness to mould the language in any way he feels necessary to do so, Titley is often regarded as an unduly difficult if not downright intimidating writer.[4]

Professor Alan Titley

The resultant comparative neglect is a serious injustice – to Titley, to literature in Irish, and to potential readers. Of course it is, as we will see below, impossible to deny the challenging nature of Titley's Irish. But that difficulty serves a crucial thematic purpose (and besides, one can hardly fault writers of all people for a love of language!).[5] Moreover, an awareness of context, a sensitivity to etymology, and sometimes a simple reading aloud can clear up many points that may initially seem unduly arcane. At other times, however, the medium is very much the message and our confusion is at the heart of our reading experience.

Titley's subject matter – cannibalism in Dublin, revolution in Africa, the adventures of a Gaelic poet on the Crusades, the

Last Judgment in the Phoenix Park[6] – fall well outside the conventional parameters of literature in Irish. But then again, the overwhelming majority of Irish people, including those with good Irish, live in a world well outside the conventional parameters of literature in Irish. Most of those who have addressed such esoteric themes in Irish – and very few have gone so far off the beaten track – have tried to make the reader forget he or she was reading Irish, attempting some sleight of mind to make that reader unconsciously suspend disbelief that Moore Street vendors or south-side Dublin civil servants, not to mention Shankill Road shipyard workers, were speaking Irish as their ordinary linguistic medium. There is, of course, nothing at all either unusual or wrong with such an approach, which writers of all languages have used with characters who would not speak the language of their books. It had, for example, certainly been standard and largely unquestioned practice for nineteenth-century Irish writers of English dealing with the Irish-speaking countryside. But it takes considerable linguistic *chutzpah* as well as technical mastery to make the language in this situation a strength not a weakness, a medium without which the story could not be told nearly as effectively. That has been the most notable of Alan Titley's many achievements as a writer of Irish willing to take on, as do writers of major languages everywhere, whatever subject inspires his creative energies.

And those subjects have, as we have seen, been eclectic and often startling. In a provocative 1981 essay entitled 'Litríocht na Gaelige, Litríocht an Bhéarla, agus *Irish Literature*' (Literature in Irish, Literature in English and *Irish Literature*), Titley argued that Irish writing in English was about Irish people while Irish writing in Irish was about people.[7] In his own fiction he has certainly set out to prove his point by creating an extraordinary range of human types, Irish and otherwise. Thus more than a decade before either Hannibal Lechter or Jeffrey Dahmer invaded our collective consciousness, Titley created a cannibalistic protagonist in his

1980 novel *Stiall Fhial Feola* (A generous slice of meat). While there is a fine satiric take here on the first stirrings of Celtic Tiger conspicuous consumption, not least in an obsession with food worthy of *Aislinge Meic Con Glinne*,[8] the novel is a disturbing read, and not simply or even primarily because of the actions of the twisted murderer, for if nothing else this cannibal knows what he believes and wants and, intuitively, according to his own twisted logic, why. It is the supposedly 'normal' characters who are most disconcerting in their isolation, fragmentation, and lack of purpose. By 1980 such a fictional universe was not entirely new in Irish-language writing, having been explored by both Máirtín Ó Cadhain and Diarmaid Ó Súilleabháin. Still, Titley's depiction of a bleak, post-Christian urban landscape must have shocked some who still looked to Irish for a sense of connection to a grounding and sheltering tradition and to a national community of shared if not entirely monolithic purpose. Everything is fair game here. The Church would seem to be on its last legs – and remember that this novel was published in 1980, the year after Pope John Paul II's triumphal visit to Ireland – its survival more a function of the apathy of both priests and their rather sheep-like congregations than of any genuine belief in its access to transcendence or even that its teaching and rituals provide any meaningful answers to modern life's questions. The state is largely irrelevant – an unimaginative employer, indifferent guardian of the public welfare, a source of distracting and quickly forgotten topics of conversation during its frequent bouts with scandal. The family is being pulled apart by centrifugal forces beyond the control of its members, were they interested.[9] The interactions among strangers, friends, and would-be lovers are driven by needs both selfish and comprehensible, though few of the characters seem to comprehend them. This is a world that earlier generations of Irish revivalists would have found their worst nightmare, and the fact that Irish – in the hands of Titley – is so capable of expressing it would have made their sense of shock more intensely painful.

Titley is by no means writing a book about the language here, however indirectly. But it is impossible for a writer in contemporary Ireland to choose to write in Irish without that decision having some influence on what and how he writes – and of course how he is read. When he chooses a setting and theme so alien to conventional expectations for post-revival Irish-language fiction, his linguistic medium of necessity becomes a central element in his work. Indeed Titley himself makes no attempt to obscure the fact that in the Dublin world of this novel all these characters would be speaking English exclusively. For example, early in the novel, Oonagh, the young woman on whose abduction and eventual murder the plot centers, takes satisfaction in her acceptance by at least some of the members of the inner-city church youth center where she volunteers, despite her 'canúint shlímshnoite bhuirgéiseach Thír an Iúir' (p. 35), ('*polished bourgeois Terenure accent*'), a kind of English they have previously heard only 'ar theilifís, ón raidió, san scoil agus ón altóir' (p. 35), ('*on television, from the radio, in school and from the altar*') and so different from 'béarlagair dícheannaithe a n-árasán dorcha féin', (p. 35), ('*the butchered jargon of their own dark flats*'). Of course in a novel in which one of whose principal themes is radical lack of communication, how could anyone see English as an unqualified success despite its unquestioned universality? In fact, Titley's use of Irish – and his characteristically challenging idiolect of the language – at times creates in the reader, I believe intentionally, that same sense of being at a slight distorting distance from this world and the people in it, forced to either grasp at most of what goes on and ignore the rest, or concentrate in a way we rarely do, to understand, or at least hear, as much as possible. In this way the Irish language is central to Titley's art in this and all his other works, its very strangeness – a strangeness he deliberately, at times aggressively cultivates – forcing us to acknowledge the impossibility of fully understanding or empathizing with his characters. Through his use of Irish we are driven into thematically rich psychic territory, sharing the well-intentioned, uneasy and frustrated incomprehension that forces his characters apart.[10]

Isolation is certainly a key note of this novel, with some characters every bit as detached as classic figures from French existentialist fiction like Roquentin in Sartre's *La nausée* or Meursault in Camus's *L'étranger*, but Titley places them in a well-defined, misleadingly familiar social context. Indeed two of the main characters are supposed to be empathetic communicators by profession, a priest and an advice columnist. But whatever they have to say is of dubious value – and they know it. Instead of a coherent and sustaining Christian philosophy, An tAthair Xavier Ó Riain has only:

a oiread sin focal ar eolas aige a bhí ag brath ar chóras iomlán tuisceana, i dtuilleamaí an ghéillte ghairmthe, a oiread sin nathanna a raibh glacantaí sármhíne mar chúlra acu, is dá mbainfeá díobh colúin sheasta na gcur-i-gcás sin nach bhfágfaí ach fuaimeanna folamha illígh trína dtiocfadh síodráil i bpoll na cluaise ach a mbeadh an chiall síothlaithe as ar nós na téipe a bheadh ag taifeadadh i ndiaidh a cúil i log an chiúnais gan bhriseadh. (p. 112).

[*as many words as depended on a comprehensive mode of understanding, a vocational obedience, as many clichés as were backed up by easy acceptance, and if you took from them the support of those assumptions nothing would be left but diverse empty sounds through which a jabbering devoid of all sense would enter the ear like a tape playing backwards in a deep, unbroken silence*].

His time in the confessional booth means nothing to him but:

an cúpla uair an chloig léitheoireachta a mbíodh fáil aige air le linn na ngníomhartha croíbhrú agus idir na paidreacha admhaithe do Dhia Uilechumhachtach a bheith á seachadadh chuige ón taobh eile den ghrátáil ... (p. 89).

[*the couple of hours for reading he would have while the acts of contrition and the prayers of confession to God were being presented to him from the other side of the grate ...*]

His pastoral advice to his good friend, Oonagh's mother Siobhán, after the young woman has vanished, is nothing but a stale blend of professional concern and a hackneyed call for submission to God's will, a fact he hopes she will not notice, for 'tréithe ab ea iad sin a mhéadaigh in éifeachtúlacht de réir is nár tugadh faoi deara iad' (p. 84). [*those were qualities that became more effective the less they were noticed*]. Even during Mass, he is well aware that while his congregation apparently still hopes he will somehow teach them the way 'ceangal a shnaidhmeadh idir a bhfocail laethúla is na focail inar cheart go mbeadh draíocht' (p. 110), [*to form a bond between their daily words and the words in which there should be magic*], that magic is 'ag cailliúint is í i ndeabhaidh achtála leis an saol' (p. 110) [*losing out in a battle to come to terms with the world*]. As a result, he finds himself obsessed with speaking clearly while knowing his words, however elegantly enunciated, will carry no real meaning. Yet he also feels he has no choice, for:

Ní bheadh sé ceart fachailí faidghreamaithe dhá mhíle bliain a streachailt anuas dá súile ar aoi go raibh léargas aige féin. Ní bheadh sé ceart damhaltaí dorcha na bréigriochta a shiúil thart i bhfíoraíocht na tuisceana dóibh a scaipeadh ar eagla go gcúbfadh siad roimh an tsaoirse imeaglach ina dtumfaí iad is roimh an eire ollmhór a chuirfí d'fhiacha orthu a iompar feasta ag iarraidh cinneadh a dhéanamh nó breith a thabhairt d'uireasa treoir gháinneoireachta ón bpuilpid nó óna comhshamhail d'aitheasclog as ar teilgeadh na slata tomhais is ón ar crochadh na cranna meá a choinneodh ar an gconair chúng dhriseach iad chun na ngeataí péarlacha a bhí mar a bheadh sciath cosanta idir iad is an neamhbhrí ... (pp. 110–1).

[*it would not be right to tear scales fixed in place for two thousand years from their eyes because he himself could see. It would not be right to scatter the dark disguised monsters that roamed in the depths of their understanding lest they shrink in face of the terrifying freedom in which they would be plunged and in face of the enormous burden they would now be obliged to carry as they tried to make a decision or give a judgment while lacking direct guidance from the pulpit or from a similar source of instruction from which had been formed the yardsticks and from which had been hung the scales that were keeping them on the narrow thorny path to the pearly gates that served as a protective shield between them and meaninglessness ...*]

The mother, who regularly offers such 'treoir gháinneoireachta' [*direct guidance*] to her readers, is no more confident in the wisdom of what she has to say, finding life full of hard and disjointed facts, so that 'ba dheacair do shúile a bheith oscailte ar an saol agus gan dá bharr ag duine ach fírinní searbha san aghaidh' (p. 27), [*it was difficult to keep your eyes open on the world when one had nothing to show for it but bitter truths to face*]. She believes only her 'creideamh láidir' [*strong faith*] keeps her from her 'ag meáisínghunnaíocht ... fan na sráideanna ar na coirpigh ramhra a beathaíodh ar neamhurchóideacht is ar mhothaolacht chailíní óga) (p. 27) [*machine-gunning through the streets at the fat criminals fed on the innocence and gullibility of young girls*]. The always dubious foundations of that faith will be exposed when her own daughter's body provides the quite literal nourishment for one of those criminals. Yet even before this atrocity, she parcels out her counsel according to a 'foirmle ... ina dtrusáileadh sí gach casadh a bhuaileadh uimpi' (p. 56) [*a formula ... in which she would trussle every twist she met*], rarely encountering questions for which she could not supply a glib answer. Her tragedy is that there are far more *fíricí* (facts) than *fírinní* (truths) in the world.

Disturbingly, the only person in the novel who has had some success in integrating the various elements of his life and world is the spoiled priest Lambe, actually the lost brother of An tAthair Ó Riain, for whom his cannibalism is an act of communion, performed with proper ritual and seen in a clear and sweeping context:

Bhí áthas air gur dhein sé duine éigin eile a theasargan ó oidhe an tsaoil. Má bhí guí amháin a d'ofráil sé suas gach lá ba é go ndíolfaí leis ar chomh-mhaith is ar chomh-charthanacht mar a dhíol seisean leis an gcine daonna ar dhíobh é ... go n-íosfaí leis an ngrá is leis an gcúram is leis an aire is leis an tuiscint chéanna é, is go bhfaighfí uaidh a raibh foghlamtha aige abhus a rachadh chun tairbhe dóibh siúd a bhí fós ag sméaracht faoi dhalladh púicín le hireas falsa ... (p. 73)

[He was happy that he had rescued some other person from life's fate. If there was one prayer he offered up every day, it was that he would be repaid with the same goodness and the same charity as he bestowed on the human race of which he was a part ... that he would be eaten with the same love and care and attention and understanding, and that there would be gotten from him what he had learned here and that it would benefit those who were still fumbling blind-folded by false faith ...]

And in his self-appointed role as messiah, he offers not only this vision of the essential spiritual unity of human beings, but also the prospect of satisfying their temporal needs here on earth:

... nuair a bheadh deireadh curtha le reiligí ... agus nuair a thaibhseofaí dóibh nach gnó chun tairbhe é corpáin a shá isteach i bpoill san aon leathacra céanna nuair a d'fhéadfaí iad a chur chun sochair na mbeo ... Múineadh dó fadó nach raibh grá níos treise ná grá an té a thugann a bheatha uaidh ar son a dheartháireacha, agus níor dheacair dó a chreidiúint gurb ionann a dheartháireacha agus iomlán an chine dhaonna ... (p. 73).[11]

[... when an end would have been put to cemetaries ... and when they would have realized that it served no purpose to stick corpses into a single half-acre when they could be put to the use of the living ... He had been taught long ago that there was no stronger love than the love of the person who gave his life for his brothers, and he had no trouble believing that everyone in the human race was his brother ...]

Fragmentation in the absence of a cohesive and generative context is a recurring image in all of Titley's fiction. Here we find most notably the dismembered body parts of Lambe's victims (pp. 104–5), but also the 'freagraí leictrecheimiceacha' ['*electrochemical responses*'] racing through the human consciousness (pp. 43–4), the intertwined limbs in a pornographic picture Lambe shows Oonagh's father Peadar in a pub (p. 48), 'an charn baictéarach, iad ina mbilliúin ag caidhp-an-chúlardaíocht san cruth ba é' ['*the heap of bacteria, billions of them dancing the high-caul cap in the form that was himself*'] of which Peadar has a vision after Lambe's departure

(p. 55), the spiders whose legs Siobhán pulled off as a child (p. 59), a decapitated stuffed toy (p. 60), the shards of dishware Peadar smashes in a rage (p. 64), the names in the phonebook suggestive of food that Lambe ponders as future victims (p. 75), the trivial consumer goods of daily life (p. 92), the shoes An tAthair Ó Riain compulsively buys (p. 93), the abstruse rituals of the Catholic Church (pp. 110–1), the blood and membrane that spill from An tAthair Ó Riain when he is stabbed on the altar by Lambe (p. 116).

Once again, this alienated post-Christian Dublin will be familiar enough territory for modern readers, including readers of Irish familiar with the London of Pádraic Ó Conaire's Micíl Ó Maoláin in *Deoraidheacht* (1910), or the Dublin of Diarmaid Ó Súilleabháin's Louis Stein in *An Uain Bheo* (1968) or Máirtín Ó Cadhain's 'N.' in *Fuíoll Fuine* (1970). What is striking here, however, is that Titley is most successful in this thoroughly contemporary novel because of, not despite, his use of Irish. And this will be every bit as true of his next novel *Méirscrí na Treibhe* or his many non-traditional short stories in *Eiriceachtaí* (Heresies) and *Leabhar Nóra Uí Anluain* (Nora O'Hanlon's book).

Méirscrí na Treibhe (The scars of the tribe) is an intellectual and stylistic *tour de force* that could be discussed from any number of perspectives. Had it been written in English it would undoubtedly be required reading in Irish Studies courses world-wide as the most provocative exploration in Irish literature, regardless of language, of the personal and cultural wounds of colonialism and unrealised liberation. For our purposes here we may look at it as a story of homecoming and self-discovery. Most simply it tells of Paul Lodabo's return to his African homeland after university education in Europe, where he has trained in the law. But as the novel develops, the meaning of home is radically problematized as this child of privilege tries to come to terms with his feelings of estrangement and alienation from the brutal dictatorship his country has become under its pompous president for life, a one-time friend of his father. He is even more troubled by the startling change in his brother, who has become a political and cultural radical in his absence. When Paul visits his brother Nicholas in his slum dwelling in the capital, Kirunda, as Nicholas now calls himself, hopes he will be able to find his way home, a remark that Paul finds 'a leithéid de ráiteas amaideach!' ['*such a foolish statement*'], thinking 'Gan amhras d'éireodh leis a shlí féin a dhéanamh abhaile. D'éireodh le héinne – dá dtaispeánfaí an bealach dó'. (p. 93). ['*Without doubt he could find his own way home. Anyone could – if he were shown the road*']. He will soon learn that it is not that easy, spending the rest of the novel until his own execution in search of that reliable guide.

Early on, however, he is only conscious of a profound dissociation from his country and its people, not least his own prosperous and compliant father Patrick (né Rubana) Lodabo.[12] That feeling is well justified. Zanidia is a squalid colonial construct of a country, ostensibly independent but in truth utterly subservient to the geo-political, economic, and military needs of the western capitalism of whose ideas, styles, and fashions it is slavishly imitative. Thus in a conversation with an authoritarian and ambitious army major – himself eventually executed – a member of the ruling class exclaims:

Ná bíodh aon bhuairt ort maidir le Rialtas na Nigéire ... Is maith atá siad in ann aire a thabhairt dóibh féin. Tá's acu cá bhfuil a gcuid margaí, cé hiad a bhfíor chairde is cad tá chun a leas, ár ndálta féin. Níl díol ró-mhaith ar earraí caiteora i siopaí Bhúdaipeist, Bhúcairist, nó Mhoscó. (p. 49).

[*Don't worry about the Government of Nigeria ... They are well able to take care of themselves. They know where their markets are, who their true friends are and what is in their interest, like ourselves. There is not much call for consumer goods in the shops of Budapest, Bucharest, or Moscow*].

And it is western money and armaments – American tanks, British armoured cars, German artillery pieces, and French ordinance – that keeps the president in power (although the rumour is that the equipment is operated by whites in blackface with African troops seated in conspicuous positions for public spectacle) (p. 4). In this climate the president's occasional assertions of national autonomy are both buffoonish self-parodies on the one hand, and on the other a cynical ploy to attract attention from the major players in the larger global power struggle, whose occasional fleeting interest is the only thing that gives Zanidia any standing in the world. Typical here are President Tumba's comments in a speech to the faculty of his university and private research institute, in which he boasts of, among other grandiose pet projects, his own research on a local mineral 'nach raibh le fáil in aon áit eile ar domhain ... acmhainní folaigh insaothraithe maidir le cumhacht mhíleata agus ó thaobh íocshláinte gach galair ann' (p. 145), ['*that could be found nowhere else in the world ... hidden resources there that could be exploited for military power and for the cure of every sickness*']. He exhorts these tame and cowed academics:

> ... meitifisic úr a bhunú ina bpósfaí an chuid ab fhearr den eagna Afraiceánach le heitic an airgid agus an nua-aosachais in aon sintéis chomhtháite amháin ... (p. 145).

> [... *to found a new metaphysics in which the best of African wisdom would be wed to the ethic of money and modernism in one coherent synthesis* ...]

He concludes this exercise in bombast with references to the fifth dimension and to his theory 'gurb iad na hAfraiceánaigh ... sliocht ceart amháin *homo sapiens* agus gur de bhrollastoc eile ar fad iad muintreacha geala agus buí an domhain go léir) (p. 145). ['*that the Africans were ... the only true line of* homo sapiens *and that all the white and yellow peoples of the world were of another species altogether*'].

All of this nonsense is for the uncomprehending edification of the native masses, perhaps to make up for the pomp and circumstance of the colonial rule that we are told they miss. In fact, the real standard of excellence for everything in Zanidia is lily white. The presidential palace is grandiosely modelled on the American White House; the central Independence Square was designed 'in ionnúil na staideanna móra peile a bhí feicthe ag an Uachtarán ar an teilifís le linn Chorn Peile an Domhain' (p. 5) ['*to match the great football stadiums the President had seen on television during the World Cup*']; the homes of the wealthy are built in 'stíl bhréag-Iodáileach', (p. 36). ['*pseudo-Italian style*']; a privileged young woman takes her fashions from '[an] stíl sin a bhíodh faoi ráchairt ag réaltscannáin na ndeich bliana roimhe sin' (p. 54). ['*that style that was in demand among the filmstars of the previous decade*']. Paul's initial pride in his education is rooted in the fact 'gur chruthaigh sé é féin i gcluiche na ndaoine geala, lena rialacha siúd, ina dtír siúd, ina measc siúd' (p. 24). [*'that he proved himself in the white people's game, by their rules, in their country, in their midst'*]. What passes for the president's political philosophy is nothing more than simplistic paeans to material progress:

> ... trínar fhás tuilleadh aerphort, bóithre leathana, réidh ag polladh na dufaire, iarnróid nua den scoth ag trasnú chumair an tuaiscirt, óstáin agus oifigí ilstóracha ag síneadh chun na spéire, tanáil na tráchtála idirnáisiúnta ag taoladh na bochtaineachta, trealamh uile an náisiúin uasail chumhachtaigh á shearradh féin as iomairí an traidisiúin thámhaigh agus ag marcaíocht go huaibhreach ar eití an ama go tairbhe an fichiú aois. (p. 19).[13]

> [*... through which grew more airports, wide, level roads penetrating the jungle, a superb new railroad crossing the northern lowlands, hotels and multi-storied office buildings stretching to the sky, the cacophony of international trade reducing poverty, the entire apparatus of the noble and powerful nation stretching itself out of the ruts of stagnant tradition and riding proudly on the wings of time to the benefits of the twentieth century*].

The hapless leader of the official opposition, who is killed by the president's troops while he is giving a speech, has modelled his stilted rhetoric on 'traidisiún roscach na bpolaiteoirí ba tháscúla in iarthar domhan ó Cicero is na SeanGhréagaigh ... abairtí meáite lucht scríofa aitheasc Uachtarán na Stát Aontaithe ó Kennedy go Carter' (pp. 62–3), ['the bombastic tradition of the most famous politicians of the western world from Cicero and the ancient Greeks ... the measured sentences of the speechwriters for presidents of the United States from Kennedy to Carter'], all delivered in 'focal ilsiollacha de fhréamh chlasaiceach, bíodh siad oiriúnach nó mí-oiriúnach' (p. 67) ['polysyllabic words of classical etymology, whether appropriate or not']. Even the genuine opposition, the guerillas whom Paul eventually joins, take a good deal of their ideology undigested from other third-world Marxists like Che Guevara or Ho Chi Minh, although, to be fair, unlike their establishment enemies they really do think and debate about how ideas originating in the industrial west can be most effectively adapted into an African context.[14]

These are, then, deracinated, fragmented people, and once again this favourite symbol of Titley's is everywhere in the novel: the mutilated bodies of those publicly executed in the opening scene (pp. 6–8), the scattered and ineffectual political cells in the capital and the countryside (p. 13), the disparate tribal groupings of Zanidia (pp. 14 and *passim*), the urban poor pictured as scurrying ants (pp. 75–6), the bits of broken conversation at a cocktail party (p. 55), the corpses and furniture strewn around a university hall after a police assault (pp. 117, 119), the torched and crumbling corpse of Paul's brother killed in this raid (p. 124), old beliefs jettisoned like so much rubbish in a dump (pp. 130, 133–4), pathogenic microbes in the jungle (pp. 161–2), miscellaneous instruments in a torture chamber (p. 261), and many more.

However horrible, this is a world we in the twenty-first century can recognize and fit into some historical context, and Titley presents it in an Irish that is generally straightforward and clear. This is particularly true of the dialogue throughout the novel, subtly reinforcing our sense that at the deepest level these people are very much like ourselves in both their evil and their heroism. But they are also very different, and, as he did in *Stiall Fhial Feola*, Titley manipulates the language for thematic purposes to deny us what would be an unforgivably facile identification with these Africans living a post-colonial nightmare even the most imperfect understanding of which white westerners have to earn, if they can get it at all. Titley's consistent use of a strikingly rich and idiosyncratic Irish to deliberately obscure our understanding of what seems to be right on the page before us in black and white is perhaps most immediately evident in his many descriptions of the jungle that is itself a central and seminal image throughout the novel, the jungle President Tumba so glibly claims he can tame and that Paul comes to love for its very reticence and mystery. Writing of *Méirscrí na Treibhe* in his monumental 1991 study *An tÚrscéal Gaeilge* (The novel in Irish), Titley stated that having himself experienced life 'ar feadh aga bhig féin i gcuid de na foraoiseacha ba thibhe fáis ar domhan' (p. 395), [*for even a little while in some of the most dense forests in the world'*], he felt obligated 'friotal a shaothrú a bheadh chomh raidhsiúil, rabairneach, raingléiseach, iomarcach, luifearnúil, drabhlásach, caiteach, neamh-chuimseach, barrbhaoiseach, antomhaiste, mímheasartha le fásra na foraoise féin' (p. 395–6), [*to develop a mode of speech that will be as profuse, prodigal, unkempt, excessive, overgrown, profligate, extravagant, immoderate, unstable, unbounded, intemperate as the vegetation of the forest itself'*]. To try to recreate the 'blas agus atmaisféar plúchtach na háite' (p. 396), [*the stifling flavour and atmosphere of the place'*] with 'uiscealach dearóil teanga na hiriseoireachta is an chuntais shimplí' (p. 396), [*the wretched diluted language of journalism and the simple account'*] would have been to falsify what he knew to be the truth of his experience and to deny readers even a vicarious opportunity to share it.[15] To give some feel for how challenging diction and dense syntax intertwine with setting and theme in these descriptions, a brief excerpt from one of the many – and by no means the most impenetrable – will have to suffice:

> Scaipthe thall is abhus bhí paistí cladraim is screalmacha a luigh isteach go nádúrtha le baill eile na cré sceilte ach go ndéanfaí deoraithe éanormalacha díobh nuair a thiocfadh an fhearthainn. Ba gheall le mion-shraoilleáil iad a d'éalaigh as

mullóga eile na gcloch arbh iad amháin a thug crothaíocht ar bith uathu don réamaire fánach as tír isteach go raibh cuimhne ar bith anseo ar an duine, nó meas ar a dhéantúis ... (p. 160).

[Scattered here and there were patches of stones and gravelly land that fit in naturally with the other parts of the stripped clay except that they became bizarrely alien when the rain came. They were like little stragglers that had escaped from the other mounds of stones that alone gave any shape at all to indicate to the odd traveller from outside that human beings had ever been thought of here, or their works considered ...].

Titley writes of a similar passage:

Tá an leabhar pulctha le sleachta dá leithéid agus a thuilleadh níos feamnaí fós agus is ann dóibh chun go rachadh an léitheoir i bhfastó iontu mar eispéireas iontu féin a fhreagródh do thaithí na háite im chuidse samhlaíochta, beag beann ar an tuarascáil neamhchas a shantaíonn an tuiscint dhíreach. B'fhéidir gurb amhlaidh nár chóir iad a léamh as intinn fhuar in aon chor ach ligean dóibh sruthlú thar an tsamhlaíocht in aon chaise leathchoineasach scuabghluaiste. (*An tÚrscéal Gaeilge*, p. 396).

[The book is packed with passages like that and others even more overgrown and they are there for the reader to get trapped in as an experience in themselves that would respond to the experience of the place in my imagination, largely regardless of the uncomplicated account the straightforward understanding desires. Perhaps they should not be read with a dispassionate mind at all but rather allowed to flow over the imagination in a single half-conscious rapidly streaming current].

Paul's real journey from smug and privileged Europhile to authentic and self-integrated African human being is, of course, a search for personal salvation. On his visit to his brother's slum apartment, one of the residents of the building casually calls him 'fear gorm geal' [*a white black man'*], with this single phrase smashing not only Paul's complacency, but his very self-concept as well. Although he has to this point seen himself as an all but anointed leader of a people he does not really know anything about, he is here instantly reduced to being another of Titley's failed communicators:

> Ghortaigh sin é. Don chéad uair bhí daoine buailte uime ar amhlachas na muintire a mb'fhéidir go mbeadh sé á gcosaint, nó a mbeadh a gcásanna á bplé aige, dá ráineodh go gcleachtfadh sé a ghairm riamh, agus don chéad uair mhothaigh sé, mar adéarfadh sé féin, neamhimleor (p. 75).

> [*That wounded him. For the first time he had met people of the kind that he would perhaps be defending or whose cases he would be pleading, if he ever were to practice his profession, and for the first time he felt, as he himself would say, inadequate*].

Despite 'blianta uile a ullmhúcháin, blianta a chleachtadh san nathaíocht dheisbhéalach agus a staidéir sa phraschaint thráthúil' (p. 75), [*all his years of preparation, his years of practice in witty eloquence and his study of felicitous repartee'*], he has no answer for this man of no importance, one of 'na daoine gioblacha, bochta, caillte, salacha, aineolacha, neamhhliteartha, graithineacha, gorma seo!' (p. 76), [*'these poor, ragged, lost, dirty, ignorant, illiterate, swarming black people!'*] who have never before entered his consciousness except as the raw material from which he could fashion a triumphant career (pp. 75–6).

They would not be getting much of a champion. Paul is such a political innocent at this point that having watched the army murder the leader of the opposition and smash up his rally, he can still think:

> gur beag é a aithne ar chúrsaí Zanidia agus gur lú ná sin a eolas ar dhlíthe na tíre, ach bhí tuairim aige dá mb'eol dó tuilleadh is dá mba leithne a léitheoireacht sna leabhair go míneodh eachtraí an lae iad féin dó. Má bhí an dlí briste acu, agus ba chosúil go raibh, bhí pionós dá réir tuillte acu, óir ba léir nár ceapadh dlí riamh gan chúis mhaith a bheith taobh thiar dó, nó b'shin é an teagasc a cuireadh air, agus ní foláir nó gurbh iad sainghnéithe na gcoinníollacha ar leith a bhí ar marthain in Zanidia ba thoisc le difríocht an chleachtadh (p. 71).

[*he knew little about the affairs of Zanidia and less than that about the laws of the country, but he was of the opinion that if he knew more and had read more widely then the events of the day would make themselves clear to him. If they had broken the law, and apparently they had, they deserved to be punished, for it was clear that no law was ever created without good cause behind it, or that is what he had been taught, and the special aspects of the unique conditions existing in Zanidia must explain the difference in practice*].

This experience, followed immediately by his brother's contemptuous dismissal of Paul's western values and *weltanschauung* set him on an odyssey every bit as daunting as his first trip through the jungle. Moreover, the insights gained by his fellow travellers, including the locally inflected Marxism of his brother, are of little use to him. In a heated argument with several of his comrades, he points out that in their allegiance to socialist orthodoxy they have made themselves members of a tribe every bit 'chomh claonta, chomh biogóideach leis an bhfrithbheartaí nó leis an asarlaí is mó amuigh', [*as biased, as bigoted as the biggest reactionary or medicine man*']. Paul himself sees no meaningful way to differentiate 'cogadh na n-aicmí ón gcogadh treibhiúil' (p. 192–3), [*'the class war from the tribal war*'].

What Paul is struggling towards is a more generous and embracing notion of human brotherhood that does not deny or suppress racial or tribal culture or tradition, but he is nowhere near being able to formulate his longing as he strives to merge aspects of his western education with his new-found commitment to elements of his tribal identity, including the language he had always ignored. Nevertheless, if the synthesis he seeks is beyond his reach, how can Titley as author or we as readers have any hope of getting more than an impression of what is going on in his mind and soul? In his own discussion of this novel in *An tÚrscéal Gaeilge*, Titley states that what he was aiming for here was a point of access into 'téamaí agus cúraimí na hAfraice mar a thuigfeadh Afraiceánach iad óna litríocht féin' (p. 397), [*'the themes and concerns of Africa as an African would understand them from his own literature'*]. In this quite extraordinary attempt 'oiread agus ab fhéidir de shaoltaithí is d'fhadhbanna comhaimseartha na hAfraice a léiriú do lucht léite na Gaeilge faoi mar a d'fhás siad as mo chleachtadh is mo shamhlaíocht féin' (p. 397), ['*to reveal to readers of Irish as much as possible of the contemporary life experience and problems of Africa as they grew out of my own experience'*], his most effective literary resource was the Irish language itself (p. 397). It is obviously a dangerous strategy to intentionally confuse the reader, but if confusion is in fact the most honest response a reader can bring to what is being presented, if transparency would entirely falsify the experience the author is trying to recreate, then a carefully managed and evocative confusion not only can but should be the goal. This point is, of course, best illustrated from the text. Haunted by his brother's death at the university, where he was shot and his body torched with a flame-thrower, Paul feels chunks of his charred flesh being branded onto his eyes, his brain, his heart:

> Ba gheall le hollchiorcalú uilechaite clúdaithe den ghrá is den fhuath in éineacht é a dhein feadáin fholamha a choirp gan tathag a chalcadh, moirtcheann pearsantachta ... (p. 124).

> [*It was like an all-consuming, all-encompassing feeling composed of love and hate together that hardened the empty insubstantial arteries of his body, a death of personality ...*]

He is, as a result, shattered:

> go dtí nach bhféadfadh sé a chloisteáil choíche, ná a mhothú feasta, ná a thadhall go deo, ná a bhlaiseadh go héag ach frithbhualadh fraochmhar na ndrumaí dúthcha i mbroinn bheireatais a shinsear ... (pp. 124–5).

> [*so that he could never again hear, or feel, or touch, or taste until death anything but the frenzied echoes of the native drums in the birth-womb of his ancestors ...*]

This initial psychic obliteration of the Paul that was is followed by the painful, tentative emergence of the new African Paul, a process Titley links with his learning his ancestral tribal language. In a passage that could have been written about an earnest student of Irish in the *Gaeltacht*, Titley captures Paul's sense of mission as he works with an elderly mentor:

Níorbh amhlaidh gur thuig sé gach uile fhocal a thagadh amach as a bhéal, ach cheana féin bhí sé ábalta ar bhunús na cainte a thabhairt leis, an méid a bhí riachtanach a réiliú óna thimpeallacht, cé gur aithin sé freisin go raibh tábhacht ag an tslí a raibh an t-eolas feistithe, tábhacht a thuigfeadh sé ina iomláine gan fial gan forscáth lá níos faide anonn (p. 179).

[*It was not that he understood every word that was coming out of his mouth, but already he was able to catch the substance of the speech, what it was necessary to distinguish from its background, although he also realized that there was an importance to the way the information was arranged, an importance he would understand without a veil, without a covering some day in the future*].

Of course this confidence is a function of Paul's *naiveté*, the *naiveté* that allows him to believe that his recently acquired ability 'duilleoga an *nwumbo* a aithint thar bhuinneáin an *anjeli*' [*'to recognize the leaves of the* nwumbo *from the shoots of the* anjeli'] gives him a claim to be:

cuid de shlampar síoraí na coille ... a chuaigh i ngreamaitheacht ó ruigile go chéile faoi mar a bheadh baint aige ó fhréimhíocht le dúchas na coille craobhiomaí, le hachtáil an bhaill bhiligh seo a raibh sé ag mothú ó sheachtain go chéile ina taobh gurbh é brú an domhain é cé nár theastaigh uaidh ach a dhearbhú go raibh páirt ag fuil a shinsear ann a d'fhéadfadh sé féin cur léi ...' (p. 181).

[*part of the eternal luxuriant growth of the forest ... that became denser with each downpour as if he were innately connected with the inherent nature of the many-branched forest, with the actuality of this heavily wooded place about which he had been feeling from week to week that it was the womb of the world although he only wanted to affirm that the blood of his ancestors had a part in it that he himself could add to ...*].[16]

More accurate is his perception:

go raibh sé ag tosú arís, go raibh ceann á chur aige ar shaol ar ndhein sé dearmad air, ar eispéiris ar chaith sé leipreach tharstu agus go rabhthas á rá leis go gcaithfeadh sé an bhearna a líonadh, an bhris a thabhairt isteach, dá dhéanaí féin, dá mhéad an mearúchán a bhí air (p. 182).

[that he was beginning again, that he was putting a start to a life that he had forgotten, to experiences that he had skipped over and that he was now being told that he would have to fill the gap, recoup the loss, however belatedly, however great his own confusion].

This process of self-actualization is, in many ways, inaccessible to language. What Paul really needs is to *live* the emerging unity as his new self comes into being, a unity that language by its very nature would attempt to dissect and analyze:

B'fhéidir gurbh é an botún a deineadh ná a cheapadh go bhfaighfí na raonta sin a thabhairt chun a chéile le focail, le hurlabhraíocht pháirtiúil bhriste, le friotal fann faoileála, nó le hionstraim ar bith ba lú ná an duine féin… (p. 204).

[Perhaps the mistake that had been made was to think that those spheres could be brought together with words, with partial broken speech, with feeble manipulative talk, or with any instrument at all less than a person himself …]

Ba mhaith leis na gléasanna eile sin a thaisceadal, ba mhaith leis fionnachtan a dhéanamh leis na goiris sin a leáfadh san áit a raibh cruas, a dhúnfadh san áit a raibh scoilt, a mhaistreodh san áit a raibh cnapa, a phollfadh san áit a raibh bac, a shoiléireodh ins an áit a raibh garbhtheilgean, a mhúdánfadh san áit a raibh ciall agus a chiallódh san áit a raibh breall. Níor thurgnamh a bhí uaidh an turas seo ach an taisteal féin a thabharfadh cuaird na limistéirí úd isteach nach raibh pas aige dóibh go dtí seo. (pp. 204–5).

[He wanted to explore those other methods, he wanted to experiment with those tools that would dissolve where there was hardness, close where there was a split, mash where there were lumps, penetrate where there was an obstruction, illuminate where there was obscurity, confuse where there was sense, make sense where there was error. It was not preparation he wanted this time, but the journey itself that would include a tour of those territories for which until now he had no passport].

Just before the initiation ritual that will make him a real member of his tribe, Paul is aware that he is facing a truth 'a bhí foghlamtha [aige] lena intinn ach nárbh fholáir dó a fhoghlaim lena chorp fós' (p. 205), [*he had learned with his mind but that he still had to learn with his body*]. What has prevented this full acceptance of his new identity has been his unwillingness, or perhaps better inability, to surrender his attachment to that linear, verbal western thought that seeks answers to such profound questions in 'slabhra na bitheolaíochta agus an tionchar cinntitheach a bhí ag geiní rialtacha agus ag crómosóim ar iompar dearfa an duine' (p. 205), [*biological chains and the determining influence that regulatory genes and chromosomes had on a person's attested behaviour*]. Although well aware by now that one cannot 'guí chun geiní' [*pray to genes*], 'sléachtadh roimh chrómosóim' (p. 205), [*genuflect to chromosomes*], or 'síciteicneolaíocht le siosúir a dhéanamh ar an teaglaim áirithe a tugadh duit' (p. 205), [*impose an artificial psycho-technological pattern on the specific combination given to you*]. Paul must still come to terms with the fact that the teaching of his tribal elders is rooted not in rational exposition, but in 'nochtadh nó foilsiú nó oscailt ba léiriú seachúil' (p. 205), [*an exposure or revelation or opening that was a transcendent manifestation*] before he can begin 'an claonadh seo ... chun réaduchtaithe a dhíbirt' (p. 205) [*to banish this propensity ... for reductionism*]. The density of Titley's Irish becomes an objective correlative for Paul's mental processes during the initiation ritual. In a moment of total surrender as the *ungwa* moves among the young men undergoing the ritual, Paul feels 'go raibh sé á stiúrú don chéad uair óna phutóga féin, go raibh forlámhas na rannóga cloíte, go raibh an duine neamhthoisí ar fáil' (p. 209), [*that he was for the first time being guided from his own bowels, that the despotism of the separate divisions had been overthrown, the essential self was present*]. Titley's genius here is to use words to capture a state in which words are irrelevant, as when Paul thinks of his new bond with his fellow initiates: 'Ní raibh an t-am tagtha fós go bhféadfadh siad labhairt le chéile ach ba dhaingne mar nasc na lámha a leagadh orthu ná na focail ba charthanaí amuigh' (p. 209), ['*The time when they could speak to each other had still not come, but the bond of the hands that were laid on them was stronger than the kindest words'*]. Indeed speech would not play any role for them 'go dtí go mbeadh obair an scamhaithe curtha i gcríoch go hiomlán' (p. 209), ['*until the work of stripping away was fully accomplished'*], when the infliction of the literal 'méirscrí na treibhe' ['*scars of the tribe'*] would establish belonging beyond question. Moreover, through this ritual Paul is transformed, no longer one of countless 'cáithníní scaipthe' ['*scattered fragments'*], but rather an integral component of 'aon chorp creathánach faoi na mílte géag' (p. 212), ['*a single quivering body with thousands of limbs'*]. And again Titley rises to the challenge to suggest the inexpressible, to use words to allow his readers to share in a state of mind cut adrift from the usual linguistic signifiers:

> Súpadh síos trína liothrach féin é, síos ar ealashruth na haimsire a d'imigh go dtí ré na réamhchuimhne go dtí an ré nach raibh aon chuimhne ann, ná dorchadas ná gile, go dtí nach bhfaigheadh sé solas a bhlaiseadh ná bia a chloisteáil ná glór a fheiceáil ná cumhra a mhothú, go dtí go raibh a chealla i dtóin an tobair, go raibh ceasnaíon ar shuthshac a chineáil, go dtí tráth roimh chogairse an chine, roimh dhaoine, roimh ainmhithe ... (p. 218).

> [*He was sucked down through his own juices, down on the swan-stream of time that went off to the time before memory to an age when there was no memory, nor darkness nor brightness, until he could not taste light or hear food or see a voice or feel a smell, until his cells were in the bottom of the well, until there was a mysterious lethargy in the embryo sac of his race, to a time before the ordering of the race, before people, before animals ...*].

This entire hallucinatory passage would be worth quoting in full, but what is presented here should suffice to illustrate how brilliantly Titley establishes the capacity of the Irish language to deal with settings, subjects, and themes 'Fear na Cathrach' could not even have imagined in his 1898 call for writers of Irish to engage more fully with the modern world.

In *An tÚrscéal Gaeilge*, Titley, albeit not altogether convincingly, claims of *Méirscrí na Treibhe* 'nach ag iarraidh aon ní a rá faoi Éirinn ná faoin Eoraip atá sé', (p. 397) [*'that it is not trying to say anything about Ireland or about Europe'*]. His third novel, *An Fear Dána* (The artist/The bold man) (1993), is, however, very much about Ireland and the role of the Irish artist. It was perhaps inevitable that a writer who, as Seán Ó Tuama noted, writes Irish as if he had millions of readers,[17] would someday take as his subject an Ireland in which a writer could find an audience in a Gaelic world that stretched from the Blaskets to the Orkneys. Still, his decision to base a novel on a figure like the thirteenth-century poet Muiríoch Albanach Ó Dálaigh is surprising. In a 1984 essay on 'An Scríbhneoir agus an Stát' (The writer and the state), he had seemed rather dismissive of the aesthetic and cultural significance of the so-called 'bardic' poets:

> Samhlaigh duit féin Dáibhí Ó Bruadair dá mba gur saolaíodh é céad bliain roimh a aimsir cheart: an aithneofaí anois é thar Mhaoilseachlainn na nÚrscéal Ó hUiginn ar bith, seachas Uilliam Mac an Bhaird eile, an mbeadh sé buailte anaithnid faon mbáthadh mór bairdne?[18]

> [*Imagine for yourself Dáibhí Ó Bruadair if he had been born a hundred years before his time: would he now be recognized from any Maoilseachlainn na nÚrscéal Ó hUiginn, from another Uilliam Mac an Bhaird, would he be buried and unknown under the great flood of bardic poetry?*].

A 1961 essay on Muiríoch Albanach Ó Dálaigh by Brian Ó Cuív seems to have inspired him to look more closely at this poet, convincing him that it was possible through 'léamh báúil tuisceanach' [*a sympathetic and discerning reading*] of the twenty-odd poems ascribed to Ó Dálaigh 'rian éigin dá scéal a fhionnadh agus pearsa bheo stairiúil a bhraith laistiar de'.[19] [*to ascertain some trace of his story and to sense a living historical person behind it*]. *An Fear Dána* is the vibrant confirmation of that insight.

A 'sympathetic and discerning reading' of the novel itself suggests two major thematic impulses behind its creation. The first is suggested by the essay in which the slighting reference to 'bardic' poets like Ó Dálaigh appeared. Written according to rigorous linguistic and stylistic conventions, and intended for the most part to glorify in at times absurdly exaggerated terms what were often little more than petty and mediocre local chieftains, the works of the 'bardic' poets are frequently regarded as formulaic to the point of impersonality, archaic if not downright irrelevant, insincere, even sycophantic – and difficult to boot.[20] The author of such verse would, to say the least, seem an improbable protagonist for a writer like Titley profoundly committed to the principle that 'córas naimhdeach braistinte agus machnaimh don pholatíocht is ea an ealaín', ['*art is a system of feeling and thought hostile to politics'*], a way of seeing life that the 'ainmhí poiblí' ['*public animal'*] would always feel the need to control, 'ceansú le mil agus le him agus le comharthaí seachtracha ómóis' ['*to tame with honey and butter and other external signs of respect'*], or attempt to ignore altogether.[21]

What probably first caught Titley's attention about this poet is the brief anecdote from the *Annals of the Four Masters*[22] that comprises most of what we know about him. Ó Dálaigh actually defied a patron, the by no means petty chieftain Dónall Mór Ó Dónaill, by killing one of Ó Dónaill's men who had insulted him. Forced to flee into a lengthy exile in which he experienced other patrons, both good and bad, he seems to have gone to Jerusalem as a crusader, and later did monastic penance as an intimate of the king of Connacht, Cathal Croibhdhearg Ó Conchúir, before finally reconciling and again breaking with Ó Dónaill to finish his life as a proudly independent artist. In other words, much like Paul Lodabo, Muiríoch Albanach Ó Dálaigh spends the novel on a voyage of self-discovery, coming gradually to an understanding of what it means to be poet, just as Paul learned what it meant to be an African. Indeed the parallel is deeper and more dramatic as both men at the end of their respective odysseys face execution for their beliefs, sustained by the identities they have forged.

Central to Ó Dálaigh's evolution are his intertwined attitudes to his craft or art, to the truth, and to his social role as a poet. He is initially ambivalent about his art, unsure whether it is, in the conventional bardic sense, a hereditary craft to be polished through lengthy apprenticeship – 'le hoidhreacht agus le hoiliúint' [*by nature and with nurture*] (p. 63) – or something much greater and more mysterious. Thus, responding to one of his students who complains he states flatly:

Ach níl rud ar bith ag tuirlingt faoim dhéin in ainneoin mo dhíchill ... (p. 54).

[*But there is nothing descending to me despite my best effort ...*]

Ní anuas a thagann filíocht ... ach aníos ... Dá mba ón spéir a fuaireamar ár mbroideadh is iomaí dán bog ar bhéal na slí a chumfaimis. Ní thagann doircheacht na ngréas snoite ach le dua (p. 54).

[*Poetry does not come from above ... but from below ... If we got our stimulation from the sky, it is many an easy poem we would compose along the way. The darkness of sculpted work comes only with difficulty*].

But then, apparently regretful of his brusque reply, he can sympathize with the young man's mumbling 'mar gheall ar dhraíocht agus bua agus fuinneamh agus deocha neamhshaolta' (p. 54), [*about magic and a gift and energy and otherworldly drinks*] and acknowledge that poetry is indeed 'deoch neamhshaolta' (p. 55), [*an otherworldy drink*], referring to the 'bua na héigse' (p. 55), [*gift of poetry*] and boasting that poets are 'siúlach ar thír amhra na sainbhuanna gan meath' (p. 55), [*able to travel over the wonderful land of unfailing special gifts*], gifted with 'foilsiú feasa agus an forosna fáistineachta mar is dual' [*the revelation of knowledge and the prophetic vision as is natural and proper*], so that 'an tinfeadh atá á lorg agat, mura bhfuil agat, ní bhfaighir é' (p. 55).[23] [*unless you have the inspiration you are seeking you will not find it*]. Thereafter, through the final two-thirds or so of the novel, this sense of his art as a personal vocation imposing on him terrific responsibilities becomes ever clearer and more insistent. This more profound understanding is particularly evident when he feels again the stirring of inspiration after a period of inarticulate numbness brought on by the loss of his wife and his Scottish patron and by the horrors of the Crusade:

Gan choinne ar an mhuir taobhsholais tháinig néal dorcha anoir lá agus múchadh an ghrian. Leis sin bhraith mé sáimhe agus sonas mar a bheinn ag cur éadaí orm a bhain liom féin. Chan fhéadfainn a rá arbh í sin an uain ball díreach ar fhill saoráid na filíochta chugam. Níorbh amhlaidh gur thug mé suas di riamh, gan amhras. Ach ní raibh an dorchadas san Éigipt ná an chothroime meoin agam ó tógadh Maol Mheá [a bhean] agus Alún [a phátrún] uaim a bhí freagrach don cheapadóireacht (p. 98).

[*Unexpectedly one day on the glinting sea a dark cloud came from the east and the sun was extinguished. With that a peacefulness and a happiness as if I were putting on clothes that were my own. I couldn't say that that was precisely the occasion that the ability to compose poetry returned to me. Doubtless I never gave it up. But there was not the darkness in Egypt nor had I had the mental equanimity necessary for composition since Maol Mheá {his wife} and Alún {his patron} were taken from me*].

The return of his poetic powers is not, however, an unmixed blessing, bringing with it a new anxiety about the authenticity of his vision, the possibility that this apparent re-awakening of his gift involves nothing but 'samhluithe gan treoir ... gur cuid díom iad idir mheabhair agus mheanma' (p. 98), [*'chaotic images ... that were part of me both in mind and spirit'*] or 'aisling mheabhail, cleas eile fós chun mé a chur i ndomheanmain agus mé ar cholbha mo chríche féin' (p. 100), [*'a deceitful vision, yet another trick to discourage me when I was on the edge of my own territory'*]. In monastic retreat in that native territory, he is given an object lesson in his poetic vocation by one of the monks, who hands him a human skull and states:

Is í an chnámh seo an fhírinne lom atá mé ag iarraidh a theagasc duit agus a lorg dom féin. Ruainne feola níl uirthi. Í gan ribe, gan ruainseachán. Tá sí díreach, crua. Tá sí geal, bán. Tá sí borb, bearrtha. Bí id chnámh. (p. 115–6).

[This bone is the bare truth that I am trying to teach you and to seek for myself. There is not a shred of flesh on it. Entirely bald, not a single strand of hair. It is straight and hard. It is bright and white. It is fierce and clean. Be a bone].

In response, Ó Dálaigh declares: 'Is maith a deilbh ... dá mba mhaith a toradh' (p. 116), [*'It looks good ... if its yield were so'*]. That, however, is a challenge that cannot be adequately answered by the artist in retreat from the world, nor is such a splendidly isolated figure Titley's concern in this novel. Rather, he wants to explore what happens when the writer tries to cultivate his personal vision in the real world with all its social and political crosscurrents. Challenged by another monk who basically accuses him of a complacent if not cowardly flight from that world, Ó Dálaigh comes to terms with the social demands of his vocation:

Cén uair is leor ár gcuid fromhtha is féachála? Le Dia féin an cás. ...Ár gcás é an dán a dhéanamh is a chur i ndlús. Ár gcás é ár ndán a chur os ard ós éigean dúinn gan a cheilt (p. 119).

[When are our testing and our trying sufficient? That is the concern of God Himself ... Our concern is to make and weave together the poem. Our concern is to proclaim the poem if we must without concealing anything].

And even if 'go grinneall na feasa ní féidir dul' [*'it is not possible to reach the bed-rock of knowledge'*], it remains

... ár ndualgas ... na cearda doilfe draíochta a thabhairt chun cruinnis. Ár ndualgas é an smúit d'inneonadh ón fhirinne. Ár ndualgas an splanc faoin cheo ar ghrís a adhaint arís (p. 119).

[... our duty ... to bring coherence to the mysterious, magical arts. Our duty to hammer the grime from the truth. Our duty to kindle again the spark under the smoke in the embers].

Returning to his original patron, Dónal Mór Ó Dónaill, Ó Dálaigh is soon forced to confront the consequences of his mature allegiance to his art and its responsibilities. Eager to break the spirit of the poet who had defied him years earlier, Ó Dónaill demands a poem in praise of the servant whom Ó Dálaigh had killed. His refusal amazes even a fellow poet, who sees it as just another example of Ó Dálaigh's old bardic *díomas* (arrogance). Moreover, he responds to Ó Dálaigh's defence that he had pledged God 'nach scríobhfainn bréag im dhán feasta' ['*that I would not write a lie in a poem from now on*'] with a logic of appeasement reminiscent of that used against St. Thomas More in Robert Bolt's 1961 play *A Man for All Seasons*, claiming glibly that what Ó Dónaill wants is only 'filíocht de chuid an tsaoil seo ... Ní mheáfaidh brobh lá an mheasta. Bréag uile é. Dia beatha mo dhánsa, agus is Dó is córa do ranna-se fónamh freisin ...' (p. 133), ['*poetry of this world ... It would not mean a thing on the day of judgement. It's all a lie. God is the life of my art, and it is Him that your verses should serve as well*']. For this poet, one's personal works could well be written with sincerity in the service of God, but 'saothar saolta' ['*worldly work*'] should command 'an mhaoin is gile' (p. 133) ['*the highest price*'].

One of Titley's most striking achievements here is his convincing recreation of an Irish bardic poet as existential saint and martyr in the cause of authenticity, for in effect that is the role Ó Dálaigh assumes in his angry response to his tempter:

Ba mhian liom a rá leis go raibh mé scíth dá scéala. Ó bhí mé san pholl seo gurbh é an lá seo ba shia liom, agus gurbh é an tráth ó tháinig sé ba ghránna liom. Go bhfaca mé naofacht ar mo chonairí ina ga tríd an doircheacht, naofacht nach bhféadfadh sé a shamhlú go brách. Nuair a bhíonn tú ar ghrinneall na mara nach féidir dul níos ísle. Nuair a bhíonn tú ar imeall an domhain nach féidir dul níos faide. Agus nuair a fheictear uachtar an tsaoil i ngrá mná, i ngáire linbh nó i ngaol flatha nach féidir dul níos airde. (p. 133).

[*I wanted to say to him that I was tired of his stories. That this was the day I found longest since I had been in this hole, and that the time since he had come was the time that I found most obnoxious. That I saw holiness on my paths as a light through the darkness, a holiness that he could never imagine. That when you are on the bottom of the sea you can go no lower. That when you are on the edge of the world you can go no farther. And that when the highpoint of life is seen in a woman's love, in a child's laugh or in the relationship with a prince one can go no higher*].

Threatened by Ó Dónaill with execution unless he produces the poem, Ó Dálaigh's response is a scathing rejection of any art created in surrender to the powers that be: 'Ní dán an aiste a scríobhfainn duitse ... Ní dán an aiste a mbeadh Fionn (an fear a maraíodh) ann. Agus ní breith orm do bhreith, a Dhónaill!' (p. 135). [*The piece I would write for you would not be a poem. The piece in which Fionn (the servant of Ó Dónaill's he had killed) appeared would not be a poem. And your judgment is no judgment on me, Dónall!*]. Facing torture and death, the poet finds serenity: 'Fós féin san fhiantas ionam bhí mé sásta. Mo leor is mo dhá leor de na daoine seo im thimpeall bhí fachta agam. Is mé a bhí bréan den bhréag'. (p. 136). [*Even with the wildness in me I was satisfied. I had seen enough and more than enough of these people around me. I was sick of lies*]. Ó Dálaigh is spared death, condemned instead to the more modern judgment on the artist that, in Ó Dónaill's words, it would be 'meath oinigh' (p. 137), [*a loss of honour*] for the state to take him that seriously. Yet even so contemptuously marginalized, the poet is unshaken:

An fear a thagras an chaint bhaoth sin ní thuigeann mórán. Sruth maoile de thuiscint anois idir mé agus leithéid Uí Dhónaill ... An mionn a ghlac mé ar mo ghlúine i láthair Dé agus na Maighdine Muire i Mainistir Chnoc Muaidhe tá ceangailte go héag anois orm. Nach scríobhfainn feasta dán ach dom féin, dom leannán taoisigh nó do Dhia. File, flaith agus fírinne. Agus ní beag sin de thríonóid. (p. 137).

[*The man who says something as foolish as that does not understand much. There is the width of the North Channel now between my understanding and that of the likes of Ó Dónaill ... The oath I took on my knees in the presence of God and the Virgin Mary in the monastery of Knockmoy now binds me until death. I would no longer write a poem except for myself, my beloved prince and God. Poet, prince and truth. And that is sufficient as a trinity*].

In 'An Scríbhneoir agus an Stát', Titley wrote that the modern writer was faced with a choice of two paths – that of state-sanctioned success or that of 'neamhspleáchas fuar an uaignis uaibhrigh' ['the cold independence of proud solitude'], adding:

> Is é baol na linne go bhfuil Autobahn an Stáit mór, fairsing, leathan, dea-dhéanta, ilchúrsach agus teanntaí iomadúla airgid laistiar de, fad is atá bóithrín an neamhspleáchais pludach, pollta, uchtógach, caol, cam, cnapánach agus ní fios cá bhfuil a thriail. [24]

> [The danger of the age is that the Autobahn of the State is large, extensive, broad, well-made, multi-directional with abundant financial supports behind it, while the boreen of independence is muddy, full of holes, uneven, narrow, crooked, bumpy, heading who knows where].

As *An Fear Dána* comes to a close, Muiríoch Albanach Ó Dálaigh proves he is one savvy and uncompromising pathfinder:

> Lúide is baol do neach a chonair féin a shiúl. É sin seachas a bholg a líonadh le gach gaoth dá dtig. Bhí mise mar sin tráth ach chan aon díobh sin atá ionam níos mó. Ionúin an mheanma dhaingean dhíreach. Fírinne na cnáimhe feasta ... (pp. 137–8).

> [It is less dangerous for one to walk his own path. That, instead of filling his belly with every wind that blows. I was like that once, but I am not one of them any longer. The firm, straight spirit is precious. The truth of the bone from now on ...].

An Fear Dána is a voyage of discovery for Titley as well, a successful engagement with what must have initially seemed one of the less promising aspects of the Irish Gaelic literary tradition. Indeed this novel with its emphasis on integrity and continuity rather than fragmentation and disruption[25] could be seen as an extended response to Thomas Kinsella's famous pronouncement that the Irish literary tradition is radically 'gapped' and 'discontinuous', leaving contemporary Irish writers of English as the culture's last best hope, standing on one side of 'a great rift' beyond which lies a Gaelic heritage that, however precious and relevant, is no longer generative in its own medium.[26] This theory has, to be fair, inspired some of Kinsella's own best work, including his magnificent translation of *Táin Bó Cúailnge* (1969) as well as some of the extraordinary poems in *In the Land of the Dead* (1973) and *One* (1974). But it has also infuriated contemporary writers of Irish like Nuala Ní Dhomhnaill, who resent being dismissed as antiquarians or cultural fossils, rather like literary coelacanths, whose survival is a source of wonder and fascination but from whom little evolutionary surprise can be expected. In *An Fear Dána* – indeed in all his work – Titley simply ignores any gap there may be as an irrelevant intellectual construct, confident that the Gaelic tradition had never been fully broken, the point that Máirtín Ó Cadhain made when he wrote: 'Tá aois na Caillí Béara agam, aois Bhrú na Bóinne, aois na heilite móire. Tá dhá mhíle bliain den chráin bhréan sin arb í Éire í ag dul timpeall i mo chluasa, i mo bhéal, i mo shúile, i mo cheann, i mo bhrionglóidí'.[27] ['*I have the age of the Hag of Beare, the age of New Grange, the age of the Irish elk. Two thousand years of that foul sow that is Ireland are going around in my ears, in my mouth, in my eyes, in my head, in my dreams*']. Indeed at several points Titley affirms the integrity of the tradition through allusion to the work of writers who would follow Ó Dálaigh – Brian Merriman, Aogán Ó Rathaille, Seosamh Mac Grianna, Seán Ó Ríordáin.[28]

In order to bring home to his readers this sense of a continuity that, while sorely threatened, was never severed, Titley adopts a quite different linguistic strategy in this novel than he had in the previous two. As noted above, the works of the so-called 'bardic' poets like Ó Dálaigh have on occasion been disparaged as impersonal, insincere, formulaic, and not infrequently impenetrable for the uninitiated reader. Taking on the challenge of making such a poet recognizable and credible as a psychic contemporary, Titley uses an Irish in *An Fear Dána* that is at once dignified, even austere, as well as straightforward, conversational, and above all immediately accessible for the reader of the modern language, with even the poems by Ó Dálaigh himself that he chooses to include rendered almost transparent by the context he creates for them. In contrast with the explosive linguistic virtuosity of his first two novels, particularly *Méirscrí na Treibhe*, what we have in *An Fear Dána* is a disciplined search for *le mot juste*, the invariable success of which is, of course, just a more subtle confirmation of Titley's extraordinary command of his linguistic and artistic medium.

Discussing *Méirscrí na Treibhe* in *An tÚrscéal Gaeilge*, Titley declared:

> Is leis an úrscéalaí Gaeilge an uile ábhar agus an uile mhúnla agus an uile théama agus an uile mheon agus an uile stíl is mian leis ó íochtar an domhain go huachtar an domhain agus níl aon chúis go dteorainneodh na gardaí liteartha lena slabhraí samhlaíochta a chuid iarrachtaí mura bhfuil sé féin sásta géilleadh dóibh (p. 401).

> [*The Irish-language novelist has a right to every subject and every form and every theme and every mental attitude and every style he wants from the bottom of the world to the top, and there is no reason why the literary police should limit his efforts with their imaginary chains unless he himself is willing to surrender to them*].

He concludes: 'Ní ghéilleann *Méirscrí na Treibhe* faic'. [Méirscrí na Treibhe *surrenders nothing'*]. Alan Titley has backed up this claim, taking the novel in Irish places no one would have expected it to go and in the process providing an irrefutable artistic response to the question 'Why Irish?' Moreover, he has thereby confirmed the faith of those like 'Fear na Cathrach', Pádraic Ó Conaire, Liam Ó Rinn and Máirtín Ó Cadhain that Irish is, as it always has been, if not 'teanga gan teorainn', at least a language whose only boundaries are those set by the human imagination.

Notes

1 Diarmaid Ó Súilleabháin, 'An Uain Bheo: Focal ón Údar', Irisleabhar Mhá Nuad, 1972, p. 67.

2 Pádraig Ua Maoileoin, 'Scríbhneoirí Chorca Dhuibhne', in Ár Leithéidí Arís (Baile Átha Cliath: Clodhanna Teoranta, 1978), p. 58.

3 Máirtín Ó Cadhain, 'Úrscéalaíocht', in Ó Cadhain, Caiscín: Altanna san Irish Times 1953/6, ed. Aindrias Ó Cathasaigh (Baile Átha Cliath: Coiscéim, 1998), p. 242.

4 For two examples of this attitude see the reviews of Stiall Fhial Feola by Alan Harrison and of Méirscrí na Treibhe by Máire Mhác an tSaoi. Harrison suggested that Titley's writing would benefit if he were willing 'to control the zest for words a bit' (an t-ampla chun focal a cheansú beagán), for 'he should not allow the natural (and cultivated) gift for language that he has to be an obstacle between the reader and the story he is reading' (níor cheart dó ligint don bhua nádúrtha {agus cothaithe} teanga atá aige a bheith ina bhac idir an léitheoir agus an scéal atá á léamh aige) (Comhar, February, 1981, p. 33). Mhac an tSaoi went even further: 'I want to do justice to the treasure-trove of words … but I cannot. According to my catechism, tautology, de Bhaldraithe's an t-athluaiteachas, is still a vice, and tautology is, in my opinion, a mortal illness here. The undergrowth chokes the narrative strand, and if not for duty I would not have cut my way through it' (Is mian liom a cheart a thabhairt do shaibhreas an stór fhocail … ach téann díom. Duáilce fós de réir mo theagaisc Chríostaíse an tautology, an t-athluaiteachas ag de Bhaldraithe, agus tá an t-athluaiteachas céanna ina ghalar báis dar liom anso. Tachtann an chaschoill snáithe na hinsinte agus mura mbeadh an dualgas ní ghearrfainn aon bhealach tríthi) (Comhar, June, 1978, p. 21).

5 In his discussion of Méirscrí na Treibhe in An tÚrscéal Gaeilge, Titley refers to 'the immoderate love I always had for the strangeness and idiosyncrasy of language' (an gean míchuibheasach a thugas riamh d'aduaine is do leithleachas teanga). See Titley, An tÚrscéal Gaeilge (Baile Átha Cliath: An Clóchomhar, 1991), p. 395.

6 For the Last Judgment story see Titley, 'An Tríú Scéal Déag' (The thirteenth story) in Eiriceachtaí agus Scéalta Eile (Baile Átha Cliath: An Clóchomhar, 1987), pp. 192–206. This is the fourteenth story in the collection!

7   Titley, 'Litríocht na Gaeilge, Litríocht an Bhéarla, agus *Irish Literature*', in *Chun Doirne: Rogha Aistí* (Ready for a fight: selected essays) (Belfast: Lagan Press, 1996), p. 73.

8   In *An tÚrscéal Gaeilge* Titley points out that virtually all of the main characters bear the names of contemporary politicians – Ó hEachaidh (Charles Haughey), Ó Riain (Richie Ryan), Ó Luineacháin (Brian Lenihan), etc. (p. 523). For a discussion of satiric and particularly rabelaisean elements in the novel see Tadhg Ó Dúshláine, 'Beckett ag Borradh Aníos: Léirmheas ar "Stiall Fhial Feola"', *Irisleabhar Mhá Nuad* (1982), p. 63.

9   Particularly relevant here is the icily disengaged Peadar Ó Luineacháin, a hedonistic pseudo-intellectual who can eat crisps and plan future seductions as he stands unmoved – bored even – at his murdered daughter's graveside. Trying to comfort Siobhán after the death of Oonagh, An tAthair Ó Riain has recourse to what he himself regards as 'truths that should be put to death' (fírinní arbh é an bás ba cheart a thabhairt dóibh), such as: 'The family is the basic unity of society, and we care about every household under our care' (Is é an chlann aonad an phobail, agus is cás linn an staid ina mbíonn gach teaghlach díobh a bhíonn faoinár gcúram) (p. 184).

10   Titley here anticipates in practice Eoghan Ó Tuairisc's 1981 comment that 'the greatest virtue with regard to Irish' (an bua is mó a bhaineann leis an Ghaeilge) is that it is 'an ancient language that comes to us as a new language. In large measure it is an alien language for us; all the better, for we are dealing today with an alien planet' (sean-teanga a thagann chugainn ina teanga nua. Cuid mhaith is teanga choimhthíoch againn í; ar fheabhas, mar tá muid ag plé sa lá inniu le plainéad choimhthíoch). See Ó Tuairisc, introductory essay in Ó Tuairisc and Rita E. Kelly, *Dialann sa Díseart* (Baile Átha Cliath: Coiscéim, 1981). n.p.

11   The 'vocation that was denied him' (an ghairm bheatha a diúltaíodh dó) is central in his thoughts as he prepares to consume Oonagh's corpse, a ceremony that concludes with his slicing her flesh 'as if it were a piece of bread' (mar a bheadh píosa aráin ann) and washing it down with the her blood, 'a swallow from the glass in which no water had been mixed' (slogóg siar as an ngloine nach raibh uisce ar bith tríd) (p. 77).

12   It is interesting that Titley uses the English and not the Irish-language forms of these names throughout.

13 See also the description of the official portrait of the president, an astonishing pastiche of African and western motifs – giraffes, snakes, nymphs, tanks, satellites – dominated, of course, by Tumbo in traditional African robes (p. 146).

14 See, for example, *Méirscrí*, pp. 13, 82, 187, 190, 192–3. Early on, Nicholas Lodabo off-handedly acknowledges that he and his comrades would use the same torture techniques inflicted on them by the state 'if I were in their place and we switched positions' (dá mbeinn ina n-áit siúd agus malairt ionaid againn) (p. 11).

15 Titley, *An tÚrscéal Gaeilge*, pp. 395–6. Responding to critics like Máire Mhac an tSaoi who felt 'that the undergrowth chokes the narrative strand' ('go dtachtann an chaschoill snáithe na hinste'), Titley sympathized with their frustration, but continued: 'I have nothing to say as an unyielding *apologia* except that I did not have any choice but to write it in that way' ('Níl agam le rá mar *apologia* neamhghéilliúil ach nach raibh an dara rogha agam ach é a scríobh ar an gcuma sin'). In his early twenties Titley had spent two years in Africa, most of it in Nigeria during its war with Biafra. There he witnessed air raids, the violent suppression of student protests, and a mass public execution, and also spent a brief time in prison for his suspected pro-Biafran sympathies (information here is from *An tÚrscéal Gaeilge*, pp. 394–5). The author himself regards this as a political novel, an aspect of the text I am not doing justice here. For instance in *An tÚrscéal Gaeilge* he is dismissive of '(an t)Eorpachas cúng seo ar cheart dúinn go léir a bheith cortha de i ndeireadh na haoise ina bhfuilimid beo' (p. 59) ['*this narrow Eurocentrism of which we ought to be weary at the end of this century in which we live*']. Titley's anti-imperialism and commitment to justice for the exploited and marginalized also find powerful expression in short pieces and fables like 'Daonlathas' (Democracy), 'Knackers', 'Maorlathas' (Bureaucracy), 'An Obair is Tábhachtaí ar Domhan' (The most important work in the world), 'An Domhan Cothrom Réidh' (The flat earth), 'Ciúnas na Clinge go Brách' (The ringing silence forever), 'An Solas ar Lasadh' (The shining light), 'An Prionsa Sona' (The happy prince), 'Nuair a d'Fhill an Saighdiúr ón gCogadh ('When the soldier returned from the war), 'Ag Cur in Aghaidh an Uilc' (Opposing evil), 'An Ceacht' (The lesson) – all from *Leabhar Nóra Uí Anluain* (Indreabhán: Cló Iar-Chonnachta, 1998) – or 'An Tríú Domhan' (The third world) 'Díoltas'

(Revenge), 'An Comhairleoir Polaiticiúil' (The political adviser),'An Chéad Chuach' (The first cuckoo) – all in *Fabhalscéalta* (Indreabhán: Cló Iar-Chonnachta, 1995).

16 For those familiar with what Myles na Gopaleen called 'the good books in Irish' (na deá-leabhair Ghaeilge), there is more than a bit of humour in the account of Paul's sessions with elderly native speakers: 'Along with that, he had to make a great effort with those of them who had no teeth or were missing a good number of them – and that was the majority of them – in order to catch the thrust of any syllable they would emit, so that there was a time that he was convinced that the old people would draw on another language altogether to save the tradition of the tribe from the foolishness of the night' (Fairis sin an méid díobha a bhí gan fiacla, nó a raibh béil mhantacha acu, agus b'shin a bhformhór, ba mhór an dua ab éigin dó a chaitheamh chun breith ar fhoirneadh aon tsiolla a chuireadh siad díobh, sa tslí go raibh an t-am ann go raibh sé sealbhaithe air ina intinn go raibh caint eile ar fad ag an sean-ghlúin a tharraingíodh siad chucu féin chun tionacal na treibhe a shlánú ó bhaois na hoíche) (p. 179). Note also Paul's pride in what he does learn, for example that there is a complex system for naming each of a cow's individual teats (p. 198).

17 Seán Ó Tuama, 'An Domhan a Chruthaigh Titley', *Comhar*, December, 1987, pp. 17–9.

18 Titley, 'An Scríbhneoir agus an Stát', in *Chun Doirne*, p. 91.

19 Titley, 'Nóta', in *An Fear Dána*, p. 141. The essay by Ó Cuív is 'Eachtraí Mhuirigh Albanaigh Í Dhálaigh', *Studia Hibernica*, No. 1 (1961), pp. 59–69. Ó Cuív's conclusion was that the accounts we have of the poet and his work contain, in all probability, a good deal of truth: 'I have mentioned thirteen of Muiríoch Ó Dálaigh's poems above, and while there are a good many things in them that agree with the story in the Four Masters I do not think there is anything in them that contradicts it. If the "Adventure" and the poetry are all fabrication, the prize must be given to their composers for how well and discretely they created the evidence' ('Trí cinn déag do dhánta Mhuireadhaigh Í Dhálaigh atá luaite agam thuas, agus bíodh go bhfuil roinnt mhaith nithe ionta a thagann le scéal na gCeithre Máistrí measaim ná fuil aon rud ionta atá contrártha leis. Más bréagchumadóireacht an fhilíocht agus an "Eachtra", ní mór an chraobh a thabhairt do lucht a

gcumtha ar a fheabhas agus a dhiscréidí a dheineadar an fhianaise a cheapadh') (p. 69).

20 See, for example, the views of Frank O'Connor in *A Short History of Irish Literature: A Backward Look* (New York: Capricorn, 1968), 85–91; and, more recently, Michelle O Riordan, *The Gaelic Mind and the Collapse of the Gaelic World* (Cork: Cork University Press, 1990), passim. Marc Caball offers a perceptive and spirited defence of the genre in *Poets and Politics: Reaction and Continuity in Irish Poetry, 1558–1625*, Field Day Monographs 8 (Cork: Cork University Press in association with Field Day, 1998).

21 Titley, 'An Scríbhneoir agus an Stát', in *Chun Doirne*, p. 88.

22 The entry in the Four Masters is for the year 1213.

23 He does insist that 'every inspiration and every spark of poetry' (gach iomas agus gach dé dána' is 'cold' (fuar) 'without the craft that will carry them' (gan an cheird a iompróidh iad), adding: 'There is no inspiration without sweat, there is no stimulation without work, there is no visionary spirit without struggle and contemplation' (Níorbh anáil go hallas, níor spreagadh go saothar, níorbh fhéith físíochta go fuirseadh agus rinnfheitheamh) (p. 55). After the death of his wife, Ó Dálaigh says that it was 'out of this agony of my pain that I had to wring poetry. For a long time I knew nothing but the door into darkness' (as cróilí seo mo chneá b'éigean dom an fhilíocht a fháisceadh aníos. Ar feadh i bhfad níorbh eol dom tada ach an doras i mbéal doircheachta) (p. 53).

24 Titley, 'An Scríbhneoir agus an Stát', in *Chun Doirne*, p. 110.

25 The sort of images of fragmentation found in *Stiall Fhial Feola* and *Méirscrí na Treibhe* are also present in *An Fear Dána* – most notably in the decapitated and castrated corpses Ó Dálaigh sees as a crusader (pp. 84–5, 90, 92) – but in this novel the poet is able to transcend the threat they symbolize.

26 See Kinsella, 'The Irish Writer', in *Davis, Mangan, Ferguson?: Tradition and the Irish Writer*, The Tower Series of Anglo-Irish Studies II (Dublin: The Dolmen Press, 1970), pp. 57–66. This piece was based on a paper read at the 1966 meeting of the Modern Language Association of America in New York.

27 Máirtín Ó Cadhain, *Páipéir Bhána agus Páipéir Bhreaca* (Baile Átha Cliath: An Clóchomhar, 1969), p. 41.

28 For Merriman, see Titley, *An Fear Dána*, p. 134 ('gleann ar ghleann' [valley after valley]). For Ó Rathaille, see p. 98 ('ba ghile ná gile an solas ...' [the light was brighter than brightness]) and

p. 131 ('faoi raibh mo shean roimh éag do Chríost' [under whom were my ancestors before the death of Christ]). For Mac Grianna, see p. 134 ('Dúirt mé mo chuid, rinne mé mo dhícheall agus ba chuma liom' [I said my share, I did my best, and I did not care]. For Ó Ríordáin, see p. 97 ('Is chonaic sé an t-uabhar i súile na staile' [And he saw the pride in the eyes of the stallion]) and p. 118 ('Cad is paidir ann? Foirfeacht filíochta? [What is prayer? The culmination of poetry?]). More surprising are echoes of Yeats and Seamus Heaney. For Yeats, see p. 119 ('Ár gcás é gach focal a lua go muirneach is go sámh, mar mháthair lena leanbh nuair is tuirseach iad a chnámha' [Our concern is to utter each word tenderly like a mother to a child when his bones are tired]); and p. 131 (the Ó Rathaille phrase used by Yeats in 'The Curse of Cromwell'). For Heaney, see p. 53 ('doras i mbéal doircheachta' [door into the darkness]). Doubtless there are more allusions that I have overlooked. For a piece in which Titley ranges across virtually the entire Irish-language literary tradition from a variety of perspectives, from serious to ironic to mischievous (although these distinctions are not always immediately or entirely obvious!), see 'Scéal Bleachtaireachta' (A detective story) in *Eiriceachtaí agus Scéalta Eile.*

Professor Philip O'Leary

An Ghaeilge mar Ábhar in Ollscoileanna Mheiriceá

Brian Ó Conchubhair
Ollscoil Notre Dame

Stair na Gaeilge i Meiriceá scéal scaipthe atá agus a bhí ann. Scéal mór é ó thaobh na tíre seo ach scéal é ar fíorbheag an taighde a dearnadh air.[1]

Ní fheadar cathain a labhraíodh an Ghaeilge den chéad uair san Oileán Úr. Má fhágtar Naomh Breandán agus a chriú arbh é, dar leis na lámhscríbhinní, a d'aimsigh Meiriceá i gcéaduair, ní foláir gurbh iad na luathlonnaitheoirí a thug teanga na nGael leo siar. Is é crochadh Anne Glover i ndeisceart chathair Boston mar chailleach sa bhliain 1688 an chéad ócáid a bhfuil neart fianaise agus cruthúnas don teanga a bheith á labhairt sna coilíneachtaí. Is nós le staraithe Ghael-Mheiriceá neamhshuim a dhéanamh de cheist seo na teanga nó í a shimpliú go mór. Léirítear na Gaeil a tháinig i dtír i Meiriceá mar Bhéarlóirí nó mar Ghaeilgeoirí a d'fhág an Ghaeilge ina ndiaidh ag gob na cé. Is annamh aon scéal chomh simplí ná chomh néata sin. Is fíor don teangeolaí Nancy Stenson a scríobh:

> Clearly, Irish speakers must have been a prominent presence among Irish immigrants in the 19th century, and one might expect their language skills to have been an important factor in their assimilation to North American life, if not in their actual departure.[2]

Tuairiscíonn an staraí Kevin Kenny:

> ... it is estimated that between one-quarter and one-third of American-bound emigrants during the famine were Irish speakers. Half of all the famine emigrants came from the two provinces of Connacht and Munster, where at least half the population still spoke Irish as late as 1851.[3]

Agus, anuas air sin:

The post-famine emigration therefore contributed significantly to the continuing decline of the Irish language while, as part of the same process, it made the language more common in many Irish-American neighbourhoods than it had been earlier in the nineteenth century, often provoking cultural conflict between the newcomers and the established community.[4]

Dar le daonáireamh na bliana 2006 tá 25,870 duine sna Stáit Aontaithe a bhfuil Gaeilge acu agus a labhraíonn an teanga ina dtithe.[5] Is ait an scéal é nach mbacann níos mó scoláirí leis an ngné áirithe seo de thaithí na nGael thar lear.[6] Tá ailt fhíorluachmhara scríofa ag an scoláire Ceiltise Kenneth Nilsen ar an bpobal Gaeilge i gcathair Nua-Eabhrac agus in Portland.[7] Is foinse luachmhar eolais é *Go Meiriceá Siar: Na Gaeil agus Meiriceá,* a chuir Stiofán Ó hAnnracháin in eagar sa bhliain 1979 do dhaoine ar spéis leo teanga agus litríocht na Gaeilge sna Stáit Aontaithe.[8] Taisce eile eolais is ea *The Irish Language in the United States: An Historical, Sociolinguistic and Applied Linguistic Survey* le Thomas Ihde[9] agus alt breá Nancy Stenson.[10]

In ainneoin na hoibre sin, áfach, agus is maith ann í, tá mórán taighde nár deineadh go fóill agus nach mór a dhéanamh sula n-inseofar scéal na nGael agus scéal na Gaeilge i Meiriceá idir thuaidh agus theas.[11] Agus an leabhar seo ag fiosrú áit na Gaeilge san acadamh go hidirnáisiúnta, in Éirinn agus i Meiriceá, is cuí sracfhéachaint a thabhairt ar stair na Gaeilge sna hollscoileanna sna Stáit Aontaithe, go háirithe na hionaid ina bhfuil sí seanbhunaithe mar ábhar léinn. Cuirtear síos san alt seo ar chás na teanga mar ábhar agus ar na hiarrachtaí a deineadh chun í a bhuanú ó ghlúin go glúin agus ar an nasc idir an teanga mar ábhar ollscoile agus meas ar phobal na teanga sin. Tarraingíodh an scéal ón iliomad foinsí agus táim faoi chomaoin ag go leor údar agus ag daoine a roinn a gcuid eolais go fial agus go flaithiúil liom.[12] Ní féidir gach aon duine a ainmniú agus is cinnte go bhfágtar daoine agus ionaid ar lár san insint. Ní féidir, de cheal ama agus ceal spáis, cur síos a dhéanamh anseo ar gach institiúid a múintear an Ghaeilge inti i láthair na huaire.[13] I measc na n-ionad ina múintear an Ghaeilge áirítear: Ionad an Léinn Cheiltigh ag Ollscoil Wisconsin, Milwaukee (Dineen Grow); Ollscoil Nua-Eabhrac (Pádraig Ó Cearúil); Coláiste Lehman ag Ollscoil Chathair Nua-Eabhrac (Thomas W. Ihde, Elaine Ní Bhraonáin, Clare Carroll) a bhfuil cúrsaí Gaeilge ar-líne á dtairiscint acu; Ollscoil Minnesota (Nancy Stenson); Coláiste Nua, California (Hetty O'Hara); Ollscoil Naomh Thomas (Fintan Moore); Ollscoil California (Joseph F. Nagy agus James McCloskey); Ollscoil Fordham (James Blake); Ollscoil Montana (Traolach Ó Ríordáin); Ollscoil William Patterson (Brian Ó Broin) agus Ollscoil Pennsylvania (Roslyn Blyn-LaDrew). Mar a deir Thomas W. Ihde 'the greatest expansion in Irish language teaching seems to be taking place in continuing education programs at two-year colleges',[14] agus tá an iomad cúrsaí oíche agus pobail in áiteanna ar nós Ollscoil Yale (Pat Whelan) chun cur síos cuimsitheach a dhéanamh orthu in alt mar seo.[15] Ní foláir a admháil, leis, nach bhfuil eagraíochtaí deonacha san áireamh anseo, eagraíochtaí ar nós Daltaí na Gaeilge a bhunaigh Ethel Brogan ó Ard Mhacha sa bhliain 1981 agus a mhúineann cúrsaí Gaeilge ó cheann ceann na tíre. Má tá faillí á déanamh i múinteoirí sna Stáit, tá neamhaird iomlán déanta ar mhuintir Cheanada ó thuaidh, tír inti féin ina múintear an Ghaeilge in Ollscoil Naomh Francis Xavier, Antigonish, Nova Scotia[16] (Kenneth Nilsen); Ollscoil Naomh Muire, Halifax (Pádraig Ó Siadhail); Ollscoil Concordia, Montréal (Martina Branigan); Coláiste Naomh Micheál, Ollscoil Toronto (Máirín Nic Dhiarmada agus Ann Dooley) agus Ollscoil Ottawa (Paul Birt agus Rosemary O'Brien).

Ós rud nár scríobhadh stair chuimsitheach na Gaeilge i Meiriceá Thuaidh go fóill, ní haon iontas é nach bhfuil stair na Gaeilge sna hollscoileanna ar fáil. Ina aiste úsáideach ón mbliain 1954, cuireann an Ciarraíoch Roland Blenner-Hassett síos ar stair an Léinn Cheiltigh sna Stáit agus i gCeanada:

Little if any serious attention was devoted to the three major Celtic languages in the United States until late in the nineteenth century. The stresses and tensions engendered by the American Civil War, and the enormous expansions of our nation from 1865 on, absorbed the major energies of the people. Until the foundation of the land grant colleges in 1890, most of the serious educational and intellectual activity of the nation centered on the older, privately endowed institutions on the eastern seaboard and the immediately adjacent hinterland.[17]

Tá an t-eolas atá ar fáil ar aon fhocal i dtaobh aon phointe amháin. Thosaigh an Léann Ceilteach, agus Léann na Gaeilge dá bharr, i Meiriceá in Ollscoil Harvard:

It was at Harvard University that the first serious and sustained interest in Celtic Studies was initiated. It is no exaggeration to say that without the consent of the authorities at Harvard and without the selfless dedication of one of its faculty members, Celtic Studies would never have achieved the position they have today in the cultural life of North America.[18]

Sa bhliain 1895, cé go mbeadh cáil mar scoláire sa Léann Ceilteach air amach anseo, ní raibh i Fred Norris Robinson (1871–1966) ach teagascóir óg i Roinn an Bhéarla in Ollscoil Harvard. Mar ba ghnách le muintir Harvard, d'imigh sé leis ar feadh bliana chun na hEorpa chun barr feabhais a chur ar a chuid léinn. Chaith sé bliain in Ollscoil Freiburg, Baden ag déanamh staidéir faoin scoláire agus faoin bhfocleolaí Rudolph Thurneysen (1857–1940). Tá David Bynum, scoláire Slavach, den tuairim gur spreag beirt ollúna – Francis J. Child (1825–96) agus George L. Kittredge (1860–1941) i Roinn an Bhéarla i Harvard – an fear óg chun an Ghaeilge a fhoghlaim mar tuigeadh dóibh a tábhacht mar áis don litríocht bhéil. Bhí spéis faoi leith ag an mbeirt sa chultúr agus sa traidisiún béil:

During the few years in the early 1890s when Child and Kittredge were together on the faculty of Harvard's English Department, several young scholars of oral traditions enjoyed the sponsorship of both men. The most eminent of these was Fred Norris Robinson of the Class of 1891. He took his Master's and Doctor's degrees at Harvard in quick succession (1892 and 1894), then Child and Kittredge sent him to Freiburg in Germany to learn the principles of Celtic philology in what was the world's foremost school of Celtic languages in that era. Child and Kittredge both regretted knowing no Celtic, and they were determined that the time had come when the Celtic component of British and other European oral traditions must be scientifically understood. The enthusiastic but inexact work in Celtic of such earlier lights as Curtin could no longer satisfy Harvard's two doyens of oral literature, and so they delegated Robinson to bring Celtic studies to Cambridge. Robinson's return to Harvard in the fall of 1896 with an appointment as instructor coincided with the death of Child, but Child like Kittredge would have been delighted with Robinson's success.[19]

Ar theacht abhaile dó, d'áitigh Robinson, agus gan é ach cúig bliana is scór, ar Charles William Eliot (1834–1926), uachtarán Ollscoil Harvard, cúrsaí sa Cheiltis agus sa Ghaeilge a thairiscint mar chuid de chlár na hollscoile. Mar sin a cuireadh tús leis an obair.

AN OLLSCOIL CHAITLICEACH, WASHINGTON D.C.

D'fhill Robinson ar Harvard ón nGearmáin tamall gearr sular bhain an tAthair Richard Henebry (1863–1916), scoláire eile a raibh seal caite aige ag foghlaim na focleolaíochta sa Ghearmáin, Meiriceá amach. Cainteoir dúchais ón Rinn ab ea Henebry a saolaíodh ar an 18 Meán Fómhair 1863 taobh le Port Lách, i gContae Phort Láirge. Oirníodh é ina shagart i Maigh Nuad sa bhliain 1892 agus ceapadh ina Ollamh le Gaeilge san Ollscoil Chaitliceach in Washington D.C. sa bhliain 1896 é. Ofráladh an post i dtús báire d'Eoin Ó Gramhnaigh (1863–99) ach dhiúltaigh sé dó ar mhaithe lena shláinte a bhí ag teip ag an am seo.[20] Mhol seisean Eoin Mac Néill a raibh leisce air áfach Éire a thréigint ar mhaithe le Meiriceá. Is ansin a deineadh tairiscint d'fhear na nDéise.[21] Ba í an Chathaoir mhaoinithe seo an chéad phost dá shórt sa tír agus ba iad Ord Ársa na nGael a dhein maoiniú uirthi. Dealraíonn sé go raibh Ó Gramhnaigh míshocair faoi thodhchaí an phoist agus go raibh imní air gurbh í an pholaitíocht seachas an léann a spreag an fhlaithiúlacht.[22]

Cuireann Charles P. Monaghan síos ar mhaoiniú na Cathaoireach ina óráid d'Uachtarán agus do bhaill an *Modern Languages Association* sa bhliain 1899:

The Ancient Order of Hibernians (of America), an organization of very poor men, subscribed $50,000 to endow the Chair of Gaelic in the Catholic University of America. The Chair was further endowed by $10,000 bequeathed in the spring of 1899 by Miss Mary Moran of Baltimore, who left the money 'to help perpetuate the language of her mother', who had been a Gaelic speaker.[23]

Cé gur tosaíodh ar airgead a chruinniú sa bhliain 1893 agus gur fógraíodh an Chathaoir sa bhliain 1896, níor thosaigh na ranganna go dtí an bhliain 1898.[24]

Nuair a ceapadh Henebry san Ollscoil, bronnadh comhaltacht air chun tabhairt faoin tSean-Ghaeilge sa Ghearmáin faoi Heinrich Zimmer (1851–1910). Chaith sé tréimhse in Ollscoileanna Greifswald agus Freiburg, áit ar bhain sé dochtúireacht amach sa bhliain 1898. Thug Henebry léachtaí sa Ghaeilge san Ollscoil Chaitliceach ó 1898 go 1900, ach d'éirigh conspóid idir é agus na húdaráis – ní fheadar fós go baileach cén bunús ná cúis a bhí léi – agus d'ardaigh sé leis a chip agus a mheanaí agus d'fhill abhaile sa bhliain 1903. Ina dhiaidh sin, bhunaigh sé *Coláiste na Rinne* agus ceapadh ina Ollamh le Sean-Ghaeilge i gColáiste na Banríona, Corcaigh é. De bharr na conspóide a luadh thuas, chlis ar Henebry a chuid ranganna a mhúineadh sa bhliain 1900–01 agus b'éigean do Fred Robinson ó Harvard an t-aistear fada idir Washington D.C. agus Cambridge, Massachusetts a chur de gach seachtain chun na ranganna a mhúineadh.

Níorbh éasca comharba Henebry a aimsiú ach sáraíodh na deacrachtaí nuair a tugadh scoláireacht do J. Joseph Dunn sa bhliain 1901 a chuir ar a chumas tamall a chaitheamh ag déanamh staidéir faoi Robinson in Harvard go dtí an bhliain 1904 agus seal a chaitheamh mar mhac léinn in Freiburg 'with Thurneysen, at Rennes with [Henri Georges] Dottin [1863–1928] and also in Aberystwyth and Edinburgh. In addition Professor Dunn, during this period, spent summers in

Ireland, perfecting his knowledge of Modern Irish'.[25] Is ábhar spéise é ceapachán Dunn ar an gcúis gurbh é an chéad fhear a rugadh agus a oileadh sna Stáit, seachas Robinson, a bheith ceaptha ina Ollamh Gaeilge. Le linn do Dunn a bheith ag foghlaim a cheird, lean Robinson ag tairiscint cúrsaí sa Ghaeilge agus sa Cheiltis san Ollscoil Chaitliceach mar léachtóir ar cuairt. Agus é cáilithe, mhúin Dunn cúrsaí Ceiltise ó 1904 go dtí 1931 nuair a chlis ar a shláinte agus b'éigean dó dul amach ar pinsean.[26] Ghlac an tAthair James Aloysius Geary (1882–1958), arbh as Worcester, Massachusetts dó, dualgas na Gaeilge air féin. Bhí bunchéim aige ón College of Holy Cross agus bhain sé dochtúireacht amach ón Ollscoil Chaitliceach sa bhliain 1931.[27] Mhúin sé an Ghaeilge den chéad uair i 1914 agus ceapadh é mar Theagascóir na Ceiltise agus na Focleolaíochta dhá bhliain ina dhiaidh sin. Lean sé air ag múineadh cúrsaí go dtí gur éirigh sé as i 1953 nuair a ghlac Robert T. Meyer na cúraimí air féin i dteannta le cúraimí na focleolaíochta comparáidí.[28] Cuireadh deireadh leis an gCathaoir sa Léann Ceilteach sa bhliain 1983 nuair a atiomnaíodh mar Chathaoir sa Léann Éireannach í agus tháinig deireadh le caibidil de stair na Gaeilge sna Stáit Aontaithe.[29]

OLLSCOIL HARVARD

Ba mhaith ann é Robinson do thodhchaí na Ceiltise san Ollscoil Chaitliceach in am an ghátair, ach ba mhó práinn a bhain leis an scéal nuair a tháinig an t-am dó féin dul amach ar pinsean. Tar éis dó tosnú amach mar theagascóir in Harvard sa bhliain 1894: 'he was promoted to full professor in 1906 and took over Kittredge's post as Gurney Professor in 1936'.[30] Mar a deir Blenner-Hassett:

It was only on his retirement in 1939 that the real nature of his contribution, in academic and personal terms, was perceived. Then, Harvard University and its Department of English were faced with a crucial decision. What was to become of Celtic Studies in the institution which was largely responsible for introducing them to America? President Conant was approached and, when a generous friend of the University placed at its disposal sufficient funds, Professor Kenneth Jackson of Cambridge, England, was installed as Associate Professor in Celtic. [31]

Réitíodh an fhadhb nuair a bhuail Henry Lee Shattuck, fear cáiliúil gnó in Boston le Dubhghlas de hÍde, scoláire Gaeilge agus Uachtarán na hÉireann. Ba é an toradh a bhí ar an gcruinniú gur fógraíodh Cathaoir mhaoinithe sa Léann Ceilteach san Ollscoil agus mar thoradh air sin bunaíodh roinn úr – Roinn Teangacha agus Litríochtaí na Ceiltise, an chéad roinn agus, go dtí an lá atá inniu ann, an t-aon roinn dá sórt sna Stáit Aontaithe.[32] Ba é Kenneth Hurlstone Jackson (1909–91) a rugadh in Croydon, Sasana, an chéad sealbhóir ar an gCathaoir úd. Stiúir sé an Léann Ceilteach in Ollscoil Harvard go dtí 1950 nuair a ceapadh Vernam Edward Nunnemacher Hull[33] (1894–1976), a bhí ina eagarthóir comhlach ar Fhoclóir an Nua-Bhéarla Mhoch in Ollscoil Michigan[34] agus ina Ollamh cúnta le Béarla in Ollscoil Nua-Eabhrac.[35] Thóg Charles W. Dunn (1916–2006) áit Hull sa bhliain 1962. Ba mhinistir Preispitéireach a athair in Albain nuair a rugadh Dunn ach d'aistrigh an teaghlach go Ceanada agus bhain an mac céim B.A. amach ó Ollscoil McMaster in Hamilton, Ontario. Dhein sé staidéar iarchéime sa Bhéarla agus sa Cheiltis faoi stiúir Robinson in Harvard agus bronnadh A.M. (1939) agus Ph.D. (1948) air.[36] D'oibrigh sé leis ó 1963 go dtí 1984 agus bhí cáil air mar mháistir tí (1966–81) ar Theach Quincy, suanlios de chuid Harvard.[37]

Is ar ainm John V. Kelleher, áfach, a chuimhneofar nuair a rianófar stair an Léinn Éireannaigh sna Stáit Aontaithe. Rugadh in Lawrence, Massachusetts ar an 8 Márta 1916 é agus thosaigh sé ar an nGaeilge a fhoghlaim agus é ina gharsún óg óna mhamó a saolaíodh i gCorcaigh. Lean sé air ag foghlaim na teanga ina dhiaidh sin faoi chúram Daniel J. O'Mahony, sagart Aibhistíneach agus col ceathar lena sheanmháthair. Tar éis dó céim bhunaidh ó Choláiste Dartmouth (1939) a chur de gan mórán stró, chláraigh sé mar Chomhalta Sóisearach sa bhliain 1940 i mbun staidéir le

Kenneth Jackson. Ba mar Chomhalta Sóisearach in aois 26 bliana a thug sé na léachtaí Lowell ar nua-litríocht na hÉireann. D'oibrigh sé sa Pentagon i rannóg na faisnéise míleata le linn an chogaidh agus bhí baint faoi leith aige leis an gCóiré. Thug sé a chéad chuairt ar Éirinn sa bhliain 1946 agus thosaigh ag múineadh cúrsaí ar stair agus ar litríocht na hÉireann an bhliain dár gcionn. Deineadh Ollamh le stair agus litríocht na hÉireann de sa bhliain 1960 agus ba mar bhall vótála de Roinn an Bhéarla agus na Staire a chaith sé a thréimhse in Harvard. Ina theannta sin, mhúin sé cúrsaí sa Scoil Fhairsingithe go bliantúil ar feadh nach mór tríocha bliain agus baint aige le Teach Lowell. Bhronn Harvard céim máistreachta oinigh air sa bhliain 1953 agus fuair sé Litt.D. oinigh ó Choláiste na Tríonóide, Baile Átha Cliath (1965) agus ó Choláiste na hOllscoile, Corcaigh (1999). Ar dhul amach ar pinsean dó, bhronn sé na mílte leabhar dá chuid féin ar leabharlanna de chuid Ollscoil Missouri, St. Louis, agus Ollscoil Southern Illinois, Carbondale. I ndiaidh Kelleher, bhí Seán Ó Coileáin i gceannas ar chúrsaí in Harvard ó 1984–85, ach ceapadh Patrick Ford mar Ollamh Margaret Brooks Robinson le Teangacha agus Litríocht na Ceiltise ó 1991–2005.[38] Nuair a d'éirigh sé as in 2005, tháinig Catherine McKenna mar chomharba air.[39]

De bharr fhlaithiúlacht Robinson, deineadh maoiniú ar an tarna Cathaoir sa Léann Ceilteach ar bhás a mhná agus tá Tomás Ó Cathasaigh as Port Láirge agus iarléachtóir sa Choláiste Ollscoile, Baile Átha Cliath agus san Institiúid Ard-Léinn sa chathaoir úd ó 1995 ar aghaidh. Is iad McKenna agus Ó Cathasaigh an bheirt ollúna[40] i Harvard faoi láthair agus i dteannta leis an scoláire Barbara Hillers, a bhfuil cúpla imleabhar de *Proceedings of the Harvard Celtic Colloquium* curtha in eagar aici, agus Margo Granfors, riarthóir na Roinne, leanann siad orthu ag múineadh agus ag déanamh taighde sa Léann Ceilteach agus ag cur leis an traidisiún seanbhunaithe in Harvard.[41]

Cé nach ollscoil ná coláiste í Institiúid Teangeolaíochta Mheiriceá, d'imir sí ról lárnach i gcur chun cinn na Gaeilge, go háirithe staidéar na teangeolaíochta Gaeilge, i measc scoláirí agus teangeolaithe Mheiriceá. Tuigeadh go forleathan sna Stáit nach raibh deis cheart ann do mhic léinn staidéar a dhéanamh ar an teangeolaíocht agus go raibh an dornán scoláirí a bhí ann scaipthe ar fud na tíre. Bunaíodh an Institiúid sa bhliain 1924 agus chuir siad rompu léirmheas a dhéanamh ar staid na disciplíne i gcoláistí agus in ollscoileanna Mheiriceá. Tugtar le fios sa tuairisc a foilsíodh 1926–27 go raibh cúrsaí sa 'Cheiltis' á dteagasc sna hionaid seo a leanas: Ollscoil Chaitliceach (4), Chicago (8), Columbia (10), Harvard (6), Nebraska (2) agus Northwestern (2).[42] Léiríodh díomá, áfach, faoi líon na gcúrsaí teangeolaíochta ar fud na tíre agus, mar leigheas ar an scéal, beartaíodh Institiúid Teangeolaíochta a bhunú in Ollscoil Yale ar feadh sé seachtaine le linn shamhradh na bliana 1928 ar chostas $40 an duine. Campa samhraidh teangeolaíochta ab ea é:

> ... to provide for students of linguistic science facilities similar to those afforded to biologists at Wood's Hole. Scholars who wished to carry on their own researches where they would have access to the needed books, and where they could experience the stimulus of discussion with other scholars of similar interests might find the Institute of advantage. There were to be also courses for graduate students, for high school and college teachers who felt the need of acquaintance with linguistic science or with the history of a particular language or group of languages, and for scholars who wished to familiarize themselves with more or less remote bits of linguistic territory in the most economical way.[43]

Ar an triúr léachtóirí is tríocha a bhí ar an bhfoireann, bhí Franz Boas (Ollscoil Columbia), Leonard Bloomfield (Ollscoil Chicago), Edward Sapir (Ollscoil Chicago) agus Joseph Dunn (An Ollscoil Chaitliceach). Cé gur bhocht an tinreamh sna blianta tosaigh, tuigeadh go maith do na heagarthóirí:

[t]he number is, in one way, not impressive, and yet in another way it is very significant. A school with only two students to every teacher must be branded a failure. But it was not as a school that the Institute was first conceived; it was planned to be a conference of scholars in a special field, and the courses were an addition to the plan to ensure the attendance of the scholars in some definite capacity, either as teachers or as pupils. And yet, as was hoped, many of the courses took the form of conferences, where in a group of two or three persons every one contributed his share and every one learned from every other, whichever one might be the nominal leader of the group. There was an unusual sympathetic scholarly atmosphere about the courses, and the remarkable earnestness of the students resulted in obviously unusual profits to them. Not the least valuable of the activities of the Institute was the gathering of small informal groups to discuss linguistic problems quite apart from the times and places of the scheduled courses; and in these, from time to time, virtually every one participated. [44]

Triúr a chláraigh do chúrsa Dunn sa Ghaeilge Mhoch: Miss Ida May Greer (South Dakota State College), Mr. J.A. Kerns (Whitman College, Washington) agus Miss Anna Irene Millar (John Hopkins). Mhéadaigh Dunn, a gcuirtear síos air mar 'Ollamh le Teangacha agus Litríochtaí Ceilteacha agus Léachtóir sna Teangacha Rómánsacha, Ollscoil Chaitliceach Mheiriceá' líon na gcúrsaí Gaeilge an bhliain dár gcionn nuair a thairg sé cúrsa sa bhreis sa Mheán-Ghaeilge. Seo mar a chuirtear síos ar an dá chúrsa úd sa chatalóg:

Old Irish – This course will serve as an introduction to Celtic Philology. It will consist of an outline of the grammar of Old Irish, a study of some Ogham inscriptions and of selections from the glosses and from the earliest literary texts. If desired, e.g. by students of the Latin language, a few lessons will be devoted to Gaulish. The course will be so arranged that a reading knowledge of French and German, while desirable, will not be necessary. Text-books: Pokorny, *A Historical Reader of Old Irish* (Niemeyer, Halle, 1923); Strachan, *Old Irish Paradigms* and *Selections from Old Irish Glosses* (Hodges, Figgis and Co. Dublin, 1909); Strachan, *Stories from the Táin* (ibid., 1908).[45]

Middle Irish – This course presupposes some knowledge of Old Irish, but, if need be, it will be shaped in accordance with the needs of beginners. It will consist of an outline of the grammar of Middle Irish, with references both to the older and to the more modern forms of the language, the interpretations of portions of the heroic saga and of ecclesiastical texts, and a paleographic and linguistic study of a short text from a photograph of the manuscript. Text-books: Dottin, *Manuel d'Irlandais Moyen* (Champion, Paris, 1913); Bergin and Meyer, *Anecdota from Irish Manuscripts*, Vol. III (Dublin and Halle, 1910).[46]

Ní raibh sé ar an bhfoireann ar chúis éigin sa bhliain 1930 in Nua-Eabhrac. Ach ba é John Lawrence Gerig (1878–1957), a gcuirtear síos air mar Ollamh le Ceiltis ó Ollscoil Columbia, an fear ionaid.[47] Is mór idir a chur síos siúd ar an gcúrsa agus bunchúrsa Dunn agus tugann sé léargas ar mhúineadh na Gaeilge in Ollscoil Columbia ag an am:

Old and Middle Irish. Mr. Gerig. – Grammar and reading of texts. This course will begin with the reading of Middle Irish texts and close with the study of Old Irish. In order to simplify the work as far as possible, the instructor will at first translate the texts and refer the students to the grammar for each word discussed. The Indo-European cognates of Celtic will be studied as far as possible. Text-books: G. Dottin, *Manuel d'Irlandais Moyen* (2 vols.), Paris (1913); J. Strachan, *Stories from the Táin*, 2nd ed., Dublin (1928).[48]

Bhí Dunn ar ais ar a sheanléim sa bhliain 1931 in Nua-Eabhrac nuair a thairg sé aon chúrsa amháin sa tSean- agus sa Mheán-Ghaeilge i dteannta a chéile.[49] Níorbh fhada áfach gur chuir líon na foirne agus laghad na mac léinn deireadh leis an scoil.[50] Beartaíodh cur chuige nua a mbeadh níos lú foirne agus níos lú léachtaí ann. Sa bhliain 1940 ag an gcomhdháil samhraidh in Ann Arbor, b'aoichainteoir é Vernam Hull ó Ollscoil Michigan, a labhair ar 'A Note on Middle Irish *sidein*'.[51] Bliain faoi leith ab ea an bhliain 1940 – ní hamháin gur cailleadh Rudolf Thurneysen, ball oinigh den Institiúid agus iartheagascóir de chuid Robinson agus Dunn, ach ba í an chéad uair go bhfacthas Myles Dillon i lár an aonaigh mar scoláire Gaeilge i Meiriceá. Níorbh fhada go raibh sé ag treabhadh leis agus labhair sé ag cruinniú bliantúil na Nollag den Institiúid in Providence ar an ábhar 'Some Irish Words'.[52] B'Ollamh é Dillon a raibh Cathaoir sa Léann Ceilteach aige in Ollscoil Wisconsin – Madison ó 1937 go dtí 1946 sular aistrigh sé go hOllscoil Chicago. Sna blianta ina dhiaidh seo, d'éirigh le Dillon tús áite a bhaint amach i measc na scoláirí san Institiúid; ba mhinic é i mbun páipéir agus ag déanamh léirmheasa ar pháipéir na comhdhála. I measc na n-aoichainteanna a thug sé don Institiúid, áirítear 'The Impersonal Transitive Verb in Irish' (1942); 'The Formation of the Subjunctive Stem in Irish and the Problem of the Indo-European Future' (1943); agus 'Textual Criticism and Literary Interpretation' (1944). Sa bhliain 1942 ceapadh Robinson ina uachtarán agus toghadh Dillon ar choiste riaracháin na hInstitiúide. Lean Dunn, Gerig agus Daniel F. Sheehan (Michigan State College) orthu ag gníomhú mar ghnáthbhaill na hInstitiúide. Nuair a chuaigh Robinson amach ar pinsean ó Harvard agus nuair a d'fhill Dillon ar Éirinn, thráigh ról na Gaeilge san Institiúid tar éis an chogaidh; mar sin féin níor chóir neamhshuim a dhéanamh de thábhacht na hInstitiúide i gcur chun cinn na Gaeilge mar ábhar taighde sna Stáit Aontaithe go háirithe i measc teangeolaithe agus lucht léinn. De réir mar a d'fhás ballraíocht na hInstitiúide ó bunaíodh í, foilsíodh sraith leanúnach alt in iris na hinstitiúide dar teideal *Language* agus de bharr ghníomhaíochtaí Dillon, Dunn agus Gerig, d'fhan an Ghaeilge os comhair teangeolaithe sna Stáit Aontaithe.

Ollscoil California, Berkeley

Más gaisce ag an Ollscoil Chaitliceach é gur acusan a bhí an chéad Chathaoir sa Cheiltis agus ag Harvard gurbh í an chéad ollscoil a thairg cúrsa sa Léann Ceilteach, ní foláir gradam faoi leith a thabhairt d'Ollscoil California, Berkeley mar an chéad ollscoil sna Stáit Aontaithe a raibh cúrsa céime sa Cheiltis aici. Is fada an nasc idir Berkeley agus an Ghaeilge agus tosaíonn an traidisiún úd ag tús na haoise seo caite le Charles Mills Gayley (1858–1932), fear ar cuireadh síos air mar 'a literary scholar distinguished for accuracy of information, clearness of method, sensitiveness of critical taste, breadth of comment, and vigor of expression'.[53] Ba eisean a bhí i gceannas ar Roinn an Bhéarla in Ollscoil California, Berkeley ó 1889 go 1919 tar éis dó Ollscoil Michigan a thréigint ar mhaithe le Berkeley sa bhliain 1889. Agus é ina pháiste, bhí tréimhsí caite aige ar saoire i nDún na nGall, Tír Eoghain agus Oileán Acla, áiteanna iad ar fad ar casadh cainteoirí Gaeilge air agus áiteanna a raibh traidisiún láidir béil fós le sonrú i measc na ndaoine. Ar nós Child agus Kittredge thoir in Harvard, thuig Gayley tábhacht an tseanchais béil agus theastaigh uaidh go mbeadh fáil ag a fhoireann ar theanga agus ar litríocht na Gaeilge. Agus fís aige do Berkeley mar ollscoil den scoth a raibh Roinn Bhéarla eiseamláireach inti, theastaigh scoláire Gaeilge uaidh mar áis don fhoireann agus do na mic léinn. Le linn dó a bheith ina cheann roinne ar Roinn an Bhéarla, d'áitigh sé ar William Whittingham Lyman Jr. (1835–1983), fochéimí ó Napa County, California, tabhairt faoin Léann Ceilteach. Tar éis do Lyman (ar a dtugtar Jack Lyman, leis) céim mháistreachta a bhaint amach, agus le cabhair agus dea-thoil Gayley, bronnadh comhaltacht air dul go Sasana ar feadh bliana chun staidéar a dhéanamh faoi stiúir Sir John Rhys in Ollscoil Oxford. Chaith sé dhá bhliain ina dhiaidh sin ag foghlaim na Gaeilge in Harvard. D'fhill sé ar an gcósta thiar agus ar phost buan mar Theagascóir le Ceiltis i Roinn an Bhéarla sa bhliain 1911–12. Sa bhliain chéanna aithníodh an Cheiltis mar phríomhábhar ceadaithe i nDámh na nEalaíon agus na hEolaíochta agus an bhliain dár gcionn ainmníodh Lyman mar chomhairleoir na mac léinn iarchéime, cúram a bhí air go dtí an bhliain 1922.[54] Ba le linn an ama seo a ceapadh Joseph O'Hagerty[55] mar 'Reader in Irish' agus tuarastal $500 aige don bhliain 1910–11, agus $600 don bhliain 1911–12. Ba mhó é seo ná an $100 a íocadh le Stanley L. Dod, Reader in Dental

Pathology and Therapeutics agus bhí sé ar cóimhéid le cúntóir sóisearach i leabharlann na hOllscoile, ach ba lú é ná an $1000–$1500 a thuill teagascóirí sna teangacha Rómánsacha, agus an $2000 a d'íoctaí le hOllúna Cúnta sa Cheimic agus sa tSanscrait. Bhí buiséad $499.92 ag Roinn na Ceiltise don bhliain 1911 agus $600 don bhliain 1912, suim i bhfad níos lú ná an $2000 a bronnadh ar chláir na dteangacha Oirthearacha, Seimíteacha agus Slavacha agus ar chlár teanga na Sanscraite.[56]

Ó 1909 i leith ba ghné lárnach de na cúrsaí a chuirtí ar fáil in Berkeley iad teangacha agus litríocht na Ceiltise. Thrácht *The Annual Report of the President of the University on behalf of the Regents* go bliantúil ar imeachtaí na Roinne agus sa bhliain 1917, dúradh: 'The Department of Celtic has pursued its usual policies throughout the last year. It suffered an indirect loss through the discontinuance, due to war conditions, of the annual contribution ($42.83 in 1911) of the Knights of St. Patrick for Celtic books for the library'.[57] Sa bhliain 1919 tuairiscíodh: 'the department has pursued its usual quiet but interesting course. The number of students enrolled in the course has not been affected by the war conditions'.[58]

Ceapadh Ella Young (1867–1956) sa bhliain 1924 in áit Lyman a bhí tar éis éirí as. B'fhile í Young a fostaíodh mar 'James D. Phelan Lecturer in Irish Myth and Lore', agus dhein sí cúram de go dtí 1934. B'Aontromach mná í ar bhall de Chumann na mBan le linn Éirí Amach na Cásca í agus ba chara leis an bPiarsach, le Maud Gonne agus le George William Russell í. B'fhearr an aithne uirthi i Meiriceá, áfach, ní mar fhile ach mar údar a d'athscríobh agus a d'athinis seanscéalta agus seanmhiotas na hÉireann i mBéarla. Scoir sí leis an léann sa bhliain 1934 agus chuir fúithi i gcoilíneacht Dhiasúnacht ar a dtugtar Halcyon, lámh le San Luis Obispo, agus b'ann a tharraing Ansel Adams an t-aon phortráid dá bhfuil againn di. Chuir sí an-spéis i gcothú na gcrónghúisí a fhásann sa cheantar agus d'fhág sí formhór a maoine lena gcothú ina huacht. Ar imeacht di ó Berkeley, ceapadh Arthur Eugene Hutson (1906–82), iarmhac léinn eile de chuid

Robinson agus thairng seisean cúrsaí sa tSean-Ghaeilge agus sa Cheiltis. Is eisean a mholtar as dlús a chur faoin mbailiúchán Ceiltise atá sa leabharlann in Berkeley. I ndiaidh Hudson, ghlac Breandán Ó hEithir (1927–91) a rugadh in Nua-Eabhrac do thuismitheoirí Éireannacha, cúram na Ceiltise agus na Gaeilge air féin. Cailleadh a athair i dtimpiste fothraenach agus cuireadh abhaile go hÉirinn chuig gaolta é le tógaint.[59] B'ann a d'fhoghlaim sé an Ghaeilge i gcéaduair. Ar theacht ar ais go Meiriceá dó, dhein sé an scrúdú ollscoile in Fordham le cúnamh scoláireacht Stáit de chuid Nua-Eabhrac. D'fhág sé an ollscoil in 1946 chun dul le baincéireacht in Baltimore ach mar sin féin d'éirigh leis a bhunchéim a chríochnú in Ollscoil Loyola sa bhliain 1953. Ba í an bhliain chéanna ar thosaigh sé ar staidéar iarchéime in Ollscoil Johns Hopkins áit ar bhain sé M.A. (1954) agus Ph.D. (1959) amach. Tháinig sé go Berkeley mar theagascóir sa bhliain 1958, agus ardaíodh go leibhéal Ollaimh Chúnta é sa bhliain 1960. In ainneoin na ndualgas i leith na Gaeilge agus na Ceiltise, spreag a chuid spéise in Joyce agus litríocht an Bhéarla an saothar *Gaelic Lexicon to Finnegan's Wake* (1967). Ní hamháin gur bhall bunaidh é den Chomhdháil Cheilteach in Ollscoil California (1979) ach ba cheannródaí é maidir leis an gClár don Léann Ceilteach in Berkeley (1989) agus ba é an chéad chathaoirleach ar an gcúrsa é. Mhúin Joan Trodden Keefe an Ghaeilge ar feadh na mblianta fada in Berkeley mar chuid den chlár seo go dtí gur éirigh sí as sna 1990í. Áirítear cúrsaí na Gaeilge – idir theanga agus litríocht – agus na Ceiltise anois in aon rannóg amháin i dteannta leis an Iodáilis agus na teangacha Lochlannacha agus Slavacha agus tá cúraimí na Ceiltise idir lámha ag Maria Teresa Agozzino, Gary Holland, Kathryn Klar, Daniel F. Melia, Esther O'Hara, Annalee C. Rejhon, Kimberly Starr-Reid, Eve Sweetser agus Kathi Brosnan ina riarthóir.

COLÁISTE BOSTON

Tá traidisiún fada cáiliúil ag Coláiste Boston mar chosantóir Léann na hÉireann sna Stáit Aontaithe. Ach mar a fheictear i saothar an tsagairt óig Michael P. Mahon ní gan stró ná anró a bunaíodh cathaoir mhaoinithe sa Ghaeilge agus dhúisigh iarrachtaí chun an Ghaeilge a fhorbairt mar ábhar léinn giorriacha as a leapacha dearga. Ní ceist airgid amháin a bhí ann i gcónaí ach bhain sé go dlúth le polaitíocht agus le ceisteanna móra sóisialta. Léiríonn aistí Mahon an deacracht a bhain le cur chun cinn na Gaeilge sna Stáit tráth a raibh amhras faoi éagsúlacht teanga agus náisiúntachtaí. Is léir an méid sin óna léacht in Ard-Eaglais Boston ar an 30 Bealtaine 1908:

> We are all, or very nearly all, from that Sainted Isle, either by birth or by descent. But we are not pilgrims. We are here to stay. We are part of the great American people, a part of the noble people of Massachusetts and of this great city. Nevertheless when we find ourselves gathered in the great metropolitan church of New England, by the special favor and gracious encouragement of our own great Archbishop, to have a heart to heart talk in our ancient tongue, we cannot help feeling some of the racial as well as spiritual exaltation that filled the soul of John MacHale at Rome.[60]

In óráid eile a thug sé i nGaeilge do Scoil Ghaeilge Boston ar an 24 Eanáir 1909, chuir sé síos ar ghaisce an Ard-Easpaig Mac hÉil agus ar iarrachtaí Chonradh na Gaeilge ar son na teanga. Ba chúis áthais dó go raibh an Ghaeilge á teagasc i gColáiste Boston i ndeisceart na cathrach:

> … has been taken up, if not literally, at least substantially, not only in his own college of St. Jarlath and in the colleges of Ireland generally; but far away from the Irish shores, in the heart of New England, under the fostering care of the greatest educational body in the world, and with the blessing of our Most Reverend Archbishop and the last wish of the Archbishop of Tuam, the desire of every enlightened and patriotic Irish mind and of every lover of the most profound linguistic study, is beginning to receive full realization. The Irish language has found its way into Boston College. May it

never leave these halls! And when our greatest Catholic educational institution of New England on University Heights is a reality, may it be our pride and our glory to furnish the means to establish and equip there a chair representing our language, literature and history, a chair filled by some Jesuit worthy of the order of which Rev. Edmund Hogan, the great Celticist of Dublin, is a member.[61]

Tagraíonn clabhsúr Mahon agus an tagairt do Hogan mar scoláire Íosánach a raibh spéis aige sa Léann Ceilteach don fheachtas chun cathaoir mhaoinithe sa Ghaeilge a bhunú sa choláiste. Ba thráthúil a leithéid dar le Mahon in óráid (30 Bealtaine, 1908) dá chuid ina ndúirt sé 'we can proudly point to the fact that the Universities of our own great land are, one by one, establishing Celtic Chairs'.[62] Lean sé air:

It has been for many years in the leading universities; and in University College, Liverpool, England, there is even a chair of modern Irish, in the care of Father Kelliher. The new Boston College cannot very well help establishing a Celtic chair, as it is safe to assume that the greatest educational body of our age will not be satisfied with having their university second to any other in this great enlightened nation … We may look to this college in the future as we now look to the Catholic university at Washington and to Dr. Robinson's 'Celtic Colony' at Harvard, to cultivate in America the enlightened taste for Celtic studies that we already find in the great European universities.[63]

In ainneoin tacaíocht Cardinal O'Connell a bheith aige, theip air. In ainneoin a chuid iarrachtaí ar fad agus a chuid óráidí agus a chuid scéimeanna tiomsaithe airgid, theip ar an iarracht chun Ollúnacht le Gaeilge a chur chun cinn. Ag deireadh na heachtra ar fad díbríodh go hiarthar an stáit é. Ceapadh uachtarán nua ar an gcoláiste sa bhliain 1907, Thomas I. Gasson SJ, a bhí ina uachtarán ar Choláiste Boston ó 1907 go 1914. B'iarollamh le heitic agus le heacnamaíocht é Gasson agus ba bheag a spéis i gcás na Gaeilge ná i moltaí ná i dtuairimí an tsagairt óig nár bhain leis an ord. Rugadh in Kent, Sasana sa bhliain 1859 é agus d'iompaigh ina Chaitliceach tar éis dó dul ar imirce go Meiriceá sa bhliain

1872. Oirníodh é mar Íosánach sa bhliain 1891, ceapadh ina léachtóir sa choláiste ceithre bliana ina dhiaidh sin é agus fógraíodh ina Uachtarán é sa bhliain 1907. Faoi cheannasaíocht Gasson d'aistrigh an coláiste, a bhunaigh na hÍosánaigh sa bhliain 1863, ón mbunláthair ar Harrison Avenue i ndeisceart na cathrach go láthair nua 31 acra taobh le teorainn Chestnut Hill/Brighton. Cé gur tosaíodh ar an bhfoirgneamh álainn den stíl Ghotach sa bhliain 1909, níor críochnaíodh é go dtí 1913 mar stopadh den tógáil tar éis dhá bhliain cheal airgid. B'éigean na páirceanna lúthchleasaíochta ar Massachusetts Avenue a dhíol chun an foirgneamh a chríochnú. De réir an bhéaloidis, cuireadh an t-airgead a bhailigh an sagart óg don Chathaoir mhaoinithe sa Ghaeilge i dtreo an fhoirgnimh nua agus gurb é atá sna manaí Gaeilge sna fuinneoga greanta a léiríonn naoimh na hÉireann sa phríomhsheomra ná tagairt faoi rún don bhunchuspóir sin.

Fíoraíodh aisling Mahon, áfach, nuair a ceapadh John Eustace Murphy (1901–85) ar an bhfoireann sa bhliain 1940. Saolaíodh in Newton Massachusetts é agus d'fhreastail sé ar scoileanna áitiúla sula ndeachaigh sé isteach sna hÍosánaigh sa bhliain 1922. Chaith sé na blianta réamhchogaidh (1935–39) i mbun staidéir in Éirinn agus sa Bhreatain Bheag, tréimhse inar bhain sé Ph.D. amach ó Ollscoil Náisiúnta na hÉireann. Agus an dochtúireacht aige, tugadh ardú dó ó bheith ina theagascóir na gClassacaí in Boston College High School go dtí Boston College, áit ar lonnaigh sé i Roinn na Litríochta Gaeilge. Sular ceapadh é mar Bhainisteoir Gnó na hOllscoile, mhúin Murphy cúrsaí rialta ar litríocht na Gaeilge trí mheán an Bhéarla mar is léir óna chartlann i leabharlann John J. Burns. Bhíodh léachtaí aige ar réimse fairsing ábhar: Caoineadh Airt Uí Laoire, Seathrún Céitinn, Aodh Mac Aingil, Seán Clárach Mac Domhnaill, Séamus Dall mac Cuarta, Donnchadh Mac Conmara, Brian Merriman, Piaras Mac Gearailt, Patrick Pearse agus Pádraic Ó Conaire i measc scríbhneoirí eile. Deimhníonn Mac Aonghusa go múintí an Ghaeilge sa choláiste idir na blianta 1944–7 agus go raibh isteach agus amach ar scór mac léinn á foghlaim.[64] Thráigh an

Ghaeilge nuair a ceapadh Murphy mar riarthóir gnó[65] ach tháinig sí chuici féin arís sa bhliain 1989 nuair a cheap Adele Dalsimer agus Kevin O'Neill scoláire Gaeilge mar chuid den chlár nua sa Léann Éireannach.[66] Ba é Philip T. O'Leary a roghnaíodh, scoláire eile a rugadh agus a tógadh in Worcester agus a bhain Ph.D. sa Cheiltis amach in Harvard. Ó shin i leith tá cúrsaí i dteanga agus i litríocht na Gaeilge á dtairiscint sa choláiste agus cruthaíodh post buan don Ghaeilge sa bhliain 2005.[67] Is é Joe Nugent, a mhúin an Ghaeilge agus a d'eagair cúrsaí samhraidh (1999–2003) in Berkeley roimhe sin, a ceapadh. Tá lucht na Gaeilge istigh le Roinn an Bhéarla agus eagraítear na cúrsaí Gaeilge mar chuid de Léann na hÉireann faoi stiúir Thomas Hachey, Majorie Howes agus Robert Savage.

A group of Irish-language students outside Bond Hall, University of Notre Dame, c. 1920, (University of Notre Dame Archives)

OLLSCOIL NOTRE DAME

Más idir Harvard, an Ollscoil Chaitliceach agus Berkeley atá an cháil don chéad institiúid chun an Ghaeilge a mhúineadh i Meiriceá, d'fhéadfadh breall a bheith ar an triúr acu. Is cosúil nach ag aon cheann acu atá an gradam seo. Más fíor don chartlann in Ollscoil Notre Dame múineadh an teanga san ollscoil chomh fada siar le 1868. Cuirtear síos ar an mBráthair Simeon mar 'Teacher of the Irish Language', a mhúin ranganna Gaeilge sa tréimhse 1868–73. Dominic Fleming as Gort Inse Guaire i ndeisceart na Gaillimhe ab ea é agus cuireann a chomh-Bhráthair O'Reilly síos air mar '... a true Irish scholar. He spoke and taught Irish. He was a man of few words, but a good religious'.[68] Tuairiscíonn an nuachtán ó Bhleá Cliath, *The Nation*, gur fhreastail breis agus 350 mac léinn ar a chuid ranganna.[69] Cruthaíonn an lámhleabhar ollscoile don bhliain 1874 go raibh an Ghaeilge ina hábhar ollscoile: 'Matriculation fee ... $5.00. Board, Bed, Bedding, Tuition (Latin and Grammar) Washing, Mending, Doctor's fees and medicine and attendance in sickness $150. French, German, Italian, Spanish, Hebrew, and Irish, each – $10.00'. Le linn don Bhráthair Simeon a bheith i mbun na Gaeilge, scríobh na mic léinn chuig Uilic de Búrca (1829–87), rúnaí Mhic Éil agus Ollamh le Gaeilge, le Loighic agus leis an Léann Daonna, agus a bhí ina uachtarán ar Choláiste Iarlatha ina dhiaidh sin.[70] Cailleadh Simeon de bharr taom croí ar an 22 Lúnasa 1873, gan é ach 35 bliain d'aois agus ba lena linn a ceapadh an Bráthair Patrick (1797–1867) mar Ollamh le Gaeilge – arbh é Michael Connelly as Contae na Mí ó dhúchas é. Bhreac Thomas J. Dundon, fochéimí ó Clarkesburg, Michigan, nóta ina dhialann faoina chuid staidéir ar an nGaeilge agus iontas a athar:

> I reserved a surprise for my father. I had not told him that I had studied the Irish language under Brother Patrick, Professor of Irish. As I was recounting to my father (during the Christmas Break) the subjects I had studied, I said, 'I can read the Irish language!' He seemed incredulous, so I got my book of poems in Irish and read 'The Bells of Shandon'. When

I had finished reading I asked him if I had done well. He made no reply but on looking up I saw a tear glistening in his eye. My father was born within hearing distance of the real 'Bells of Shandon'.[71]

Ba dhlúthchuid den chlár léinn in Notre Dame í an Ghaeilge ó na 1870í ar aghaidh, dáta atá an-luath agus an-suntasach ó taobh stair na teanga sna Stáit Aontaithe agus rud a chiallaíonn murab é Notre Dame an chéad ollscoil a múintí an teanga inti, is cinnte go raibh sí i measc na chéad choláistí a ghlac cúram na teanga orthu féin. Tar éis bhás an Bhráthar Simeon, thráigh an Ghaeilge go dtí gur tháinig an Bráthair Finan C.S.C. ar an bhfód i dtúsbhlianta na fichiú haoise (1901–05). Cuirtear síos air mar theagascóir agus mar Ollamh le Gaeilge; ba é stiúrthóir Shuanlios Carroll é freisin idir na blianta 1901–05. Is mó rud a bhaineann leis an nGaeilge a thit amach idir na blianta seo. Bunaíodh craobh de Chonradh na Gaeilge san Ollscoil sa bhliain 1901 agus foilsíodh éileamh i nuachtán na hollscoile, *The Scholastic*, go mbunófaí Cathaoir i dTeanga agus i Litríocht na Gaeilge. Thug Dubhghlas de hÍde, duine de bhunaitheoirí Chonradh na Gaeilge agus fear a cheapfaí ina chéad uachtarán ar Éirinn, cuairt ar an ollscoil idir 27–29 Eanáir 1906 mar chuid dá thuras tiomsaithe airgid. Ba chuimhin leis ina dhírbheathaisnéis *Mo Thuras go Meiriceá*, gur fháiltigh an tOllamh Hugh O'Neill, an tOllamh MacGahan agus fear darbh ainm O'Sullivan, ar chainteoir dúchais é, dar leis an gCraoibhín roimhe.[72] Thug sé léacht uair go leith ar sheanscéalta na Gaeilge do chúig chéad ban i gColáiste Mhuire [Saint Mary's College] agus léacht eile ar bhéaloideas do mhic léinn Notre Dame a foilsíodh sa *Notre Dame Scholastic*. Dar leis an bpáipéar sin:

> Dr. Hyde is a speaker interestingly powerful and powerfully interesting … no one who had heard him but was glad to have had the opportunity, and realized that such experiences come but once or twice, if at all, in the run of a long college career.[73]

Chaith de hÍde an oíche ag comhrá le baill foirne agus leis an Athair John W. Cavanaugh, Uachtarán na hOllscoile ó 1905–19. Lá arna mhárach bhronn an tAthair John Augustine

Zham[74] C.S.C. (1851–1921) cóip de dhánta Dante ar de hÍde agus d'impigh air iad a aistriú go Gaeilge, an t-aon teanga Eorpach dar leis nach raibh siad le fáil inti. Chuir sé deireadh lena chuairt ar Notre Dame le léacht i gcathair South Bend sular thug sé bóthar Chicago air féin.

Tairgeadh ranganna Gaeilge le linn an tsamhraidh sa bhliain 1910 ach ba bheag a tharla go rialta go dtí 1919. B'shin an bhliain ar tháinig an tAthair Hugh S. Gallagher C.S.C. (1873–1949) go Notre Dame ó Ollscoil Columbia in Portland, áit a raibh sé ina leasuachtarán ar an ollscoil agus ar cuireadh síos air mar Ollamh le Ceiltis a raibh Gaeilge, Breatnais agus Briotáinis aige. Dhein Gallagher athbheochan ar an nGaeilge san ollscoil agus ceapadh breis teagascóirí, ina measc an tAthair Jeremiah Harrington agus John Joseph O'Hagerty. Is suntasach an rud é O'Hagerty a bheith ar an bhfoireann in Notre Dame toisc é a bheith ag múineadh Gaeilge roimhe sin in Berkeley, rud a thugann le fios go raibh daoine ag aistriú ní hamháin ó Harvard go hollscoileanna eile ach go raibh teagmháil éigin idir na hinstitiúidí. Eagraíodh cúrsaí samhraidh do mhic léinn idir 1920–24 i dteanga, i litríocht, i stair agus i mbéaloideas na hÉireann. Fógraíodh sa *Scholastic*:

> Notre Dame is fast becoming one of the best centers of Irish learning in the country. An Irish library has been collected, which, if the present plans develop, will be in time one of the finest libraries in this country. During this school year Professor J.J. O'Hagerty, formerly of the University of California, has been in charge of the courses in Irish language, history, and literature. He will be assisted during the summer school by the Rev. Hugh Gallagher, C.S.C., a specialist in the Gaelic language and Irish history, and by Rev. Jeremiah C. Harrington, of the St. Paul Seminary, also a noted Irish scholar. Elementary, intermediate and special courses in Gaelic will be offered, the last for those who can speak the language but have had little opportunity to read and write it … The object of these courses is to give the student a correct understanding of the language, history and life of the Irish people from the earliest time to the present day.[75]

Mar aon le cúrsaí ar nós 'Irish Influence on European Civilization', 'The Music of Ireland', 'History of the Gaelic Literature in Ireland', agus 'Irish Political Movements in the 19th Century', thairg an roinn dar theideal 'the Gaelic Department of the Notre Dame Summer School' trí chúrsa teanga agus is fiú cur síos an nuachtáin ar na cúrsaí a léamh ar mhaithe leis an léargas a thugann siad ar chur chuige agus meon na linne:

> Elementary Gaelic: the initial mutations, aspirations and eclipses, declensions, conjugations and as much of the etymology of the language as can be covered with thoroughness. This course aims to fit the student for a good understanding of simple texts in Gaelic. Two hours a day: Eight hours a week.

> Intermediate Irish: for those who have had at least a half-year in Gaelic. This course will include a brief review of course I, the completion of etymology, syntax, the reading of Gaelic texts, translation from English into Gaelic, and conversation practice in Gaelic. Two hours a day: Eight hours a week.

Pé rud é faoi na cúrsaí úd is é an tríú cúrsa an ghné is spéisiúla ar fad. Faoin teideal 'Special Course in Gaelic' tá sé intuigthe uaidh go raibh pobal labhartha Gaeilge in aice láimhe a raibh labhairt na teanga acu ach iad aineolach nó dall ar léamh agus ar scríobh na teanga:

> Special Course in Gaelic: for those who speak the language but who have had little or no opportunity to read or write it. There will be in this course as much application of grammar as the needs of the student may demand. One hour a day; Four hours a week.

Ba líonmhair na huaisle ó Éirinn a thuirling in Notre Dame le linn an 19ú agus 20ú haois. Bhí Cathaoir i Roinn an Bhéarla ag an léirmheastóir agus údar Shane Leslie (1885–1971) sa bhliain 1935; ba mhinic Seamus Mac Manus (1869–1960) ar cuairt mar theagascóir agus mar aoichainteoir sna 1920í agus 1930í agus dóbair don drámadóir Críostóir Ó Floinn (1927–) teacht go Notre Dame ar scoláireacht sa bhliain 1960. Ach is ar éigean aon duine acu inchurtha le hÉamon de

Valera – 'the uncrowned king of Ireland' mar a tugadh air le linn a chuairte sa bhliain 1919.

Tar éis dó éalú ó phríosún Lincoln i Sasana ar an 3 Feabhra 1919, bhuail imní an IRA go mbainfí an bonn den bholscaireacht dá ngabhfaí an athuair é. Seoladh go Meiriceá é dá bharr chun cás na hÉireann a chur chun cinn, argóint a dhéanamh ar mhaithe leis an bhfeachtas saoirse agus airgead a bhailiú. Shir sé soir agus siar ar fud na tíre ar son na cúise sin agus lá dá raibh tharla in South Bend agus in Ollscoil Notre Dame, Indiana é. Thug *The Scholastic* le fios gur ghlac de Valera le cuireadh ón Athair Burns, Uachtarán na hOllscoile, chun labhairt leis an mic léinn ar an gCéadaoin 15 Deireadh Fómhair:

> Elaborate preparations are being made at the university by the committees acting with the local branch of the Friends of Irish Freedom for the reception of the distinguished visitor. If the necessary arrangements can be made, the students will be asked to turn out *en masse* for a parade, and the school's newly-organized band will be expected to add 'tone' to the reception.[76]

Éamon de Valera, Notre Dame Scholastic
(Courtesy of University of Notre Dame Archives)

Thug eagrán na chéad seachtaine eile le fios gur chóir meas a léiriú ar an gcuairteoir: 'Notre Dame's welcome should be worthy of the eminence of her guest'. Níor ghá a bheith inmíonoch. Dar leis an *Ave Maria*:

> It was characteristically gracious of Dr. Eamon de Valera, 'King of Ireland', as one youthful admirer calls him to assure the students of the University of Notre Dame that he would remember as 'his happiest day in America' the one when he visited them. The address in which he made this statement evoked such applause as the eminent Irishman seldom hears, it was so spontaneous, continuous and uproarious. He was listened to with breathless attention, every one present seemingly eager to catch every word that fell from his lips. But his personality made even a deeper impression – his gravity when speaking of serious things, his reverence when referring to holy things. Few failed to observe how recollectedly he said grace at table, and how thoroughly absorbed he seemed to be while kneeling before the Blessed Sacrament. A good as well as a great man, a leader who inspires the highest respect and the fullest confidence, is President Eamon de Valera.[77]

Bhain óráid de Valera, a foilsíodh sa nuachám *The Scholastic*, le dearcadh na hÉireann i leith Léig na Náisiún, moráltacht an Éirí Amach agus na féidearthachtaí go mbeadh comhoibriú síochánta idir Caitlicigh agus Protastúnaigh. Scríobh T.J. Tobin:

> From the time sixteen hundred Notre Dame men joined in a big U.N.D. for De Valera, till Doctor Burns bade him bon voyage on leaving, the visitor smiled his satisfaction. … Upon his arrival, Mr. De Valera received one of the greatest ovations that Notre Dame has ever accorded a visitor. After exchanging greetings with Very Reverend Provincial Morrissey and the members of the faculty, he proceeded to the statue of Father Corby, at the foot of which he laid a wreath bearing the inscription 'From Eamon De Valera in loving tribute to Father Corby who gave general absolution to the Irish Brigade at Gettysburg'. After he had spoken briefly upon the importance of the role played by army chaplains, he was taken to the University Library and shown the Gaelic collection in which are the sword of General Meaghar and the flag of the Irish Brigade. From the Library he went to the center of the

quadrangle and there planted a tree as a memorial of his visit.[78]

D'fhill de Valera ar Éirinn um Nollaig 1920 agus bhí sé ina cheannasaí ar an dream a throid i gcoinne an Chonartha Angla-Éireannaigh. Gabhadh arís é agus rinneadh cime de ag iarchomrádaithe seachas ag Gaill. Nuair a bhuail imní a lucht leanúna go rabhthas ag tabhairt drochíde dó, d'iarr siad ar Notre Dame teacht i gcabhair orthu: 'to use its influence to obtain immediate information regarding the present condition and whereabouts of the distinguished scholar and statesman its President and faculty took pride in honoring if for no other reason that to alleviate the suffering and anxiety of his sorrowing wife (or perhaps widow) and family and to join in the nation wide demand for his release, if still alive'.[79] Saothar in aisce é, áfach, d'aon duine an crann a chuir de Valera le linn a chuairte ar an ollscoil a lorg sa lá atá inniu ann. Seachtain tar éis dó é a chur, stróiceadh aníos ón talamh é agus caitheadh sa loch é atá taobh leis an uaimh. Aontachtaí míshásta ba chúis leis.

Le bás Gallagher sa bhliain 1949, tháinig meath nach mór iomlán ar theagasc na Gaeilge go dtí tús na 1990í nuair a thug Christopher Fox i Roinn an Bhéarla faoin Léann Éireannach a bhunú san Ollscoil. Is é a chuir tús leis an bhfiontar ar a dtugtar Institiúid Mhic Eochaidh-Uí Neachtain um an Léann Éireannach.[80] I dtús báire cheap sé Seamus Deane agus an scoláire Gaeilge Peter McQuillan, a rugadh i nDún Dealgán agus a oileadh in Harvard. Bhí cúrsaí Gaeilge ar fáil do mhic léinn arís agus McQuillan ar an láthair mar bhall de Roinn an Bhéarla sa bhliain 1992. De thoradh fhís agus fhuinneamh Fox, bunaíodh Roinn Theanga agus Litríocht na Gaeilge ar 1 Deireadh Fómhair 2004, an t-aon roinn dá sórt sna Stáit agus ba é an tUasal Noel Fahy, Ambasadóir na hÉireann i Stáit Aontaithe Mheiriceá, a labhair ag an ócáid. Ghlac Breandán Ó Buachalla, ball d'Acadamh Ríoga na hÉireann, leis an gCathaoir mhaoinithe i dTeanga agus i Litríocht na Gaeilge sa bhliain 2002 agus ceapadh Sarah McKibben agus Brian Ó Conchubhair mar ollúna cúnta ina dhiaidh sin.[81] Tá fás leanúnach ar líon na mac léinn ag clárú le ranganna na Roinne ó shin i leith.[82] Sa bhliain 2005, céad is a deich mbliana ó d'fhág Fred Robinson Harvard chun staidéar a dhéanamh faoi Thurneysen, cheadaigh Dámh na nDán agus na hEolaíochta in Notre Dame Mionúr i dTeanga agus Litríocht na Gaeilge, an chéad cháilíocht dá sórt sna Stáit.

CONCLÚID

Chuir Blenner-Hasset tús lena aiste ón mbliain 1954 trí chaighdeán na scoláirí sa Léann Ceilteach a mholadh. Chaoin sé a laghad daoine a bhí ag gabháil don léann sin agus cháin sé easpa suime an phobail san ábhar:

> Though their numbers are few, it may be said that the Celticists in this country constitute a unique body of scholars. All of them, despite the handicaps of limited resources, give generously of their time and energies to promote the cause of Celtic Studies. All of them stand ready to place their knowledge and training at the disposal of students in related disciplines. Most regrettable is the apathy displayed towards Celtic Studies by the majority of people of Celtic origins in the United States. One might reasonably suppose that, in view of their numerical strength and the prominence they have achieved in all walks of life, Americans of Celtic origin would display a far more active and generous interest than they have thus far in the cultures of the lands of their forebears. The great revival of interest in Celtic culture in the homelands has not yet been, but may eventually be, reflected in America.[83]

Déantar staidéar ar an nGaeilge ar fud na Stát Aontaithe anois; i gcoláistí Caitliceacha agus i gcoláistí pobail, i gcoláistí stáit agus i gcoláistí príobháideacha. Eagraíonn *The Celtic Studies Association of North America*, (CSANA), a bunaíodh sa bhliain 1976, seisiúin gach bliain ag an gcomhdháil idirnáisiúnta de léann na Meán-Aoiseanna agus ag comhdháil bhliantúil an *Modern Language Association* um Nollaig. Ina theannta sin eagraítear comhdháil Cheilteach go bliantúil in California mar aon leis an *Harvard Celtic Colloquium*. Ní hionann an scéal inniu agus an t-am a bhí Blenner-Hasset i mbun pinn. Sa staidéar a dhein E.B. Wells i 2002 ar chlárú mac léinn do theangacha iasachta sna Stáit Aontaithe don *Association of Departments of Foreign Languages Bulletin* bhí sí den tuairim gur múineadh an Ghaeilge i dtrí institiúid déag sna Stáit le 705 mac léinn. Is méadú é seo ar an 326 a dhein staidéar uirthi i 1998, an 133 i 1995 agus an 121 i 1990. Tá fás leanúnach ann ó shuirbhéanna eile a deineadh ó thús na 1970í. Beifear ag súil leis, más féidir brath ar na figiúirí seo, go mbeidh méadú suntasach ar na figiúirí seo an chéad uair eile a fhoilseofar iad, is é sin ag deireadh 2008. Is cinnte go bhfuil líon na mac léinn i mbun na Gaeilge íseal i gcomparáid leis na mórtheangacha a ndeintear staidéar orthu sna Stáit, mar atá, an Spáinnis, an Fhraincis, an Ghearmáinis, an Iodáilis, teanga chomharthaíochta Mheiriceá, an tSeapáinis, an tSínis, an Laidin, an Rúisis, an tSean-Ghréigis, Eabhrais an Bhíobla, Arabais, Nua-Eabhrais, an Phortaingéilis agus an Chóiréis. Ach i gcomparáid le go leor teangacha Ceilteacha eile agus teangacha mór-le-rá ón Eoraip, cruthaíonn an Ghaeilge go maith nó níos fearr ná iad. Is mó mac léinn aici ná ag teangacha ar nós na Tuircise, na Cróitise, na Bulgáirise, na Seicise, na hOllainnise, na Fionlainnise agus na Slóvaicise.[84]

Thug an Ghaeilge na cosa léi san aois seo caite in ollscoileanna agus i gcoláistí Mheiriceá. Má tá fiúntas ar bith i scéalta béil, ba chóir go mbeadh borradh mór i líon na mac léinn atá ag déanamh staidéir ar an nGaeilge sa chéad suirbhé eile a fhoilseofar sa bhliain 2008. Ag tús na haoise seo tá sruth leanúnach teagascóirí óga líofa cáilithe ar fáil ó scéim de chuid an Fulbright Commission Foreign Language Teaching Assistants, agus ó Chiste na Gaeilge ón Roinn Gnóthaí Pobail, Tuaithe agus Gaeltachta.[85] Tá stair agus traidisiún ag baint le teagasc na Gaeilge sna Stáit Aontaithe mar ábhar inti féin nó mar dhlúthchuid den Léann Ceilteach nó de Léann na hÉireann, ach níos tábhachtaí ná sin tá todhchaí chinnte dhearfach aici. Má tá éiginnteacht ann faoi cé a chéadlabhair, cár labhraíodh nó cén chanúint inar labhraíodh an Ghaeilge den chéad uair san Oileán Úr, is cinnte go labharofar, go múinfear agus go ndéanfar staidéar ar an nGaeilge go ceann i bhfad sna Stáit Aontaithe.

Nótaí

1 Proinsias Mac Aonghusa, 'An Ghaeilge i Meiriceá', *Go Meiriceá Siar: Na Gaeil agus Meiriceá*, eag. Stiofán Ó hAnnracháin (Baile Átha Cliath: An Clóchomhar, 1979), lth. 13.

2 Nancy Stenson, 'Speaking Irish in America: language and identity', *Global Eurolinguistics: European languages in North America, Migration, Maintenance and Death*, eag. P. Sture Ureland (Tubingen, Niemeyer, 2001), lgh. 435–59.

3 Kevin Kenny, *The American Irish: A History* (Harlow: Pearson Education, 2000), lth. 99.

4 Kenny, *ibid.*, lth. 138.

5 http://factfinder.census.gov/home/saff/main.html?_lang=en

6 Eisceacht anseo is ea Kevin Kenny, *The American Irish: A History* (Harlow: Pearson Education Inc., 2000) agus Úna Ní Bhroiméil, *Building Irish Identity in America 1870–1915: The Gaelic Revival* (Dublin: Four Courts Press, 2003).

7 Kenneth E. Nilsen, 'The Irish Language in New York, 1850–1900', *The New York Irish*, eag. R. H. Bayor agus T. J. Meagher (Baltimore: The Johns Hopkins University Press, 1996), lgh. 252–274. Féach, Kenneth E. Nilsen, 'The Irish Language in Nineteenth Century New York City', *The Multilingual Apple: Languages in New York City*, eag. O. García & J. A. Fishman (New York: Mouton de Gruyter, 1997), lgh. 52–69; agus Kenneth E. Nilsen, 'Thinking of Monday: Irish speakers of Portland, Maine', *Éire-Ireland*, Iml. 25, Uimhir 1 (1990), lgh. 6–19.

8 *Go Meiriceá Siar: Na Gaeil agus Meiriceá*, eag. Stiofán Ó hAnnracháin (Baile Átha Cliath: An Clóchomhar, 1979).

9 Thomas Ihde, *The Irish Language in the United States: An Historical, Sociolinguistic and Applied Linguistic Survey*, (Westport; CT: Bergin & Garvey, 1994). I measc na n-aistí eile a bhaineann leis an nGaeilge sna Stáit Aontaithe, tá: J. Callahan, 'Gaeilge i bhPhiladelphia', *An Teanga Mharthanach*, Uimhir 2 (1990), gan lth; D. Clark, 'Muted History: Gaelic in an American City', *Éire-Ireland*, Iml. 6, Uimhir 1 (1971), lgh. 3–7; R. Crow, 'Teaching Irish at Antioch College', *Journal of Celtic Language Learning*, Uimhir 2 (1996), lgh. 77–78; Thomas W. Ihde, 'Language Report: Irish

Language Courses at American Colleges', *Éire-Ireland,* Iml. 30, Uimhir 4 (1996), lgh. 181–186; J.L. Kallen, 'Language and ethnic identity: The Irish language in the United States', *Language Across Cultures,* eag. L. Mac Mathúna agus D. Singleton (Dublin: Irish Association for Applied Linguistics, 1983), lgh. 101–12; J.L. Kallen, 'Language Maintenance and Loss: An International Perspective', *Teanga,* Uimhir 13 (1983), lgh. 100–14; L.M. Lynch, 'Gaelic Language in America', *Irish America* Iúil-Lúnasa (1987), lgh. 42–43; Séamas Mac Bloscaidh, 'An Ghaeilge i Nua Eabhrac', *An Teanga Mharthanach,* Iml. 4 (1989), gan lth.; L.P. Murray, 'A Louth manuscript in New York', *County Louth Archaeological Journal,* Uimhir 3 (1912–1915), lgh. 318–22; Kenneth E. Nilsen, 'A Nineteenth-Century Irish Life of St. Margaret', *Harvard Celtic Colloquium,* Uimhir 4 (1984), lgh. 82–104; Kenneth E. Nilsen, 'Three Irish Manuscripts in Massachusetts', *Harvard Celtic Colloquium,* Uimhir 5 (1985), lgh. 1–21; I. O'Carroll, 'The Boston Gaeltacht', *Irish Voice,* 16 Iúil (1986), lth. 16; J. Ridge, 'The Hidden Gaeltacht in Old New York: Nineteenth-Century preaching in the Irish Language', *New York Irish History,* Uimhir 6 (1991–2), lgh. 13–17; G. Schoepperle, 'Irish Studies at the University of Illinois', *Studies* Iml. 7, Uimhir 25 (1918), lgh. 100–11; Nancy Stenson, 'The Use of Irish Among Immigrants to the United States', *New Hibernia Review,* Iml. 2, Uimhir 2 (1998), lgh. 116–31; Nancy Stenson, 'Cúrsaí Gaeilge i Meiriceá Thuaidh', *Teagasc na Gaeilge,* Uimhir 7 (2000), lgh. 107–113; Fionnula Uí Fhlannagáin, *Mícheál Ó Lócháin agus 'An Gaodhal'* (Baile Átha Cliath: An Clóchomhar, 1990); E.J. Walsh, 'The Language Problem of Irish Immigrants at the Time of the Great Famine', *St. Meinrad Essays,* Iml. 12, Uimhir 1 (1959), lgh. 60–75.

10 Nancy Stenson, lgh. 435–459.

11 Tá teacht ar bhreis eolais ar theagasc na Gaeilge sna Stáit Aontaithe san alt a scríobh Thomas W. Ihde: 'A Hundred Years: Irish Language Courses in American College', *Éire-Ireland,* Iml. 30, Uimhir 4 (1996), lgh. 181–6.

12 Ní foláir a admháil gur baineadh an-leas as an eolas atá ar fáil ag na ranna agus ag na hollscoileanna féin, na suímh seo a leanas ach go háirithe:
http://www.fas.harvard.edu/~celtic/storyofceltic/index.htm
agus
http://ls.berkeley.edu/dept/celtic/celtic_study_berkeley.html

13 Is mó duine a roinn a chuid eolais go fial liom agus mé i mbun na haiste seo. Ní aiste chríochnúil ar stair na Gaeilge sa chóras oideachais ach iarracht ar a bhfuil ar eolas a chruinniú le chéile in aon áit amháin í seo.

14 Thomas W. Ihde: 'A Hundred Years: Irish Language Courses in American College', *Éire-Ireland*, Iml. 30, Uimhir 4 (1996), lgh. 181–6.

15 Patricia Bellew Gray, "Tis True: Irish Gaelic Still Charms', *New York Times*, 12 Márta 2006.

16 Tá stair an Léinn Cheiltigh in Ollscoil Naomh Francis Xavier le fáil ag http://people.stfx.ca/knilsen/celtics.html

17 Roland Blenner-Hassett, 'A Brief History of Celtic Studies in North America', *Proceedings of the Modern Language Association*, Iml. 69, Uimhir 4, Cuid 2: forlíonadh (Meán Fómhair, 1954), lth. 8.

18 Blenner-Hassett, lth. 8.

19 David E. Bynum, 'Four Generations of Oral Literary Studies at Harvard University – Oral Literary Studies at Harvard Since 1856'. Féach http://www.chs.harvard.edu/mpc/about/bynum.html

20 Proinsias Mac Aonghusa, lth. 25.

21 Seán Ó Ceallaigh, *Eoghan Ó Gramhnaigh: Beathaisnéis* (Baile Átha Cliath: Oifig an tSoláthair, 1968), lth. 61.

22 Ó Ceallaigh, lgh. 67–8.

23 Charles P. Monaghan, 'The Revival of the Gaelic Language', *Proceedings of the Modern Languages Association*, Iml. 14, Aguisín I agus II (Proceedings 1899), lth. xxxvii.

24 Blenner-Hassett, lth. 13.

25 *Ibid.*

26 D'eagraigh Dunn seimineáir do mhic léinn arbh as Yale a bhformhór tar éis dó dul amach ar pinsean.

27 D'oibrigh sé i nDeoise Portland (Maine) agus i Springfield (Massachusetts) ar feadh ceithre bliana – dhá pharóiste a bhfuil líon ard de Ghaeilgeoirí iontu – sular thug sé faoi iarchéim san Ollscoil Chaitliceach. (1911–1916).

28 Blenner-Hassett, lgh. 12–13.

29 Tá cúrsa sa Ghaeilge fós ar fáil mar chuid de Léann na hÉireann san Ollscoil Chaitliceach.

30 Daniel Donohue, 'The History of English Medieval Studies at Harvard University', *Medieval English Studies Newsletter* (Center

for Medieval English Studies, University of Tokyo), Uimhir 28 (Meitheamh 1993), lth. 2.

31 Blenner-Hassett, lgh. 9–10.

32 Gheofar níos mó eolais ar bhileog na Roinne nó ar an suíomh idirlín: http://www.fas.harvard.edu/~celtic/

33 Bhronn Prifysgol Cymru *D.Litt honoris causa* air in 1963.

34 'List of Members', *Bulletin of the Linguistic Society*, Iml. 15, Uimhir 12 (Eanáir-Márta, 1930), lth. 42.

35 'List of Members 1940', Supplement to *Language: Journal of the Linguistic Society of America*, Iml. 17, Uimhir 1 (Eanáir-Márta 1941), lth. 32.

36 Ba chomh-Ollamh le Béarla in Ollscoil Toronto (1946–56) agus Ollamh le Béarla in Ollscoil Nua-Eabhrac (1956–63) roimhe sin é.

37 Ken Gewertz, 'Celtic Dept. Chair, Housemaster Dunn dies at 90', *Harvard University Gazette*, 2 Lúnasa, 2006.

38 Tá céimeanna ag an Ollamh Ford ó Ollscoil Stát Michigan University (1959) agus dochtúireacht ó Harvard (1969). Mhúin sé roimhe sin in Ollscoil Stanford agus in Ollscoil California, Los Angeles.

39 Bhain An tOllamh McKenna dochtúireacht amach sa Léann Ceilteach i 1976 agus sular fhill sí ar Harvard ba Stiúrthóir í ar an Léann Éireannach in Ollscoil na Banríona Nua-Eabhrac ó 1984 go 1997.

40 Sa bhliain 1966, dhein Robinson maoiniú ar an tarna Cathaoir sa Léann Ceilteach i gcuimhne ar a bhean chéile – Margaret Brooks Robinson – agus cruthaíodh Cathaoir mhaoinithe sa Léann Éireannach – an Chathaoir Shattuck. Ba é Kellehar an chéad ollamh a luadh leis an gcathaoir áirithe seo.

41 I measc na dteagascóirí eile a mhúin an Ghaeilge in Ollscoil Harvard tá: John Armstrong, Bruce Boling, John Carey, Kate Chadbourne, Elizabeth Gray, Karrina Hollo, John Koch agus William Mahon. I measc na gcuairteoirí chuig an Roinn bhí: David Greene, Proinsias Mac Cana, Brian Ó Cuív agus Angela Bourke.

42 Féach, Roland G. Kent agus E.H. Sturtevant, 'Survey of Linguistic Studies: Opportunities for Advanced Work in the United States', *Linguistic Society of America: Bulletin*, Uimhir 1 (Nollaig, 1926), lgh. 3–14. Féach Tábla 1: General Linguistics and Miscellaneous Indo-European.

43 'History of the Linguistic Institute', *Bulletin of the Linguistic Society*, Uimhir 2, (1928), lth. 4.

44 *Ibid.* lgh. 9–10.
45 'Announcement of the Linguistic Institute, 1929', *Bulletin of the Linguistic Society*, Uimhir 3 (1929), lth. 10.
46 *Ibid.* lth. 11. Chláraigh Cross agus Curtis don dá chúrsa agus roghnaigh Strodach an cúrsa ar an tSean-Ghaeilge amháin. Ina ainneoin seo, ba mhó mac léinn ag Dunn ná go leor cúrsaí eile.
47 'Announcement of the Linguistic Institute, 1930', *Bulletin of the Linguistic Society*, Uimhir 5 (Márta, 1930), lth. 10. Rugadh i Columbia, Missouri é agus bhain sé B.A. agus M.A. amach in Ollscoil Missouri (1898) agus M.A. (1899). Bhronn Ollscoil Nebraska Ph.D. air sa bhliain 1902. Ceapadh mar bhall foirne in Ollscoil Columbia i 1911 é.
48 *Ibid.* lth. 10.
49 Ba é an Dr. B.J. Olli (College of the City of New York) an t-aon mhac léinn a bhí ag Dunn. Chláraigh an mac léinn áirithe seo do chúig chúrsa ar fad. Féach *Bulletin of the Linguistic Society*, Uimhir 8 (Meán Fómhair, 1931), lth. 10.
50 Féach 'Report of the Special Committee on the Linguistic Institute', Forlíonadh le *Language: Journal of the Linguistic Society of America*, Iml. 16, Uimhir. 1 (Eanáir-Márta 1940), lgh. 83–101.
51 Forlíonadh le *Language: Journal of the Linguistic Society of America*, Iml 17, Uimhir 1 (Eanáir-Márta 1941), lth. 13.
52 *Ibid,* lth. 32.
53 Féach http://www.ourstory.info/library/2-ww1/Gayley/Gayley4.html
54 *Ibid.*
55 Is cosúil gurbh é seo an J.J. O'Hagerty a bhí in Ollscoil Notre Dame sna 1920í.
56 Féach *Annual Reports of the President of the University on behalf of the Regents to His Excellency the Governor of the State of California, 1911–12.* Oriental ($3,008.22), Sanskrit ($1,8000.00), Semitic ($1,999.97), Slavic ($2,225.52)
57 Ba nós leo $100 a thabhairt in aghaidh na bliana ar mhaithe leis an leabharlann. Féach *Annual Report of the President of the University on behalf of the Regents to His Excellency the Governor of the State of California, 1917.*
58 *Annual Reports of the President of the University on behalf of the Regents to His Excellency the Governor of the State of California, 1919.*
59 *New York Times,* 20 Márta 1991.

60 Michael P. Mahon, 'The Irish Language: A Language of Prayer', *Ireland in Religion and Letters: Discourses and Writings of Catholic and Irish Interest* (Boston: Thomas J. Flynn & Co., 1919), lth. 45.

61 Mahon, 'A Gaelic Chair in the New Boston College', lth. 67.

62 Mahon, 'The Irish Language: A Language of Prayer', lth. 46.

63 Mahon, 'Tribute in Solemn High Mass for Dead Veterans', lth. 52 (30 Bealtaine 1910).

64 Proinsias Mac Aonghusa, lth. 29. Luann sé an Ghaeilge á múineadh in Ollscoil Binghampton, Nua-Eabhrac ag Seán Ó Nualláin.

65 Reid Oslin, *The Boston College Chronicle*, Iml. 13, Uimhir 3 (7 Deireadh Fómhair, 2004).

66 Niall O'Dowd, 'Boston College: Guardian of Irish Culture', *Irish America* (Aibreán-Bealtaine, 2007), lgh. 63–70.

67 Ba mhinic na teagascóirí Gaeilge mar bhaill de Roinn na dTeangacha Slavacha. I measc na ndaoine a mhúin an Ghaeilge ann tá: Kate Chadbourne, Michael Connolly, John Koch, William Mahon, Ken Nilsen, Brian Ó Conchubhair agus Donna Wong. D'fhreastail Seán Ó Tuama (1984), Nuala Ní Dhomhnaill (1998–99) agus Breandán Ó Buachalla (2001–02) mar Scoláire an Léinn Éireannaigh i Leabharlann Burns.

68 Brother Aidan O'Reilly, C.S.C., *Story of Notre Dame, Brother Aidan's Extracts* (Brothers of Holy Cross: Notre Dame, Indiana, 1951). http://archives.nd.edu/aidan/aidan515.htm

69 'The Irish Class', *Notre Dame Scholastic* (30 Deireadh Fómhair, 1869), Iml. III, Uimhir 4, lth. 28.

70 *Notre Dame Scholastic*, Iml. III, Uimhir 16 (16 Aibreán 1870), lth. 126.

71 Rugadh Januarius Aloysius MacGahan 12 Meitheamh 1844 trí mhíle taobh ó dheas de New Lexington. B'as Doire dá athair agus ba é féin an t-iriseoir ba mhó le rá lena linn. Thuill sé an-cháil de bharr ar scríobh sé faoin slad sa Bhulgáir.

72 An Craoibhín Aoibhinn, *Mo Thuras go Meiriceá: I Measg na nGael ins an Oileán Úr* (Baile Átha Cliath: An Gúm, 1937), lgh. 75–6.

73 'Dr. Hyde's Lecture', *Notre Dame Scholastic*, Iml. XXXIX, Uimhir 16 (3 Feabhra 1906), lgh. 274–5.

74 Rugadh John Augustine Zahm i New Lexington, Ohio. Tá cáil air as an Eaglais Chaitliceach a fhorbairt sna Stáit Aontaithe. Cuimhnítear air i Notre Dame mar ollamh a raibh an-spéis aige san eolaíocht agus i saothar Dante ach go háirithe.

75 F.S.F., 'Summer Courses in Irish Subjects', *Notre Dame Scholastic,*
    Iml. LIII, Uimhir 29, (22 Bealtaine, 1920), lth. 476. Is í Aedín Ní
    Bhroithe Clements atá i gceannas ar an mbailiúchán Gaeilge faoi
    láthair.

76 *Notre Dame Scholastic,* Iml. III, Uimhir 4 (5 Meán Fómhair, 1919),
    lth. 26.

77 Eagarthóir, 'Notes and Remarks', *Ave Maria* luaite sa *Notre Dame
    Scholastic,* Iml. LIII, Uimhir 8 (15 Samhain, 1919), lth. 118.

78 T.J. Tobin, 'President De Valera at Notre Dame,' *Notre Dame
    Scholastic,* Iml. LIII, Uimhir 4 (18 Deireadh Fómhair, 1919)., lth.
    58.

79 Cartlann Notre Dame, Bosca 18, Comhad 10.

80 Féach Niall O'Dowd, 'Waking Up the Irish Echoes', *Irish-America*
    (Feabhra-Márta 2007) lgh. 26–8.

81 Ceapadh Tara MacLeod sa Roinn sa bhliain 2005 mar Speisialtóir
    Teanga Cúnta agus thosaigh an Dr. Hugh Fogarty ag múineadh
    ann i 2006. In imeacht na mblianta tá ranganna Gaeilge múinte
    ag Ciara Conneely, Breandán Mac Suibhne, Elaine Naughton,
    Éamonn Ó Ciardha, Tomás Ó Murchú, Traolach Ó Ríordáin agus
    Peadar Ó Muircheartaigh. I measc na gcuairteoirí a mhúin cúrsaí
    ar litríocht na Gaeilge, tá: Angela Bourke, Nuala Ní Dhomhnaill,
    Bríona Nic Dhiarmada, Diarmuid Ó Doibhlin, Diarmuid Ó
    Giolláin agus Philip T. O'Leary.

82 An bhliain acadúil agus líon na mac léinn in aghaidh na bliana:
    1997–98 (44), 1998–99 (62), 1999–00 (78), 2000–01 (101), 2002–02
    (98), 2002–03 (114), 2003–04 (147), 2004–05 (173), 2005–6 (294),
    2006–07 (401).

83 Blenner-Hassett, lgh. 19–20.

84 Féach Elizabeth B. Welles, 'Foreign Language Enrollments in
    United States Institutes of Higher Education, Fall 2002',
    Association of Departments of Foreign Languages Bulletin, Iml. 35,
    Uimhir 1–2, (Geimhreadh-Earrach 2004), lgh. 7–26.

85 Ba iad na daoine seo a leanas a roghnaíodh mar chúntóirí teanga
    de chuid Fulbright don bhliain 2006–07: Francesca McCully,
    Laoise Ní Thuairisg, Maeve Nic An Airchinnigh agus AibhistínÓ
    Coimín. Ba iad Edward Kelleher, Sinéad Ní Mhaolmhicíl, Ailbhe
    Ní Ghearbhuigh, Tomás Ó Murchú agus Mairéad McKendry a
    roghnaíodh don bhliain 2007–08.

THE IRISH LANGUAGE IN AMERICAN UNIVERSITIES

Brian Ó Conchubhair
University of Notre Dame

Stair na Gaeilge i Meiriceá scéal scaipthe atá agus a bhí ann. Scéal mór é ó thaobh na tíre seo ach scéal é ar fíorbheag an taighde a dearnadh air.[1]

When precisely the Irish language first graced the shores of America is unknown. Discounting Saint Brendan who, manuscripts allege, first 'discovered' America, Irish, presumably, was initially spoken in the 'new world' by early settlers. The execution of Anne Glover as a suspected witch in South Boston in 1688 is, however, well documented and provides an early recorded instance of Irish in the colonies. Historians of Irish-America frequently simplify matters and present Irish emigrants as monoglot English-speakers or as entirely abandoning Irish on embarkation. Human behaviour is rarely so neat or convenient. As linguist Nancy Stenson correctly observes:

> Clearly, Irish speakers must have been a prominent presence among Irish immigrants in the 19th century, and one might expect their language skills to have been an important factor in their assimilation to North American life, if not in their actual departure.[2]

According to historian Kevin Kenny:

> ...it is estimated that between one-quarter and one-third of American-bound emigrants during the famine were Irish speakers. Half of all the famine emigrants came from the two provinces of Connacht and Munster, where at least half the population still spoke Irish as late as 1851.[3]

and:

> the post-famine emigration therefore contributed significantly to the continuing decline of the Irish language while, as part of

the same process, it made the language more common in many Irish-American neighbourhoods than it had been earlier in the nineteenth century, often provoking cultural conflict between the newcomers and the established community.[4]

Bizarrely, however, this particular feature of the Irish-American experience attracts little scholarly attention.[5] Celtic Studies scholar Kenneth Nilsen has published significant articles detailing the existence and survival of Irish-language communities and networks in New York and Portland.[6] Stiofán Ó hAnnracháin's 1979 *Go Meiriceá Siar: Na Gaeil agus Meiriceá* is an indispensable collection of essays on Irish-speakers and their literary production in the United States and essential reading for anyone concerned with Irish-America or the Irish diaspora.[7] Similarly Thomas Ihde's *The Irish Language in the United States: An Historical, Sociolinguistic and Applied Linguistic Survey*[8] is requisite reading, as is Nancy Stenson's aforementioned seminal essay.[9]

Yet much work on the Irish language and Irish-speakers in North and South America remains undone.[10] This essay seems an opportune point to trace the history of Irish in some third level institutions in the United States that have taught the language over a long period. It charts the fluctuating fortunes of Irish in universities and the efforts to preserve and develop an ethnic identity through the prestige and cultural capital associated with universities and higher education. As a synthetic narrative, it sketches in very broad strokes a truncated history of Irish-language teaching in the United States drawing on many sources; formal and informal, written and oral as well as relying on the work and knowledge of scholars and friends too numerous to name. It in no way presents itself as a definitive or conclusive history.[11] Of necessity it neglects and overlooks the story of Celtic Studies and Irish Studies at many other institutions.

Space does not allow for mention of all colleges and universities currently offering Irish.[12] Such include: the Centre for Celtic Studies at the University of Wisconsin, Milwaukee (Dineen Grow); New York University (Pádraig Ó Cearúil);

Lehman College at the City University of New York (Thomas W. Ihde, Elaine Ní Bhraonáin, Clare Carroll) who also offer Irish-language courses on-line; University of Minnesota (Nancy Stenson); New College, California (Hetty O'Hara); University of Saint Thomas (Fintan Moore); University of California (Joseph F. Nagy and James McCloskey), Fordham University (James Blake); University of Montana (Traolach Ó Ríordáin); and University of Pennsylvania (Roslyn Blyn-LaDrew). Community and out-reach programs based in universities such as Yale (Pat Whelan) are too numerous to cite,[13] despite Ihde's conclusion that 'the greatest expansion in Irish language teaching seems to be taking place in continuing education programs at two-year colleges'.[14] Nor does this article consider voluntary groups, such as *Daltaí na Gaeilge*, founded by Ethel Brogan in 1981 – that teach adults throughout the United States. In omitting many in the States, this essay makes no pretence to address Irish-language teaching in Canada where Irish is taught at Saint Francis Xavier University, Antigonish, Nova Scotia[15] (Kenneth E. Nilsen); Saint Mary's University, Halifax (Pádraig Ó Siadhail); Concordia University, Montreal (Martina Branigan); Saint Michael's College, University of Toronto (Máirín Nic Dhiarmada and Ann Dooley) and the University of Ottawa (Paul Birt and Rosemary O'Brien).

Since a detailed history of the Irish language in North America remains largely unwritten, it is unsurprising that the language's history in institutes of higher education is also mostly unknown. In his seminal but singular 1954 essay on the history of Celtic Studies in the United States and Canada, Roland Blenner-Hassett explains:

> Little if any serious attention was devoted to the three major Celtic languages in the United States until late in the nineteenth century. The stresses and tensions engendered by the American Civil War, and the enormous expansions of our nation from 1865 on, absorbed the major energies of the people. Until the foundation of the land grant colleges in 1890, most of the serious educational and intellectual activity of the nation centered on the older, privately endowed institutions

on the eastern seaboard and the immediately adjacent hinterland.[16]

A survey of the literature provided by universities involved in promoting Celtic and Irish Studies reveals some commonly accepted facts. Irish-language teaching, as part of Celtic Studies, began, it appears, in North America with Harvard University:

> It was at Harvard University that the first serious and sustained interest in Celtic Studies was initiated. It is no exaggeration to say that without the consent of the authorities at Harvard and without the selfless dedication of one of its faculty members, Celtic Studies would never have achieved the position they have today in the cultural life of North America.[17]

In 1895 Fred Norris Robinson (1871–1966), who would become synonymous with Celtic Studies in America, was a young instructor in the English Department at Harvard University in Cambridge, Massachusetts. Availing of the traditional opportunity afforded Harvard faculty he travelled to Germany where he studied at the University of Freiburg in Baden with the great Celtic scholar and philologist Rudolph Thurneysen (1857–1940). Slavic-language scholar, David Bynum suggests that Harvard English Department professors Francis J. Child (1825–96) and George L. Kittredge (1860–1941) regretted their lack of knowledge of the living Celtic languages while understanding their value for researching oral literature, a research interest both scholars shared:

> During the few years in the early 1890s when Child and Kittredge were together on the faculty of Harvard's English Department, several young scholars of oral traditions enjoyed the sponsorship of both men. The most eminent of these was Fred Norris Robinson of the Class of 1891. He took his Master's and Doctor's degrees at Harvard in quick succession (1892 and 1894), then Child and Kittredge sent him to Freiburg in Germany to learn the principles of Celtic philology in what was the world's foremost school of Celtic languages in that era. Child and Kittredge both regretted knowing no Celtic,

and they were determined that the time had come when the Celtic component of British and other European oral traditions must be scientifically understood. The enthusiastic but inexact work in Celtic of such earlier lights as Curtin could no longer satisfy Harvard's two doyens of oral literature, and so they delegated Robinson to bring Celtic studies to Cambridge. Robinson's return to Harvard in the fall of 1896 with an appointment as instructor coincided with the death of Child, but Child like Kittredge would have been delighted with Robinson's success'.[18]

On his return, the twenty-five-year-old Robinson persuaded Charles William Eliot (1834–1926), then President of Harvard University, to offer courses in the Celtic languages, including Irish, at Harvard. Thus began the tradition.

CATHOLIC UNIVERSITY, WASHINGTON D.C.

Robinson's return to Harvard from Germany predates, by a few years, the arrival in the United States of the Reverend Richard Henebry (1863–1916), another scholar who familiarized himself with philology and Celtic Studies in Germany. A native Irish-speaker from Waterford, Henebry was appointed to the newly created chair in Irish language and literature at the Catholic University, Washington D.C. in 1896. The chair was initially offered to Father Eoin Ó Gramhnaigh/Eoghan O'Growney (1863–99) who declined on grounds of ill-health.[19] Ó Gramhnaigh recommended Eoin Mac Néill who was disinclined to leave Ireland and Henebry was then offered the position.[20] This position, endowed by the generosity of the Ancient Order of Hibernians, was the first such academic position in North America. Ó Gramhnaigh, it appears, harboured grave doubts about the Chair's viability and feared its sponsors were more concerned with political rather than educational ends.[21] In an address to the President and members of the Modern Languages Association in 1899, essayist Charles P. Monaghan describes how:

> The Ancient Order of Hibernians (of America), an organization of very poor men, subscribed $50,000 to endow

the Chair of Gaelic in the Catholic University of America. The Chair was further endowed by $10,000 bequeathed in the spring of 1899 by Miss Mary Moran of Baltimore, who left the money 'to help perpetuate the language of her mother', who had been a Gaelic speaker.[22]

While fund-raising began in 1893, and the chair was formally announced in 1896, formal instruction in Irish only commenced in 1898.[23]

Henebry was born 18 September 1863 near Portlaw, county Waterford and ordained a Catholic priest at Maynooth seminary in 1892. On his appointment, the university awarded him a fellowship to complete his Old Irish studies in Germany under Heinrich Zimmer (1851–1910), at Greifswald University and also Freiburg, where he received his doctorate in 1898. Henebry taught courses in Irish at Catholic University from 1898 to 1900, but after a dispute – the origins and the exact nature of which remain unclear – returned to Ireland. Subsequently he helped establish *Coláiste na Rinne* prior to accepting the Chair of Old Irish at University College Cork. The aforementioned dispute prevented Henebry from conducting his teaching duties for 1900–01 and Fred Robinson of Harvard reputedly travelled on a weekly basis to Washington to teach his classes.

Appointing Henebry's replacement posed a difficulty. The Catholic University surmounted the problem by awarding J. Joseph Dunn a fellowship in Celtic Studies in 1901, thus allowing him to study with Robinson at Harvard until 1904 as well as undertaking study in 'Freiburg with Thurneysen, at Rennes with [Henri Georges] Dottin [1863–1928] and also in Aberystwyth and Edinburgh. In addition Professor Dunn, during this period, spent summers in Ireland, perfecting his knowledge of Modern Irish'.[24] Dunn's selection is significant as it marks the emergence of native scholars trained in the United States and points to a maturing of the discipline. During the period of Dunn's fellowship, Robinson continued to offer brief courses of instruction at Catholic University as a visiting lecturer. On completion of his training, Dunn taught

Irish from 1904 to 1931 when ill-health forced his retirement.[25] Irish was subsequently taught by the Reverend James Aloysius Geary (1882–1958), a native of Worcester, Massachusetts; who had studied at the College of Holy Cross and earned a doctorate in 1931 from Catholic University.[26] He first taught Irish in 1914 and was appointed Instructor of Celtic and Comparative Philology two years later. Geary offered courses in Irish and Celtic Studies until his retirement in 1953 when the onus fell on Robert T. Meyer, who also combined Celtic with Comparative Philology.[27] In 1983, the endowed Chair in Irish was rededicated as a Chair of Irish Studies, thus closing a chapter in the history of Irish-language studies.[28]

HARVARD UNIVERSITY

If Robinson's availability saved Irish at Catholic University, his own retirement posed a more urgent challenge to the future of Irish and Celtic Studies at Harvard. Having joined the Harvard faculty as an instructor in 1894, 'he was promoted to full professor in 1906 and took over Kittredge's post as Gurney Professor in 1936'.[29] As Blenner-Hassett notes:

> It was only on his retirement in 1939 that the real nature of his contribution, in academic and personal terms, was perceived. Then, Harvard University and its Department of English were faced with a crucial decision. What was to become of Celtic Studies in the institution which was largely responsible for introducing them to America? President Conant was approached and, when a generous friend of the University placed at its disposal sufficient funds, Professor Kenneth Jackson of Cambridge, England, was installed as Associate Professor in Celtic.[30]

A meeting between Henry Lee Shattuck, a distinguished Bostonian, and Douglas Hyde, an Irish-language scholar and President of Ireland, resulted in an endowed Chair in Celtic Studies at Harvard.[31] This gift led to the formation of the Department of Celtic Languages and Literatures, the first and only such institution in the United States and ensured the regular teaching of Irish language and literature. The first incumbent of this prestigious Chair was Kenneth Hurlstone Jackson (1909–91), a native of Croydon, England, who directed Celtic Studies at Harvard until 1950. Vernam Edward Nunnemacher Hull[32] (1894–1976), formerly Associate Editor of the Early Modern English Dictionary at the University of Michigan[33] and Assistant Professor of English, New York University[34] succeeded Jackson, and in turn was followed in 1962 by Charles W. Dunn (1916–2006). Dunn was born in Arbuthnott, Scotland to a Presbyterian minister and earned a B.A. from McMaster University in Hamilton, Ontario as result of his family's decision to move initially to Boston and later Canada. He pursued graduate work in English and Celtic philology under Robinson and earned an M.A. (1939) and a Ph.D. (1948) from Harvard.[35] He served not only as Chairman of the Department of Celtic Languages and Literatures until his retirement in 1984 but also as master of Quincy House (1966–81). In 1955, he received the Canada Award of the Federation of Gaelic Societies.[36]

However, modern Celtic Studies and the emergence of Irish Studies as a discipline in America are, and will be, forever linked with the name of John V. Kelleher. Born in Lawrence, Massachusetts on 8 March, 1916, he began learning Irish as a child from his Cork-born grandmother and continued lessons with his grandfather's cousin, Augustinian priest Daniel J. O'Mahony. With a degree in English from Dartmouth College (1939), he entered Harvard in 1940 as a Junior Fellow in the Society of Fellows and studied with Kenneth Jackson. It was as a Junior Fellow at the tender age of 26 that he delivered the Lowell Lectures, on modern Irish literature. During World War II, Kelleher served in military intelligence assigned to the Korea Desk at the Pentagon. After visiting Ireland for the first time in 1946, he began his long teaching career in Irish history and literature the following year. In 1960, he became professor of modern Irish history and literature at Harvard. A voting member of the departments of English and History, he also taught highly popular Extension School courses every year for nearly three decades and was a faculty associate of Lowell House. A second chair, the Shattuck Chair in Irish Studies, was endowed by Robinson's generosity on his death and Kelleher was the inaugural professor. During his career he was awarded an honorary M.A. by Harvard (1953) and honorary Litt.D.s by Trinity College, Dublin (1965) and the National University of Ireland, Cork (1999). Kelleher, having retired in 1986, donated thousands of scholarly books from his own collection to libraries at the University of Missouri, St. Louis, and Southern Illinois University, Carbondale. After Kelleher's retirement, Seán Ó Coileán taught at Harvard (1984–85), before the appointment of Patrick Ford as Margaret Brooks Robinson Professor of Celtic Languages and Literatures from 1991–2005.[37] On retiring, he was replaced by Catherine McKenna.[38]

The Shattuck Chair is now occupied by Tomás Ó Cathasaigh, a native of county Waterford and formerly of University College Dublin and the Dublin Institute for Advanced Studies, since 1995. McKenna and Ó Cathasaigh are the two current endowed chairs of Celtic and Irish at Harvard.[39] Together with scholar Barbara Hillers, who has edited several volumes of the *Proceedings of the Harvard Celtic Colloquium*, and administrator Margo Granfors, they continue a distinguished tradition of teaching and researching Celtic Studies at Harvard.[40]

LINGUISTIC SOCIETY OF AMERICA

While neither a university nor a college, the Linguistic Society of America played a significant role in promoting the Irish language, particularly the linguistic study of Old and Middle Irish, among American academics and linguists. Formed in 1924 as a result of the general opinion that opportunities for training in linguistic science were inadequate and very unevenly distributed, the society surveyed universities and colleges to gauge the status of linguistic study. Its report from 1926–27 reveals that 'Celtic' language courses were offered at Catholic University (4), Chicago (8), Columbia (10), Harvard (6), Nebraska (2) and Northwestern (2).[41] Disappointed with their findings a Linguistic Institute was organised at Yale University for a six week period in 1928 at a cost for $40 per course:

> ... to provide for students of linguistic science facilities similar to those afforded to biologists at Wood's Hole. Scholars who wished to carry on their own researches where they would have access to the needed books, and where they could experience the stimulus of discussion with other scholars of similar interests might find the Institute of advantage. There were to be also courses for graduate students, for high school and college teachers who felt the need of acquaintance with linguistic science or with the history of a particular language or group of languages, and for scholars who wished to familiarize themselves with more or less remote bits of linguistic territory in the most economical way.[42]

Among the thirty-three faculty slated for the first institute were Franz Boas (Columbia University), Leonard Bloomfield (University of Chicago), Edward Sapir (University of Chicago) and Joesph Dunn (Catholic University). While enrollments in the initial years were disappointing the organizers correctly noted that:

> [t]he number is, in one way, not impressive, and yet in another way it is very significant. A school with only two students to every teacher must be branded a failure. But it was not as a school that the Institute was first conceived; it was planned to be a conference of scholars in a special field, and the courses were an addition to the plan to ensure the attendance of the scholars in some definite capacity, either as teachers or as pupils. And yet, as was hoped, many of the courses took the form of conferences, where in a group of two or three persons every one contributed his share and every one learned from every other, whichever one might be the nominal leader of the group. There was an unusual sympathetic scholarly atmosphere about the courses, and the remarkable earnestness of the students resulted in obviously unusual profits to them. Not the least valuable of the activities of the Institute was the gathering of small informal groups to discuss linguistic

problems quite apart from the times and places of the scheduled courses; and in these, from time to time, virtually every one participated.[43]

Three registrants selected Dunn's course on Early Irish – Miss Ida May Greer (South Dakota State College), Mr. J.A. Kerns (Whitman College, Washington) and Miss Anna Irene Millar (Johns Hopkins). Dunn, described as Professor of Celtic Languages and Literatures and Lecturer in Romance Languages, Catholic University of America, increased his course offerings the following year to include Middle Irish. The catalogue advertised the courses as follows:

Old Irish – This course will serve as an introduction to Celtic Philology. It will consist of an outline of the grammar of Old Irish, a study of some Ogham inscriptions and of selections from the glosses and from the earliest literary texts. If desired, e.g. by students of the Latin language, a few lessons will be devoted to Gaulish. The course will be so arranged that a reading knowledge of French and German, while desireable, will not be necessary. Text-books: Pokorny, *A Historical Reader of Old Irish* (Niemeyer, Halle, 1923); Strachan, *Old Irish Paradigms* and *Selections from Old Irish Glosses* (Hodges, Figgis and Co. Dublin, 1909); Strachan, *Stories from the Táin* (*ibid.*, 1908).[44]

Middle Irish – This course presupposes some knowledge of Old Irish, but, if need be, it will be shaped in accordance with the needs of beginners. It will consist of an outline of the grammar of Middle Irish, with references both to the older and to the more modern forms of the language, the interpretations of portions of the heroic saga and of ecclesiastical texts, and a paleographic and linguistic study of a short text from a photograph of the manuscript. Text-books: Dottin, *Manuel d'Irlandais Moyen* (Champion, Paris, 1913); Bergin and Meyer, *Anecdota from Irish Manuscripts*, Vol. III (Dublin and Halle, 1910).[45]

Dunn did not feature as a faculty member at the 1930 Linguistic Institute hosted by College of the City of New York, but John Lawrence Gerig (1878–1957), described as Professor of Celtic, Columbia University, acted as substitute.[46]

His course description differs considerably from Dunn and offers an insight, perhaps, into the teaching of Irish at Columbia:

> Old and Middle Irish. Mr. Gerig. – Grammar and reading of texts. This course will begin with the reading of Middle Irish texts and close with the study of Old Irish. In order to simplify the work as far as possible, the instructor will at first translate the texts and refer the students to the grammar for each word discussed. The Indo-European cognates of Celtic will be studied as far as possible. Text-books: G. Dottin, *Manuel d'Irlandais Moyen* (2 vols.), Paris (1913); J. Strachan, *Stories from the Táin*, 2nd ed., Dublin (1928).[47]

Dunn returned in 1931 when the institute was at New York and offered a combined course in Old and Middle Irish.[48] The imbalance between faculty and students and the financial burden, however, proved insurmountable and mandated a format change that focused on particular topics thus requiring fewer lectures and courses.[49] In the 1940 Summer Meeting at Ann Arbor, Vernam Hull (University of Michigan) delivered one of the key papers, 'A Note on Middle Irish *sidein*'.[50] 1940 is also remarkable as not only does it witness the death of Rudolf Thurneysen, an honorary member of the Society and mentor of Robinson and Dunn, but for the appearance of Myles Dillon as an Irish-language scholar in America when he delivered a paper to Society's seventeenth annual meeting, 30–31 December at Providence on 'Some Irish Words'.[51] Dillon held a chair in Celtic Studies at the University of Wisconsin – Madison from 1937–46 before he moved to the University of Chicago. In future years Dillon became a leading member of the society not only delivering plenary papers but acting as respondent and also discussant to plenary papers. Among his keynote addresses were: 'The Impersonal Transitive Verb in Irish' (1942); 'The Formation of the Subjunctive Stem in Irish and the Problem of the Indo-European Future' (1943); 'Textual Criticism and Literary Interpretation' (1944). In 1943 the Society appointed Fred Robinson as President and Myles Dillon to the Administrative Committee of the Linguistic Society while Dunn, Gerig and

Daniel F. Sheehan (Michigan State College) continued as active members. The presence of Irish wanes with Robinson's retirement and Dillon's return to Ireland in the post-war era. Yet the role of the Institute in popularizing Irish-language studies among American academics and scholars cannot be overemphasised. As the Society's membership grew, attendance at the Institute increased, and a steady flow of Irish related articles appeared in the journal *Language*. The combined efforts of Dillon, Dunn and Gerig kept Irish close to the centre of linguistic study in America.

UNIVERSITY OF CALIFORNIA, BERKELEY

If Catholic University boasts the first endowed Chair of Irish Language and Literature, and Harvard claims to be the first university to offer Celtic Studies, then the honour of having the first degree-granting program in Celtic languages and literatures in North America belongs to the University of California, Berkeley. Berkeley's association with the Irish language and Celtic Studies traces back to the early years of the twentieth century, the spur being Charles Mills Gayley (1858–1932) 'a literary scholar distinguished for accuracy of information, clearness of method, sensitiveness of critical taste, breadth of comment, and vigor of expression'[52] who chaired the English Department of the University of California, Berkeley from 1889 to 1919. Having left the University of Michigan, he came to Berkeley in the fall of 1889. Gayley had previously spent childhood holidays in Donegal, Tyrone and Achill Island where he encountered both native Irish-speakers and a vibrant oral culture. Just as Child and Kittredge did at Harvard, Gayley appreciated the value of Irish oral literature and epic tales. In his quest to make Berkeley a great university and a leading department of English literary studies he wanted an Irish-language scholar on the faculty. Gayley, the educational visionary, saw the value of such a resource for graduate students and faculty. At Berkeley he persuaded William Whittingham Lyman Jr. (1835–1983), an undergraduate born in Napa County,

California, to pursue Celtic Studies. On receiving a Masters in English from Berkeley, Lyman (aka Jack Lyman) secured, through Gayley's assistance, a university fellowship that allowed him a year's study with Sir John Rhys at Oxford. He spent two further years studying Irish at Harvard before returning to a tenure-track position as Instructor in Celtic in the English department in 1911–1912. In the following year Lyman is named as 'Graduate Adviser' in Celtic, a position funded by the Knights of Saint Patrick.[53] He taught and acted as Graduate Adviser in Celtic until 1922. During this period Berkeley's English Department appointed Joseph O'Hagerty[54] as 'Reader in Irish' on a salary of $500 in 1910–11, and $600 for 1911–12, considerably more than the $100 paid to Stanley L. Dod, 'Reader in Dental Pathology and Therapeutics' and on a par with a Junior Assistant in the university library, but less that the $1000–$1500 paid to Instructors in Romance languages and the average $2000 paid to Assistant Professors in Sanskrit and Semitic. The department had an annual budget of $499.92 for the year 1911 and $600 for 1912, considerably less that the average $2000 allotted to Oriental, Sanskrit, Semitic and Slavic language programs.[55] Lynam returned as Instructor in Celtic in 1911–12 and subsequently Celtic appears on the list of approved majors in the College of Letters and Science.

Since 1909 Celtic languages and literature have formed a staple element of the academic fare offered by the University of California, Berkeley. The *Annual Report of the President of the University on Behalf of the Regents* that comments annually on departmental activities noted in 1917 that:

> The Department of Celtic has pursued its usual policies throughout the last year. It suffered an indirect loss through the discontinuance, due to war conditions, of the annual contribution ($42.83 in 1911) of the Knights of St. Patrick for Celtic books for the library.[56]

In 1919 it reported that 'the department has pursued its usual quiet but interesting course. The number of students enrolled in the course has not been affected by the war conditions'.[57]

Berkeley appointed Ella Young (1867–1956) in 1924 to replace Lyman. A poet, she was hired as the 'James D. Phelan Lecturer in Irish Myth and Lore', a position she occupied until 1934. A native of county Antrim and a member of Cumann na mBan during the 1916 Rising, she numbered Patrick Pearse, Maud Gonne and George William Russell among her friends and acquaintances, but was best known in the United States for her retellings of Irish myths and legends. On leaving her position at Berkeley in 1934, she spent some years at a Theosophical colony known as Halcyon, near San Luis Obispo, where Ansel Adams drew the only extant portrait of her. She became active in preserving the California Redwoods and on her death in 1956 donated the bulk of her estate to their preservation. On her departure, Arthur Eugene Hutson (1906–82), a student of Robinson's began to offer courses in Old Irish and Celtic Studies and is widely acknowledged as the driving force behind UC, Berkeley's Celtic library holdings. After Hudson the onus fell largely on Brendan O'Hehir (1927–1991), who was born in New York City to Irish-immigrant parents.[58] On the death of his father in a subway accident in 1931, the future scholar was sent to live with relatives in Ireland where he first learned Irish. On returning to the United States he matriculated at Fordham with the help of a New York State Scholarship. Despite leaving in 1945 to pursue a banking career in Baltimore, he finished his undergraduate degree at Loyola University in 1953. That same year he began graduate work at Johns Hopkins University, where he took an M.A. (1954) and a Ph.D. (1959). He joined the Berkeley faculty in 1958 as an instructor, with promotion to assistant professor in 1960. In addition to teaching Irish-language and Celtic Studies, his interest in Joyce and Anglo-Irish literature led to the publication of *Gaelic Lexicon to Finnegan's Wake* (1967). Not only was he a founding member of the University of California Celtic Conference (1979), but an initiator of the Celtic Studies Program at Berkeley (1989) and also the program's first chair.

Joan Trodden Keefe taught Irish for many years at Berkeley until her retirement in the late 1990s. Irish-language courses and the Celtic Studies program that incorporates Irish-language studies is now grouped with Italian, Scandinavian and Slavic as a department and directed by Maria Teresa Agozzino, Gary Holland, Kathryn Klar, Daniel F. Melia, Esther O'Hara, Annalee C. Rejhon, Kimberly Starr-Reid, Eve Sweetser and administrator Kathi Brosnan.

BOSTON COLLEGE

Boston College has long been a bastion of Irish Studies and Irish heritage in the United States. Yet a study of the writings of the Reverend Michael P. Mahon reveals that the foundation of Irish-language programs and endowed chairs was not always a straight-forward task governed by the academic politics of the ivory tower. Mahon's writings reveal the social and historical difficulties in promoting Irish and Irish-language studies in America at a time when ethnic diversity and celebration were frowned on and frequently resented. His lecture in the Boston Cathedral (30 May 1908) enunciates the context:

> We are all, or very nearly all, from that Sainted Isle, either by birth or by descent. But we are not pilgrims. We are here to stay. We are part of the great American people, a part of the noble people of Massachusetts and of this great city. Nevertheless when we find ourselves gathered in the great metropolitan church of New England, by the special favor and gracious encouragement of our own great Archbishop, to have a heart to heart talk in our ancient tongue, we cannot help feeling some of the racial as well as spiritual exaltation that filled the soul of John MacHale at Rome.[59]

In a similar address in Irish, delivered to the Boston Gaelic School on 24 January 1909 in which he recapped the feats of Archbishop MacHale and those of the Gaelic League, Mahon rejoiced that the cause of the Irish language has taken root in Boston College in South Boston. The Irish language, he announced:

... has been taken up, if not literally, at least substantially, not only in his own college of St. Jarlath and in the colleges of Ireland generally; but far away from the Irish shores, in the heart of New England, under the fostering care of the greatest educational body in the world, and with the blessing of our Most Reverend Archbishop and the last wish of the Archbishop of Tuam, the desire of every enlightened and patriotic Irish mind and of every lover of the most profound linguistic study, is beginning to receive full realization. The Irish language has found its way into Boston College. May it never leave these halls! And when our greatest Catholic educational institution of New England on University Heights is a reality, may it be our pride and our glory to furnish the means to establish and equip there a chair representing our language, literature and history, a chair filled by some Jesuit worthy of the order of which Rev. Edmund Hogan, the great Celticist of Dublin, is a member.[60]

Mahon's closing comments and reference to Hogan (1831-1917) as a Jesuit scholar of Celtic Studies reveals his efforts to create, fund and fill a Chair of Irish language and literature at Boston College at the start of the twentieth century, a time in which, according to Mahon in an Irish-language address at the Boston Cathedral (30 May 1908) 'we can proudly point to the fact that the Universities of our own great land are, one by one, establishing Celtic Chairs'.[61] He continues:

It has been for many years in the leading universities; and in University College, Liverpool, England, there is even a chair of modern Irish, in the care of Father Kelliher. The new Boston College cannot very well help establishing a Celtic chair, as it is safe to assume that the greatest educational body of our age will not be satisfied with having their university second to any other in this great enlightened nation.

We may look to this college in the future as we now look to the Catholic university at Washington and to Dr. Robinson's 'Celtic Colony' at Harvard, to cultivate in America the enlightened taste for Celtic studies that we already find in the great European universities.[62]

Despite apparently having Cardinal O'Connell's support, Mahon's plans were ultimately doomed. The chair, despite his fundraising, never materialized and he was relocated from Boston. A new college president and former professor of ethics and economics, with little interest in Irish and even less in Mahon's suggestions, was appointed in 1907. The Reverend Thomas I. Gasson, SJ, president of Boston College from 1907 to 1914, was born in Kent, England in 1859 and only converted to Catholicism having emigrated to the United States in 1872. Ordained in 1891, he began teaching at Boston College in 1895 and was appointed president in 1907. With Gasson at the helm, Boston College, founded by the Society of Jesus in 1863, relocated from its original site on Harrison Avenue in the South End of Boston to Chestnut Hill/Brighton. It was under Gasson's leadership that a new thirty-one acre site was identified, purchased and developed. Although construction commenced on the impressive gothic-styled building in 1909, it did not open until 1913 as construction halted midway through the four-year process. A lack of funds necessitated selling an athletics field on Massachusetts Avenue and folklore suggests that the funds raised by Mahon for a chair in Irish language were funneled into the completion of the new building. The Irish-language inscriptions on the stain glass windows featuring Irish saints in the new building's main room being an oblique tribute to the fund's original purpose.

Mahon's aspirations would, however, reach partial fulfillment when John Eustace Murphy (1901–85) joined the faculty in 1940. Born to two Irish emigrants in Newton, Massachusetts he attended local schools before entering the Society of Jesus in 1922 and spent the pre-war years (1935–39) studying in Ireland and Wales where he earned a doctorate from the National University of Ireland. With doctorate in hand, Murphy was promoted from classics teacher at Boston College High School to university professor at Boston College where he taught in the Department of Gaelic Literature. Prior to his appointment as Business Manager of the University,

Murphy taught regular course on Irish-language literature in translation. His courses featured texts and authors such as: Caoineadh Airt Uí Laoire, Seathrún Céitinn, Aodh Mac Aingil, Seán Clárach Mac Domhnaill, Séamus Dall mac Cuarta, Donnchadh Mac Conmara, Brian Merriman, Piaras Mac Gearailt, Patrick Pearse and Pádraic Ó Conaire among others. Mac Aonghusa confirms that Boston provided courses in Irish from 1944–7 to approximately twenty students.[63] Irish-language study declined with Murphy's appointment to an administration position,[64] but were put on a firm footing once again in 1989 when Adele Dalsimer and Kevin O'Neill appointed Philip T. O'Leary, another Worcester native and Harvard graduate, as part of their Irish Studies program.[65] Since that time Boston College has offered regular courses in Irish language and literature[66] and in 2005 this post became a tenure track position occupied by Joe Nugent, who in addition to earning a doctorate at UC, Berkeley also previously taught Irish there and organized several summer sessions between the years 1999–2003. The Irish-language faculty at Boston College – O'Leary and Nugent - are located in the Department of English and offer courses for Irish Studies Program under the directorship of Thomas Hachey, Majorie Howes and Robert Savage.

THE UNIVERSITY OF NOTRE DAME

Founded in 1842, the university archives reveal that Irish was taught at Notre Dame as early as 1868. Brother Simeon, described as 'Teacher of the Irish Language', conducted Irish language classes at Notre Dame in the period 1868–73. Simeon, originally Dominic Fleming from Gort, County Galway, is described by Brother O'Reilly as ' ... a true Irish scholar. He spoke and taught Irish. He was a man of few words, but a good religious'.[67] His lectures, as described in the Dublin-based newspaper *The Nation*, attracted in excess of 350 students.[68] The 1874 Notre Dame academic guide also attests to Irish at Notre Dame: 'Matriculation fee ... $5.00. Board, Bed, Bedding, Tuition (Latin and Grammar) Washing,

Mending, Doctor's fees and medicine and attendance in sickness $150. French, German, Italian, Spanish, Hebrew, and Irish, each – $10.00'. During Brother Simeon's time at Notre Dame, students corresponded with Father Ulick Bourke (1829–87), private secretary to Archbishop MacHale.[69] It was during the tenure of Brother Simeon (who died suddenly on 22 August 1873, aged thirty-five), that a Brother Patrick (1797–1867), originally Michael Connelly, born in County Meath, described as a 'Professor of Irish', also taught the language at Notre Dame. Thomas J. Dundon, an undergraduate from Clarkesburg, Michigan, vividly recalled informing his father of his language study:

> I reserved a surprise for my father. I had not told him that I had studied the Irish language under Brother Patrick, Professor of Irish. As I was recounting to my father (during the Christmas Break) the subjects I had studied, I said, 'I can read the Irish language!' He seemed incredulous, so I got my book of poems in Irish and read 'The Bells of Shandon'. When I had finished reading I asked him if I had done well. He made no reply but on looking up I saw a tear glistening in his eye. My father was born within hearing distance of the real 'Bells of Shandon'.[70]

Irish was a standard feature on the Notre Dame curriculum from the early 1870s. This is a remarkably early date for a North American university, making Notre Dame, if not the earliest, then certainly among the earliest institutions to offer the language. After Brother Simeon a lull came in Irish-language teaching before Brother Finan, C.S.C. revived it in the early years of the twentieth century. Described both as 'Professor' and 'Instructor of Irish', he also served as Director of Carroll Hall, a dormitory on the university campus, for the years 1901–05. Finan's tenure at Notre Dame was marked by a burst of activity; in 1901 a branch of the Gaelic League was founded on campus and the university newspaper *The Scholastic* called for a chair in Irish language and literature. Douglas Hyde, founder of the Gaelic League and future President of Ireland, visited Notre Dame from 27–

29 January 1906 as part of his American fund raising tour for the Irish language. In his memoir *Mo Thuras go Meiriceá*, 'An Craoibhín Aoibhinn' recalled that on arrival, he was greeted by Professor Hugh O'Neill, Professor MacGahan and one O'Sullivan, referred to by Hyde as 'an Irish speaker'.[71] He delivered a ninety-minute lecture on Irish Sagas to five hundred female students at Saint Mary's and later another lecture on Irish folklore, published in the *Notre Dame Scholastic*, to five-hundred male students at Notre Dame. The *Scholastic* commented that:

> Dr. Hyde is a speaker interestingly powerful and powerfully interesting ... no one who had heard him but was glad to have had the opportunity, and realized that such experiences come but once or twice, if at all, in the run of a long college career.[72]

Hyde spent the night in conversation with Father John W. Cavanaugh, University President (1905–19), and faculty members. The following morning Father John Augustine Zham[73] C.S.C. (1851–1921) presented Hyde with a copy of Dante's poetry and urged him to translate it into Irish.

Irish language summer classes were offered in 1910, and after a brief hiatus, were again offered from 1919 to 1923 by Reverend Hugh S. Gallagher, C.S.C. (1873–1949). Gallagher transferred to Notre Dame from Columbia University of Portland where he had served as Vice-President and is described as a Professor of Celtic Languages including Irish, Welsh and Breton. During Gallagher's tenure Irish underwent a revival and additional instructors included Reverend Jeremiah Harrington and John Joseph O'Hagerty. O'Hagerty's arrival at Notre Dame is of note as it demonstrates a transfer of faculty from UC, Berkeley. In addition to regular courses, Notre Dame offered summer courses in 1920–24 in language, literature, folklore and history. The *Scholastic* reports:

> Notre Dame is fast becoming one of the best centers of Irish learning. An Irish library has been collected, which, if the present plans develop, will in time be one of the finest libraries in this country. During this school year Professor J.J.

O'Hagerty, formerly of the University of California, has been in charge of the courses in Irish language, history, and literature. He will be assisted during the summer school by the Rev. Hugh Gallagher, C.S.C., a specialist in the Gaelic language and Irish history, and by Rev. Jeremiah C. Harrington, of the St. Paul Seminary, also a noted Irish scholar. Elementary, intermediate and special courses in Gaelic will be offered, the last for those who can speak the language but have had little opportunity to read and write it … The object of these courses is to give the student a correct understanding of the language, history and life of the Irish people from the earliest time to the present day.[74]

In addition to courses such as 'Irish Influence on European Civilization', 'The Music of Ireland', 'History of the Gaelic Literature in Ireland', and 'Irish Political Movements in the 19th Century', the Gaelic Department of the Notre Dame Summer School offered three courses in the language. The course descriptions provide an insight into the scope of such courses and their intent:

Elementary Gaelic: the initial mutations, aspirations and eclipses, declensions, conjugations and as much of the etymology of the language as can be covered with thoroughness. This course aims to fit the student for a good understanding of simple texts in Gaelic. Two hours a day: Eight hours a week.

Intermediate Irish: for those who have had at least a half-year in Gaelic. This course will include a brief review of course I, the completion of etymology, syntax, the reading of Gaelic texts, translation from English into Gaelic, and conversation practice in Gaelic. Two hours a day: Eight hours a week.

Perhaps the offering of most interest is the third course entitled 'Special Course in Gaelic' as it presupposes the existence of Irish-speakers without literary skills:

Special Course in Gaelic: for those who speak the language but who have had little or no opportunity to read or write it. There will be in this course as much application of grammar as the needs of the student may demand. One hour a day; Four hours a week.

Notre Dame served as a port of call for many famous Irish-language dignitaries throughout the nineteenth and twentieth centuries. Critic and author Shane Leslie (1885–1971) held a chair in the English Department in the spring of 1935; Seamus Mac Manus (1869–1960) was a regular visitor in the 1920s and 1930s. Yet of the many illustrious Irish-language dignitaries to visit Notre Dame, none were more famous or perhaps better received than Éamon de Valera – 'the uncrowned king of Ireland'.

De Valera escaped in dramatic fashion from Lincoln Prison, England on 3 February 1919. The Irish Republican Army, fearing the propaganda boost his re-arrest would provide England in the Anglo-Irish War, dispatched him to the United States to promote Irish independence, acquire US support and raise funds. One such promotional trip took him to South Bend, Indiana and the University of Notre Dame. *The Scholastic* reported that de Valera had accepted an invitation from Father Burns, University President, to address the student body on Wednesday 15 October:

> Elaborate preparations are being made at the university by the committees acting with the local branch of the Friends of Irish Freedom for the reception of the distinguished visitor. If the necessary arrangements can be made, the students will be asked to turn out *en masse* for a parade, and the school's newly-organized band will be expected to add 'tone' to the reception.[75]

The following week's edition counseled that 'Notre Dame's welcome should be worthy of the eminence of her guest'. Any fears were unfounded. The *Ave Maria* newspaper described:

> It was characteristically gracious of Dr. Eamon de Valera, 'King of Ireland', as one youthful admirer calls him to assure the students of the university of Notre Dame that he would remember as 'his happiest day in America' the one when he visited them. The address in which he made this statement evoked such applause as the eminent Irishman seldom hears,

it was so spontaneous, continuous and uproarious. He was listened to with breathless attention, every one present seemingly eager to catch every word that fell from his lips. But his personality made even a deeper impression – his gravity when speaking of serious things, his reverence when referring to holy things. Few failed to observe how recollectedly he said grace at table, and how thoroughly absorbed he seemed to be while kneeling before the Blessed Sacrament. A good as well as a great man, a leader who inspires the highest respect and the fullest confidence, is President Eamon de Valera.[76]

De Valera's speech, subsequently published in *The Scholastic*, concerned Ireland's favorable attitude to the League of Nations, the morality of the 1916 Rising, and the potential for peaceful political co-operation between Catholic and Protestant. T.J. Tobin commented that:

From the time sixteen hundred Notre Dame men joined in a big U.N.D. for De Valera, till Doctor Burns bade him bon voyage on leaving, the visitor smiled his satisfaction. ... Upon his arrival, Mr. De Valera received one of the greatest ovations that Notre Dame has ever accorded a visitor. After exchanging greetings with Very Reverend Provincial Morrissey and the members of the faculty, he proceeded to the statute of Father Corby, at the foot of which he laid a wreath bearing the inscription 'From Eamon De Valera in loving tribute to Father Corby who gave general absolution to the Irish Brigade at Gettysburg'. After he had spoken briefly upon the importance of the role played by army chaplains, he was taken to the University Library and shown the Gaelic collection in which are the sword of General Meaghar and the flag of the Irish Brigade. From the Library he went to the center of the quadrangle and there planted a tree as a memorial of his visit.[77]

De Valera would return to Ireland in December 1920 and later lead the anti-treaty forces in the Irish Civil War during which he would again be arrested and imprisoned, on this occasion by his former comrades. His supporters appealed to Notre Dame 'to use its influence to obtain immediate information regarding the present condition and whereabouts of the distinguished scholar and statesman its President and faculty took pride in honoring if for no other reason than to alleviate the suffering and anxiety of his sorrowing wife (or perhaps widow) and family and to join in the nation wide demand for his release, if still alive'.[78] Twenty-first century visitors to Notre Dame on game weekend seeking the tree planted by de Valera, however, will seek in vain. A mere week after the future Irish president's departure, a student of 'the Unionist persuasion' pulled the sapling roots and all, and deposited it in one of the placid lakes flanking the holy grotto.

With Gallagher's death in 1949, Irish-language study became largely dormant at Notre Dame until the early 1990s when Christopher Fox in the English Department embarked on constructing what is now the Keough-Naughton Institute for Irish Studies.[79] As part of the initial steps in initiating an Irish Studies program, Fox appointed Seamus Deane and Dundalk-born and Harvard-trained Irish-language scholar, Peter McQuillan. With McQuillan's arrival on campus in 1992 as a member of the Department of English, Irish was again offered on a regular basis. Fox's vision and energy saw the establishment of a Department of Irish Language and Literature officially launched at Notre Dame on 1 October 2004 by Mr. Noel Fahy, Irish Ambassador to the United States. McQuillan was joined by Breandán Ó Buachalla, a member of the Royal Irish Academy as the first Thomas and Kathleen O'Donnell Chair of Irish Language and Literature in 2002. Sarah McKibben and Brian Ó Conchubhair were subsequently hired as Assistant Professors.[80] Enrollment in departmental courses has consistently improved over the past decade.[81] In 2005, one hundred and ten years after Fred Robinson left Harvard to study with Thurneysen in Germany, the University of Notre Dame approved a Minor in Irish Language and Literature, the first such qualification in the United States.

CONCLUSION

Blenner-Hasset begins his 1954 essay by praising the quality of Celtic scholars, yet lamenting their relatively low number and deploring the lack of popular interest in Celtic Studies:

> Though their numbers are few, it may be said that the Celticists in this country constitute a unique body of scholars. All of them, despite the handicaps of limited resources, give generously of their time and energies to promote the cause of Celtic Studies. All of them stand ready to place their knowledge and training at the disposal of students in related disciplines. Most regrettable is the apathy displayed towards Celtic Studies by the majority of people of Celtic origins in the United States. One might reasonably suppose that, in view of their numerical strength and the prominence they have achieved in all walks of life, Americans of Celtic origin would display a far more active and generous interest than they have thus far in the cultures of the lands of their forebears. The great revival of interest in Celtic culture in the homelands has not yet been, but may eventually be, reflected in America.[82]

American students and scholars now study Irish throughout the United States in colleges and universities; public and private, Catholic and nondenominational. The Celtic Studies Association of North America, (CSANA) founded in 1976 sponsors yearly sessions at the International Congress of Medieval Studies, and it collaborates with the MLA's Celtic Discussion Group, the annual University of California Celtic Colloquium, the annual Harvard Celtic Colloquium. In her 2002 report on foreign language enrolment, E.B. Welles calculates that Irish was taught at thirteen institutes to 705 students. This is an increase from the 326 studying in 1998, 133 in 1995 and 121 in 1990. This number is again an increase on the data available from similar surveys collected since the early 1970s. If anecdotal evidence conveys any elements of truth then the next survey due to be collected in 2007 and published in 2008 will reveal a surge in the number of registrations in Irish courses. While these numbers may appear low and indeed are low in comparison to the major foreign languages studied in the United States they are nevertheless impressive when placed in context.[83] Irish, in contrast to other Celtic languages and prestigious European languages, more than holds its own. Indeed it betters many, including Turkish, Croatian, Bulgarian, Czech, Dutch, Finnish and Slovakian in terms of student enrollment in institutes of higher learning in the United States.[84]

Irish-language teaching at American universities has survived and thrived throughout the twentieth century. At the start of the twenty-first century the Fulbright Commission's Foreign Language Teaching Assistants, combined with the Department of Community, Rural and Gaeltacht Affairs' *Ciste na Gaeilge* funding subvents a steady stream of young trained language assistants to teach Irish in universities and colleges in the United States.[85] Irish-language teaching as part of Celtic Studies, Irish Studies or Irish-language studies in the United States has a distinguished history and a promising future. Regardless of when Irish was first spoken or taught in the 'new world', it would appear that it will continue to be spoken, taught and studied in the United States for the foreseeable future.

Notes

1   Proinsias Mac Aonghusa, 'An Ghaeilge i Meiriceá', *Go Meiriceá Siar: Na Gaeil agus Meiriceá*, ed. Stiofán Ó hAnnracháin (Baile Átha Cliath: An Clóchomhar, 1979), p. 13.

2   Nancy Stenson, 'Speaking Irish in America: language and identity', *Global Eurolinguistics: European languages in North America, Migration, Maintenance and Death*, ed. P. Sture Ureland (Tubingen: Niemeyer 2001), pp. 435–59.

3   Kevin Kenny, *The American Irish: A History* (Harlow: Pearson Education, 2000), p. 99.

4   Kevin Kenny, p. 138. The 2006 census reports 25,870 Irish-speakers residing in the United States. See http://factfinder.census.gov/home/saff/main.html?_lang=en

5   Notable exceptions include Kevin Kenny, *The American Irish: A History* and Úna Ní Bhroiméil, *Building Irish Identity in America 1870–1915: The Gaelic Revival* (Dublin: Four Courts Press, 2003).

6   Kenneth E. Nilsen, 'The Irish Language in New York, 1850–1900', *The New York Irish*, ed. by R. H. Bayor and T. J. Meagher (Baltimore: The Johns Hopkins University Press, 1996), pp. 252–274. See also Kenneth E. Nilsen, 'The Irish Language in Nineteenth Century New York City', *The Multilingual Apple: Languages in New York City*, ed. O. García & J. A. Fishman (New York: Mouton de Gruyter, 1997), pp. 52–69; and Kenneth E. Nilsen, 'Thinking of Monday: Irish speakers of Portland, Maine', *Éire-Ireland*, Vol. 25, No. 1 (1990), pp. 6–19.

7   *Go Meiriceá Siar: Na Gaeil agus Meiriceá*, ed. Stiofán Ó hAnnracháin (Baile Átha Cliath: An Clóchomhar, 1979).

8   Thomas Ihde, *The Irish Language in the United States: An Historical, Sociolinguistic and Applied Linguistic Survey* (Westport, CT: Bergin & Garvey 1994).

9   Nancy Stenson, pp. 435–459.

10 Other essays that detail the history of the Irish language in America include the following: J. Callahan, 'Gaeilge i bhPhiladelphia', *An Teanga Mharthanach* (Summer 1990) No. 2, n.p.; D. Clark, 'Muted History: Gaelic in an American City', *Éire-Ireland* Vol. 6, No. 1 (1971), pp. 3–7; R. Crow, 'Teaching Irish at Antioch College', *Journal of Celtic Language Learning*, Vol. 2 (1996), pp. 77–78; Thomas W. Ihde, 'Language Report: Irish Language Courses at American Colleges', *Éire-Ireland*, Vol. 30, No. 4 (1996), pp. 181–186; J.L. Kallen, 'Language and ethnic identity: The Irish language in the United States', *Language Across Cultures*, ed. L. Mac Mathúna and D. Singleton (Dublin: Irish Association for Applied Linguistics 1983), pp. 101–12; J.L. Kallen, 'Language Maintenance and Loss: An International Perspective', *Teanga*, Vol. 13 (1983), pp 100–114; L.M. Lynch, 'Gaelic Language in America', *Irish America* (July-August 1987), pp. 42–43; Séamas Mac Bloscaidh, 'An Ghaeilge i Nua Eabhrac', *An Teanga Mharthanach* (1989) No. 4, n.p.; L.P. Murray, 'A Louth manuscript in New York', *County Louth Archaeological Journal*, No. 3 (1912–1915), pp. 318–22; Kenneth E. Nilsen, 'A Nineteenth-Century Irish Life of St. Margaret', *Harvard Celtic Colloquium*, Vol. 4 (1984), pp. 82–104; Kenneth E. Nilsen, 'Three Irish Manuscripts in Massachusetts', *Harvard Celtic Colloquium*, Vol. 5 (1985), pp. 1–21; I. O'Carroll, 'The Boston Gaeltacht', *Irish Voice* (16 July 1986) p.

16; J. Ridge, 'The Hidden Gaeltacht in Old New York: Nineteenth-Century preaching in the Irish Language', *New York Irish History*, No. 6, (1991–2), pp. 13–17; G. Schoepperle, 'Irish Studies at the University of Illinois', *Studies*, Vol. 7, No. 25 (1918), pp. 100–11; Nancy Stenson, 'The Use of Irish Among Immigrants to the United States', *New Hibernia Review*, Vol. 2, No. 2 (1998), pp. 116–131; Nancy Stenson, 'Cúrsaí Gaeilge i Meiriceá Thuaidh', *Teagasc na Gaeilge*, Vol. 7 (2000), pp. 107–113; Fionnula Uí Fhlannagáin, 'Mícheál Ó Lócháin agus "An Gaodhal"' (Baile Átha Cliath: An Clóchomhar 1990); E. J. Walsh, 'The Language Problem of Irish Immigrants at the Time of the Great Famine', *St. Meinrad Essays*, Vol. 12, No. 1 (1959), pp. 60–75.

11 I am deeply indebted to the many people who generously shared their knowledge with me while researching this topic. This essay is in no way a complete history of Irish in the American educational system, rather it is a synthetic history relying extensively on information provided in several sites and by numerous individuals. Particularly important are the pamphlets and websites produced by Harvard University http://www.fas.harvard.edu/~celtic/storyofceltic/index.htm and UC Berkeley http://ls.berkeley.edu/dept/celtic/celtic_study_berkeley.html

12 Further information on the contemporary teaching of Irish in the United States is to be found in Thomas W. Ihde's informative article, 'A Hundred Years: Irish Language Courses in American College', *Éire-Ireland*, Vol. 30, No. 4 (1996) pp. 181–6. Ihde concludes that '... the greatest expansion in Irish language teaching seems to be taking place in continuing education programs at two-year colleges. Although courses taken through continuing education do not offer credit, they do provide opportunities for non-degreed, fluent teachers to share their communicative skills in Irish with their students in an institutional setting'.

13 Patricia Bellew Gray, "'Tis True: Irish Gaelic Still Charms', *New York Times*, 12 March 2006.

14 Thomas W. Ihde, 'A Hundred Years', p. 186.

15 A history of Celtic Studies at Saint Francis Xavier University is available at http://people.stfx.ca/knilsen/celtics.html

16 Roland Blenner-Hassett, 'A Brief History of Celtic Studies in North America', *Proceedings of the Modern Language Association*, Vol. 69, No. 4, Part 2: Supplement (September 1954), p. 8.

17 *Ibid.* p. 8.

18 David E. Bynum, 'Four Generations of Oral Literary Studies at Harvard University – Oral Literary Studies at Harvard Since 1856'. See http://www.chs.harvard.edu/mpc/about/bynum.html

19 Proinsias Mac Aonghusa, p. 25.

20 Seán Ó Ceallaigh, *Eoghan Ó Gramhnaigh: Beathaisnéis* (Baile Átha Cliath: Oifig an tSoláthair, 1968), p. 61.

21 Ó Ceallaigh, pp. 67–8.

22 Charles P. Monaghan, 'The Revival of the Gaelic Language', *Proceedings of the Modern Languages Association*, Vol. 14, Appendix I and II, Proceedings 1899, p. xxxvii

23 Blenner-Hassett, p. 13.

24 *Ibid.*

25 On retiring, Dunn conducted seminars in Middle Irish with students, mostly from Yale.

26 He completed four years of parish work in the Diocese of Portland (Maine) and of Springfield (Massachusetts) – two parishes strongly associated with Irish-speakers – before undertaking graduate work at the Catholic University of America (1911–1916).

27 Blenner-Hassett, pp. 12–13.

28 The Irish Studies program at Catholic University continues to offer an Irish-language course.

29 Daniel Donohue, 'The History of English Medieval Studies at Harvard University', *Medieval English Studies Newsletter* (Center for Medieval English Studies, University of Tokyo) No. 28 (June 1993) p. 2.

30 Blenner-Hassett, pp. 9–10.

31 For more detailed information, see the informative leaflet on the history of Celtic Studies at Harvard that is also available on the department's website. http://www.fas.harvard.edu/~celtic/

32 Prifysgol Cymru/The University of Wales awarded Hull a D.Litt. *honoris causa* at the International Congress of Celtic Studies in 1963. Hull also endowed an annual award at the University of Wales.

33 'List of Members', *Bulletin of the Linguistic Society*, Vol. 15, No. 12 (January-March 1930), p. 42.

34 'List of Members 1940', Supplement to *Language: Journal of the Linguistic Society of America*, Vol. 17, No. 1 (January-March 1941), p. 32.

35 He had previously served as Associate Professor of English, University of Toronto (1946–56), and Professor of English, New York University (1956–63).

36 Ken Gewertz, 'Celtic Dept. Chair, Housemaster Dunn dies at 90', *Harvard University Gazette* (2 August 2006).

37 Professor Patrick Ford holds a degrees from Michigan State University (1959) and a Harvard doctorate (1969). He previously taught at Stanford University and University of California, Los Angeles.

38 Professor Catherina McKenna received her Ph.D. in Celtic Studies in 1976 and prior to returning to Harvard served as director of Queens College NY's Irish Studies Program from 1984 to 1997. She was also the coordinator of CUNY's Medieval Studies Certificate Program and a visiting adjunct professor at New York University.

39 In 1966 Robinson endowed a second chair of Celtic. This second endowed chair, the Shattuck chair, was designated for Irish and Kelleher was the first professor to hold the position.

40 Others instructors in Irish at Harvard include the following: John Armstrong, Bruce Boling, John Carey, Kate Chadbourne, Elizabeth Gray, John Koch and Willie Mahon. Irish-language scholars who have held visiting positions at the Department include: David Greene, Proinsias Mac Cana, Brian Ó Cuív and Angela Bourke.

41 Roland G. Kent and E.H. Sturtevant, 'Survey of Linguistic Studies: Opportunities for Advanced Work in the United States', *Linguistic Society of America: Bulletin* No. 1 (December 1926), pp. 3–14. See Table 1: General Linguistics and Miscellaneous Indo-European, in particular.

42 'History of the Linguistic Institute', *Bulletin of the Linguistic Society*, No. 2 (1928), p. 4.

43 *Ibid*. p. 9–10.

44 'Announcement of the Linguistic Institute, 1929', *Bulletin of the Linguistic Society*, No. 3 (1929), p. 10.

45 'Announcement of the Linguistic Institute, 1929', *Bulletin of the Linguistic Society*, No. 3 (1929), p. 11. A Mr. Cross and a Mr. Curtiss registered for both courses on offer while a Mr. Strodach limited his focus to Old Irish. Despite these numbers, Dunn's courses attracted more students than most of his colleagues.

46 'Announcement of the Linguistic Institute, 1930', *Bulletin of the Linguistic Society*, No. 5 (March 1930), p. 3. Born in Columbia,

Missouri, he earned an B.A. from the University of Missouri (1898), an M.A. (1899), and a Ph.D. from the University of Nebraska (1902). He was appointed to the faculty at Columbia University in 1911.

47 'Announcement of the Linguistic Institute, 1930', *Bulletin of the Linguistic Society*, No. 5 (March 1930), p. 10. Gerig's sole student was a Mr. Healy.

48 Dunn's single student was Dr. B.J. Olli (College of the City of New York) who registered for five courses. See *Bulletin of the Linguistic Society*, No. 8 (September 1931), p. 10.

49 See 'Report of the Special Committee on the Linguistic Institute', Supplement to *Language: Journal of the Linguistic Society of America*, Vol. 16, No. 1 (January-March 1940), p. 83–101.

50 Supplement to *Language: Journal of the Linguistic Society of America*, Vol. 17, No. 1 (January-March 1941), p. 13.

51 *Ibid*. p. 32.

52 http://www.ourstory.info/library/2-ww1/Gayley/Gayley4.html

53 *Ibid*.

54 This appears to be the same J.J. O'Hagerty who reappears at Notre Dame in the 1920s.

55 *Annual Reports of the President of the University on behalf of the Regents to His Excellency the Governor of the State of California 1911–12*. Oriental ($3,008.22), Sanskrit ($1,8000.00), Semitic ($1,999.97), Slavic ($2,225.52).

56 It had been their habit to provide $100 per year for library purchases. See *Annual Report of the President of the University on behalf of the Regents to His Excellency the Governor of the State of California, 1917*.

57 *Annual Reports of the President of the University on behalf of the Regents to His Excellency the Governor of the State of California, 1919*.

58 *New York Times*, 20 March 1991.

59 Michael P. Mahon, 'The Irish Language: A Language of Prayer', *Ireland in Religion and Letters: Discourses and Writings of Catholic and Irish Interest* (Boston: Thomas J. Flynn & Co., 1919), p. 45.

60 Mahon, 'A Gaelic Chair in the New Boston College', p. 67.

61 Mahon, 'The Irish Language: A Language of Prayer', p. 46.

62 Mahon, 'Tribute in Solemn High Mass for Dead Veterans', p. 52 (30 May 1910).

63 Proinsias Mac Aonghusa, p. 29. This article also cites Irish being taught at the University of Binghampton in New York State by Seán Ó Nualláin.

64 Reid Oslin, *The Boston College Chronicle*, Vol. 13, No. 3 (7 October 2004).

65 Niall O'Dowd, 'Boston College: Guardian of Irish Culture', *Irish-America* (April-May 2007), pp. 63–70.

66 Irish-language instructors were regular appointed as members of the Department of Slavic Languages. Among those who taught Irish at Boston College are counted: Kate Chadbourne, Michael Connolly, John Koch, Willie Mahon, Ken Nilsen, Brian Ó Conchubhair, Donna Wong. Seán Ó Tuama (1984), Nuala Ní Dhomhnaill (1998–99) and Breandán Ó Buachalla (2001–02) held the John J. Burns Chair in Irish Studies.

67 Brother Aidan O'Reilly, C.S.C., *Story of Notre Dame, Brother Aidan's Extracts* (Brothers of Holy Cross, Notre Dame, Indiana, 1951). http://archives.nd.edu/aidan/aidan515.htm

68 'The Irish Class', *Notre Dame Scholastic*, Vol. III, No. 4 (30 October 1869), p. 28.

69 John E. Garrity, 'The Gaelic Language', *Notre Dame Scholastic*, Vol. III, No. 16 (16 April 1870), p. 126.

70 Januarius Aloysius MacGahan was born 12 June 1844, three miles south of New Lexington, Ohio. His father, James MacGahan, was a native of County Derry, Ireland. Regarded as the most distinguished newspaper correspondent of his time, his newspaper accounts of the Bulgarian atrocities attracted international attention.

71 An Craoibhín Aoibhinn, *Mo Thuras go Meiriceá: I Measg na nGael ins an Oileán Úr* (Baile Átha Cliath: An Gúm, 1937), p. 75–6.

72 'Dr. Hyde's Lecture', *Notre Dame Scholastic*, Vol. XXXIX, No. 16 (3 February 1906), pp. 274–5.

73 John Augustine Zahm born in New Lexington, Ohio, is strongly associated with Americanizing the Catholic Church in the United States. At Notre Dame he developed the teaching of science and initiating the Dante collection.

74 F.S.F., 'Summer Courses in Irish Subjects', *Notre Dame Scholastic*, Vol. LIII, No. 29 (22 May 1920), p. 476. The Irish language collection at Notre Dame is now administered by Aedín Ní Bhroithe Clements and boasts the Ristéard Ó Glaisne collection as well as the Tomás de Bhaldraithe collection.

75 *Notre Dame Scholastic* Vol. LIII, No. 2 (5 October 1919), p. 26.

76 Editor, 'Notes and Remarks', *Ave Maria* cited in *Notre Dame Scholastic*, Vol. LIII, No. 8 (15 November 1919), p. 118.

77 T.J Tobin, 'President De Valera at Notre Dame', *Notre Dame Scholastic*, Vol. LIII, No. 4 (18 October 1919), p. 58.

78 Notre Dame Archives, Box 18, Folder 10.

79 Niall O'Dowd, 'Waking Up the Irish Echoes', *Irish-America* (February-March 2007), pp. 26–8.

80 Tara MacLeod joined the Department in 2005 as an Assistant Professional Specialist and Dr. Hugh Fogarty has offered courses in Irish language Studies since 2006. Ciara Conneely, Breandán Mac Suibhne, Elaine Naughton, Éamonn Ó Ciardha, Tomás Ó Murchú, Traolach Ó Ríordáin and Peadar Ó Muircheartaigh have also taught Irish-language courses at the university. Recent visitors to teach literature courses in the Department include Angela Bourke, Nuala Ní Dhomhnaill, Bríona Nic Dhiarmada, Diarmuid Ó Doibhlin, Diarmuid Ó Giolláin and Philip T. O'Leary.

81 Academic year and enrollment: 1997–98 (44), 1998–99 (62), 1999–00 (78), 2000–01 (101), 2002–02 (98), 2002–03 (114), 2003–04 (147), 2004–05 (173), 2005–6 (294), 2006–07 (401).

82 Blenner-Hassett, pp. 19–20.

83 The most popular foreign language studied in the United States are: Spanish, French, German, Italian, American Sign language, Japanese, Chinese, Latin, Russian, Ancient Greek, biblical Hebrew, Arabic, Modern Hebrew, Portuguese and Korean.

84 See Elizabeth B. Welles, 'Foreign Language Enrollments in United States Institutes of Higher Education, Fall 2002', *Association of Departments of Foreign Languages Bulletin*, Vol. 35, No. 1–2 (Winter-Spring 2004) pp. 7–26.

85 Fulbright Foreign Language Teaching Assistants (FLTAs) for the Irish language in 2006–07 were Francesca McCully, Laoise Ní Thuairisg, Maeve Nic An Airchinnigh and Aibhistín Ó Coimín. FLTAs for 2007–08 were Edward Kelleher, Sinéad Ní Mhaolmhicíl, Ailbhe Ní Ghearbhuigh, Tomás Ó Murchú and Mairéad McKendry.

CUR CHUN CINN NA GAEILGE AR FUD NA CRUINNE

An tAire Éamon Ó Cuív, T.D.

Roinn Gnóthaí Pobail, Tuaithe agus Gaeltachta
Rialtas na hÉireann

Is mór an onóir dom a bheith anseo inniu in Ollscoil Notre Dame, ollscoil a bhfuil an-cháil uirthi go hacadúil agus ó thaobh na peile de. Go mórmhór, tá cáil ar an ollscoil seo de bharr an leasainm a bhí ar an bhfoireann peile – *The Fighting Irish.*

Éamon Ó Cuív, T.D. ag comhrá leis an Ath. John Jenkins, C.S.C.,
Uachtarán Ollscoil Notre Dame

Tá áthas orm a bheith anseo inniu freisin de bharr an ceangal a bhí ag mo sheanathair leis an ollscoil seo, agus an chuairt stairiúil a thug sé uirthi sa bhliain 1919. Ar ndóigh, tá an tír ina bhfuil cónaí ormsa anois mar thír neamhspleách an-difriúil ón Éirinn a bhí ann i 1919. Chun an rud nach ndúirt Mark Twain a rá, tá áibhéil mhór ag baint leis na ráflaí atá ann faoi bhás na Gaeilge. Is rud maith é seo mar go bhfuil tábhacht mhór le héagsúlacht teangacha an domhain, ó tharla go bhfuil próisis smaointeoireachta uathúla ag baint le gach teanga, agus cuireann siad sin le feasacht agus le taithí an duine. Is le blianta beaga anuas atá sochaithe ag fáil tuiscint cheart ar an tábhacht a bhaineann le héagsúlacht teangacha don oidhreacht chultúrtha agus do shaibhreacht an chine dhaonna sa lá atá inniu ann. Nuair atá tú ag breathnú ar cheist na Gaeilge sa lá atá inniu ann, níor mhór breathnú i dtús báire ar cheist na Gaeilge sa naoú haois déag. Chuaigh an Ghaeilge i léig go tapaidh sa naoú haois déag agus faoi dheireadh an chéid sin ní raibh ach 1% de na cainteoirí nach raibh acu ach Gaeilge amháin. Tá sé seo thar a bheith tábhachtach mar, ag an am sin, nuair a rinneadh cainteoirí dátheangacha de dhaoine, d'aistrigh daoine go tapaidh go teanga amháin – an Béarla – sa ghlúin a tháinig ina dhiaidh sin.

Tháinig athrú ó bhonn ar rudaí nuair a bunaíodh Conradh na Gaeilge ag deireadh an naoú haois déag agus nuair a bunaíodh an Stát ag tús na fichiú haoise. Thug an dá dhream seo faoi athbheochan na Gaeilge agus bhí sé mar aidhm acu an Ghaeilge a chur in áit an Bhéarla in Éirinn in athuair. Níl aon amhras orainn anois ach go raibh an polasaí sin a bhí ag an Stát ar dtús beagán simplíoch agus ródhíograiseach ach, é sin ráite, baineadh torthaí amach ag an am céanna.

Cé go bhfuilim ag labhairt in ollscoil, caithfidh mé a rá gurb í mo spéis féin sa teanga ná í a chloisteáil in úsáid mar theanga dhúchais laethúil sa saol nua-aimseartha, agus tábhacht náisiúnta agus stairiúil na teanga á tabhairt san áireamh. Tuigeann Stát na hÉireann an tábhacht a bhaineann leis an nGaeilge ó thaobh léargas bríomhar a thabhairt ar ár bhféiniúlacht náisiúnta, ar ár gcultúr Gaelach agus ar ár gcuid cluichí, ar ár gcuid damhsaí, ar ár gcuid ceoil, srl. Déanfaidh mé iarracht anois míniú símplí a thabhairt ar cá seasann an Ghaeilge sa lá atá inniu ann.

I mí an Mheithimh 2005 cuireadh an Ghaeilge ar ais san áit ar cheart di a bheith san Eoraip. An mhí sin, d'aontaigh Comhairle Eorpach na nAirí go mbeadh an Ghaeilge ar an bhfichiú teanga oifigiúil agus oibre den Aontas Eorpach ón gcéad lá d'Eanáir 2007 ar aghaidh. Mar atá faoi láthair, is í an Ghaeilge an chéad teanga oifigiúil in Éirinn agus aithnítear seo i mbunreacht na tíre. In 2003, glacadh le hAcht Teanga den chéad uair, rud a chiallaíonn go bhfuil éifeacht dhlíthiúil ag an bhforáil i mbunreacht na hÉireann agus bunaíodh Oifig an Choimisinéara Teanga chun a chinntiú go gcloífí le forálacha an Achta agus go gcuirfí i bhfeidhm iad. Glacadh le reachtaíocht eile le gairid ina bhfuil forálacha tábhachtacha a bhaineann leis an nGaeilge. Ina measc sin tá an tAcht Oideachais 1998, an tAcht Pleanála 2000 ina bhfuil forálacha speisialta a bhaineann le pleanáil i gceantair Ghaeltachta agus i gceantair ina labhraítear Gaeilge, agus an tAcht um Chomhaontú na Breataine-na hÉireann 1999 faoinar bunaíodh an Foras Teanga. Faoin Acht deireanach sin rinneadh foráil speisialta go mbunófaí foras teanga uile-Éireann, Foras na Gaeilge. Tháinig sé seo as forálacha Chomhaontú Aoine an Chéasta. Tá forálacha tábhachtacha san Acht Craolacháin 2003 freisin a bhaineann leis an nGaeilge.

Éamon de Valera agus Harry Boland ar an mbealach go Notre Dame
(le caoinchead ó Chartlann Ollscoile Notre Dame)

Ó bunaíodh an Stát tá obair mhór déanta chun foclóirí, gramadach, stór focal, téarmaíocht agus logainmneacha a sholáthar. Ar cheann de phríomhghníomhaíochtaí Rialtas na hÉireann bhí simpliú ar litriú agus ar ghramadach na teanga, chomh maith le bunú eagraíochta ar a bhfuil freagracht ar leith as cúrsaí téarmeolaíochta. Tá rannóg ar leith i mo Roinnse a dhéanann taighde ar logainmneacha na hÉireann agus a chuireann comhairle ar fáil domsa maidir le leaganacha cinnte de na logainmneacha sin. Tagann formhór logainmneacha Béarla in Éirinn, ar a n-áirítear *Galway, Dublin, Cork*, srl. as an leagan Gaeilge.

Maidir leis na meáin chumarsáide, tá cainéal teilifíse ar leith ann don Ghaeilge a bunaíodh i 1996, ar a dtugtar TG4. Bunaíodh Raidió na Gaeltachta i 1973 chun freastal ar na ceantair ina labhraítear Gaeilge, ach craoltar go náisiúnta anois é fiche a ceathair uair an chloig in aghaidh an lae. Tá an péire acu seo faoi úinéireacht an Stáit.

Luaigh mé níos luaithe nach raibh ach 1% den daonra in Éirinn ag labhairt Gaeilge amháin ag deireadh an naoú haois. Inniu, éilíonn 43% den phobal go bhfuil siad in ann Gaeilge a labhairt agus labhraíonn 5% de dhaoine fásta an teanga ar bhonn laethúil. Measann 90% de mhuintir na hÉireann go bhfuil tábhacht náisiúnta leis an nGaeilge nó go bhfuil sí tábhachtach dóibh féin go pearsanta. Is figiúirí thar a bheith tábhachtach iad seo nuair a smaoiníonn duine ar an meath as ar tháinig an t-athfhás seo a thosaigh beagán os cionn céad bliain ó shin. Níl aon amhras ann ach go mbeadh an Ghaeilge básaithe i bhfad ó shin murach an tacaíocht a fuair sí ón Stát.

Dúshlán mór eile a bhí san athrú a tháinig ar phobal labhartha na Gaeilge ó phobal bocht, tuaithe go pobal meánaicmeach. Ba dhúshlán a bhí i gcaomhnú na teanga agus an t-athrú sin ag tarlú. Ní féidir aon bhuanseasmhacht a bhaint amach do thodhchaí na teanga mura bhfuil pobal meánaicmeach ann a labhraíonn Gaeilge, ní hamháin sa Ghaeltacht ach ar fud na tíre. Tá borradh freisin le blianta beaga anuas faoin oideachas trí mheán na Gaeilge. Mar shampla, i 1972, ní raibh ach sé déag scoil lán-Ghaeilge sa tír ar fad, taobh amuigh den Ghaeltacht. Tá sé sin méadaithe go 184 scoil sa lá atá inniu ann.

Éamon de Valera ag caint ag Ollscoil Notre Dame, 1919
(le caoinchead ó Chartlann Ollscoile Notre Dame)

Tá sé tábhachtach go dtabharfaidh mise léargas daoibh inniu ar fhís an Rialtais agus an Stáit i leith na Gaeilge. Tá an Rialtas tiomanta do chur le húsáid na Gaeilge ar bhonn náisiúnta. É sin ráite, ba mhaith liom béim a chur inniu freisin, go háirithe i ngeall ar an gcéad pholasaí riamh a bhí ag an Rialtas i leith na Gaeilge, nach bhfuil sé mar chuid d'aidhm Rialtas an lae inniu fáil réidh leis an mBéarla ná an t-eolas atá ag saoránaigh ar an teanga sin a laghdú ar aon bhealach. Chun é a chur ar bhealach eile, is éard atáimid ag iarraidh a bhaint amach ná an dátheangachas feidhmiúil, nuair atá daoine ábalta an dá theanga a labhairt go héasca. Tá sé mar chuspóir ag an Rialtas freisin an pobal go ginearálta a dhéanamh níos compordaí leis an nGaeilge. Tá sé seo á bhaint amach trí na meáin (TG4, Raidió na Gaeltachta) agus tríd an Acht Teanga. Tá an Rialtas tiomanta freisin do threisiú na gceantar Gaeltachta, nó na ceantair ina labhraítear Gaeilge, ó thaobh na heacnamaíochta, na sochaí agus na teangeolaíochta de. Agus mar chríoch, tá sé mar bhunaidhm ag an bhfís pholaitiúil an líon daoine a labhraíonn Gaeilge ar bhonn laethúil a mhéadú. Chun na haidhmeanna sin a bhaint amach i saol daonlathach, oscailte an aonú haois is fiche, níor mhór don Rialtas iarracht a dhéanamh an pobal a thabhairt leo. Ní féidir iallach a chur ar dhaoine rud a dhéanamh, mar gur éifeacht diúltach a bheadh aige seo. Tá sé riachtanach freisin go lorgódh an Rialtas tacaíocht uathu siúd nach bhfuil Gaeilge acu, mar go bhfuil tacaíocht ón bpobal go ginearálta riachtanach do thodhchaí na teanga.

Ba mhaith liom cúpla focal a rá faoi stádas na Gaeilge sa domhan. Nuair a tháinig sí ar cuairt go hÉirinn, rinne Dyane Adams, Coimisinéir Teanga Cheanada, comparáid idir staid na Gaeilge in Éirinn agus staid na Fraincise i gCeanada. Dúirt sí freisin, dá bhfaigheadh an Fhraincis bás i gCeanada bheadh sí fós ina teanga mhór idirnáisiúnta, ach dá bhfaigheadh an Ghaeilge bás mar theanga dhúchais in Éirinn bheadh deireadh léi mar theanga dhúchais sa domhan seo.

Dúirt sí freisin go bhfuil an Ghaeilge ina cuid d'oidhreacht an domhain agus nach tábhacht náisiúnta amháin a bhaineann léi, ach tábhacht dhomhanda. Tá sé seo amhlaidh, ach go háirithe, mar gurb í an Ghaeilge an teanga dhúchais scríofa is sine san Eoraip le saibhreas láidir litríochta a théann siar chomh fada leis an gcúigiú haois. Is í seo an litríocht is sine san Eoraip ó thuaidh de na hAlpa. Tá a stór filíochta agus litríochta ina cuid lárnach de stair agus de chultúr oileán na hÉireann agus tá sé mar chuid de chomhoidhreacht chultúrtha an chine dhaonna.

Mar a luaigh mé ag tús na hóráide, tháinig Éamon de Valera anseo ag lorg tacaíochta i 1919. Tagaimse ar ais chugaibh inniu mar Aire i Rialtas neamhspleách na hÉireann. Tá sé seo ina ábhar mór sásaimh pearsanta domsa ar ndóigh.

Ach, tá a fhios agam freisin go bhfuil Éire, lena stádas mar náisiún, faoi chomaoin ag an gcuid eile den domhan. Mar sin, chun ár ndualgas ina leith seo a chomhlíonadh, táimid ag iarraidh an Ghaeilge a chur chun cinn ar fud na cruinne. Múintear an Ghaeilge i gcaoga is a haon choláiste tríú leibhéal ar fud an domhain. Tá an-áthas orm inniu go bhfuilim in ann ciste atá maoinithe ag an Rialtas a sheoladh. Is é aidhm an chiste seo na nascanna idir Éire agus ollscoileanna a mhúineann an Ghaeilge ar fud an domhain a threisiú agus a chur chun cinn.

Mar a dúirt mé, tá líon mór coláistí agus ollscoileanna tríú leibhéal i Stáit Aontaithe Mheiriceá, i dtíortha san Eoraip, agus in áiteanna eile nach iad, atá cheana féin gníomhach i soláthar clár sa Léann Ceilteach agus sa Ghaeilge ina gcuid institiúidí agus spéis léirithe acu i bhforbairt na gcláranna seo. Ina measc seo tá coláistí ar nós Ollscoil Humbolt sa Ghearmáin, Ollscoil Nua-Eabrach agus sibh féin anseo i Notre Dame i Meiriceá Thuaidh. Táim sásta go bhfuilim in ann cabhrú leis an bhforbairt shuntasach seo. Cothaíonn na cláir seo tuiscint níos fearr ar Éirinn agus ar ár gcultúr lasmuigh den oileán. Tugann go leor de na mic léinn atá páirteach sna cláir seo cuairt ar Éirinn agus cruthaíonn a rannpháirtíocht siúd nascanna le hÉirinn chomh maith le spéis agus le tuiscint ar ár gcultúr uathúil a fhanfaidh leo ar feadh a saoil.

Is é €300,000 nó $360,000 an méid a bheidh sa chiste gach bliain agus tá súil agam go dtabharfaidh an ciste seo spreagadh dóibh siúd a bhfuil suim acu inár dteanga, chun í a mhúineadh do ghlúin óg mac léinn ar fud an domhain.

Ar deireadh, is féidir liom a rá libh go bhfuil Coimisiún Fulbright S.A.M.-Éire tar éis tús a chur le comhráití idir mo Roinnse agus Roinn Stáit SAM maidir le tionscnamh chun teagasc na Gaeilge a chur chun cinn i gcoláistí agus in ollscoileanna i Meiriceá trí Chlár Fulbright. Tá an dá thaobh ag súil le fógra oifigiúil a dhéanamh ina leith seo go luath.

Arís, ba mhaith liom mo bhuíochas a chur in iúl as cuireadh a thabhairt dom bheith i láthair anseo inniu agus as an onóir agus as an bhfáilte a chuir sibh romham.

Foreign Language Teaching Asssistants (2007-08): Minister Éamon Ó Cuív (Irish Government), Dr. Bríona Nic Dhiarmada (Senior Fulbright Scholar), Edward Kelleher, Sinéad Ní Mhaolmhicíl, H.E. Thomas C. Foley (US Ambassador), Ailbhe Ní Ghearbhuigh, Tomás O Murchú

Foreign Language Teaching Asssistants (2006-2007): Francesca McCully, Laoise Ní Thuairisg, Fr. Monk Malloy (President Emeritus, University of Notre Dame), Minister Éamon Ó Cuív (Irish Government), Maeve Nic An Airchinnigh and Aibhistín Ó Coimín.

Promoting the Irish Language Worldwide

Minister Éamon Ó Cuív, T.D.

Department of Community, Rural and Gaeltacht Affairs
Government of Ireland

Is mór an onóir dom a bheith anseo inniu in Ollscoil Notre Dame, ollscoil a bhfuil an-cháil uirthi go hacadúil agus ó thaobh na peile de. Go mórmhór, tá cáil ar an ollscoil seo de bharr an leasainm a bhí ar an bhfoireann peile – *The Fighting Irish*.

Tá áthas orm a bheith anseo inniu de bharr an ceangal a bhí ag mo sheanathair leis an ollscoil seo, agus an chuairt stairiúil a thug sé uirthi sa bhliain 1919. Ar ndóigh, tá an tír ina bhfuil cónaí ormsa anois mar thír neamhsplách an-difriúil ón Éirinn a bhí ann i 1919.

To misquote Mark Twain, rumours of the demise of the Irish language have been vastly exaggerated. This is a good thing, as world linguistic diversity is of great importance, because each language involves a unique thought process that add to human knowledge and experience. The importance of linguistic diversity to the cultural heritage and present-day richness of all humanity is something that societies have only begun to understand and appreciate in recent years. When we look at the situation in relation to the Irish language today, one must first look at the situation of the language in the nineteenth century. Irish declined rapidly in the nineteenth century, and by the end of that century, only 1% of the speakers were monolingual Irish. This is of particular significance, as at that time, once people became bilingual, there was a rapid transition in the following generation to monolingual English.

The foundation of the Gaelic League in the late nineteenth century, and the foundation of the Irish State in the early twentieth century changed things radically. Both of these organisations set about reviving the fortunes of the Irish language with the aim of supplanting English in Ireland with Irish once again. There is no question about it from this vantage point but that the original policy of the State was simplistic and over ambitious, but that it also did achieve results.

Although I am speaking in a University, I must declare that my interest in the Irish language is the use of Irish as a modern vernacular in every-day life, recognising at the same time its national and historical significance. The Irish State recognises the importance of the Irish language as a vibrant expression of national identity, and of Irish culture, along with our games, dance, music etc. I will try to set out very simply where the Irish language stands today.

In June 2005, Irish was once again restored to its rightful position in Europe. In this month, the European Council of Ministers agreed that as and from 1 January 2007, Irish would become the twentieth official and working language of the European Union. As it is, Irish is the first official language of the Irish State, and is recognised as such in the Irish constitution. In 2003, a Languages Act was passed for the first time, giving legislative effect to the provision in the Irish constitution, and providing for the establishment of the Office of the Language Commissioner, or *Coimisinéir Teanga*, to enforce and ensure compliance with the provisions of the Act. There is other legislation passed recently with significant provisions in relation to the Irish language. These included the Education Act 1998, the Planning Act 2000, which has special provisions in relation to planning in Irish-speaking, or *Gaeltacht* areas, and the British – Irish Agreement Act 1999, under which the Language Body was set up. This last Act made special provision for the setting up of an all-Ireland Irish language body, *Foras na Gaeilge*. This arose out of the provisions of the Good Friday Agreement. There are also significant provisions in the Broadcasting Act 2003 in relation to the Irish language.

Since the foundation of the State, major work has been done on the provision of dictionaries, grammars, vocabulary, terminology and placenames. One of the major exercises carried out by the Irish Government was the simplification of the spelling and grammar of the language, and also the setting up of a body with special responsibility for terminology. My Department has a special section in it that researches Irish placenames, and provides advice to me on definitive versions of these placenames. The vast majority of placenames in Ireland, including names such as Galway, Dublin, Cork etc. originate from the Irish language.

In relation to the media, there is a specially dedicated Irish language channel, called TG4, which was set up in 1996. *Raidió na Gaeltachta* was set up initially in 1973 to service the Irish-speaking areas, but is now broadcast nationally, and broadcasts 24 hours a day. Both of these are state owned.

I mentioned earlier that only 1% of the population of Ireland were monolingual at the end of the 19th century. Today, 43% of the public claim that they can speak Irish, while 5% of adults use it as a daily language. 90% of Irish people feel that Irish is important nationally, or personally to them. These are very significant figures when one considers the baseline of decline from which this re-growth began just over 100 years ago. There is no doubt but that without State support, Irish would have died a long time ago.

Another big challenge has been the transformation of the Irish-speaking community from a poor, rural community to an effectively middle-class community, and the maintenance of the language in the transition. No stability can be reached in relation to the future of the language unless there is an Irish speaking middle-class, not only in the *Gaeltacht*, but throughout the country. There has also, in recent years, been a significant interest in growth in all-Irish medium education. For example, in 1972, there were only 16 all-Irish primary schools in the country, outside of *An Ghaeltacht*, and this has since increased to 184 schools.

It is important for me to outline the political vision of the Government and the State in relation to the Irish language. The Irish State is committed to increasing the use of Irish nationally. However, I would also like to emphasise, particularly in view of the State's original policy in relation to Irish, that it is not part of the Government's object to get rid of, or in any other way decrease the knowledge of English amongst our citizens. In other words, what we are striving to achieve is functional bilingualism, where people will use both languages with ease. It is also an objective of the Government to increase the comfort of the community at large with the Irish language. This is being done, primarily through the media (*TG4, Raidió na Gaeltachta*) and through the Language Act. The Government are also committed to strengthening the Irish-speaking, or *Gaeltacht* areas, economically, socially and linguistically. And finally, it is a basic aim of the political vision to increase the numbers of daily Irish speakers.

To achieve these aims, living in a modern, open democracy in the twenty-first century, Government must seek to bring the community with them, and cannot resort to dictation/coercion, which would have negative effects. It is also vital for Government to encourage, and seek support, from those who do not know the Irish language, as broad community support for the language is vital to its future.

I would like to say a short word in relation to the position of the Irish language in the world. The Canadian Language Commissioner, on a visit to Ireland, compared the situation of Irish in Ireland with French in Canada. She also pointed out that if the French language were to die in Canada, it would still survive as a major world language, but if the Irish language were to die as a vernacular in Ireland, then it would cease to exist as a vernacular language anywhere in the world.

She went on to further point out that the Irish language is part of a world heritage that is not only of national importance, but of world importance. This is particularly so because the Irish language is the oldest written vernacular language in Europe, with a very rich literature stretching back to the fifth century. This is the oldest literature in Europe north of the Alps. Its poems and literature are the repository of a major part of the history and culture of the island of Ireland and are part of the common cultural heritage of all humanity.

As I mentioned in Irish at the beginning of my speech, Éamon de Valera came here looking for support in 1919. I come back to you today as a Minister in a Sovereign Irish Independent Government. This, of course, is a matter of great personal satisfaction to me, but I am also aware that Ireland now has obligations to the world due to its status as a nation. We, therefore, in fulfilling this obligation, seek to promote the Irish language worldwide. There are fifty-one third-level colleges teaching Irish worldwide. I am delighted to be able today to launch a Government-sponsored fund to cement and promote the ties between Ireland and Universities that teach Irish around the world.

As I said, a significant number of third level Colleges and Universities in the United States and countries in Europe and elsewhere are already actively involved in the provision of an Irish language and Celtic Studies programme within their institutions and have indicated an interest in developing these programmes. These include Colleges such as Humbolt University in Germany, NYU and yourselves here in Notre Dame in North America. I am happy to be able to support this very significant development. These programmes foster a greater appreciation of Ireland and our culture outside the island. Many of the students taking these programmes visit Ireland and participation leads to lifelong links with Ireland and a lifelong interest in and understanding of our unique cultural contribution.

The amount of the fund is €300,000, or $360,000, per annum, and I hope that this fund will be an incentive to those who are interested in our language, to teach it to a young generation of students across the globe.

Finally, I can inform you that the US-Irish Fulbright Commission has initiated discussions between my Department and the U.S. Department of State for an initiative to promote Irish language instruction in US Colleges and Universities through the Fulbright Program. Both sides look forward to making a formal announcement in this regard soon.

Again, my many thanks for the invitation to be with you, and for the honour and hospitality that you have bestowed on me.

JAMES MCCLOSKEY is a leading theoretician in linguistics who specializes in bringing the facts of Irish and the facts of Hiberno-English to bear on the shaping of general theories of human language. Educated at Saint Columb's College Derry, University College Dublin, and the University of Texas at Austin, he has held research positions at the Center for Cognitive Science at MIT, at the Center for Advanced Study in the Behavioral Sciences at Stanford, and at the Zentrum fur allgemeine Sprachwissenschaft in Berlin. Originally based in the Department of Irish at University College Dublin, he has, since 1988, been Professor of Linguistics at the University of California, Santa Cruz. Apart from his work in linguistic theory, he has written on the politics of language from a variety of perspectives, most recently in the highly-acclaimed bilingual monograph *Guthanna in Éag/Voices Silenced* (2001).

TOMÁS Ó CATHASAIGH, a native of Tramore, County Waterford, Ireland, received B.A. and M.A. degrees from University College Cork. He was a junior research assistant at the Dublin Institute for Advanced Studies in 1972 and subsequently a member of the Department of Early and Medieval Irish Language and Literature, University College Dublin (1972–1995). He became the Henry L. Shattuck Professor of Irish Studies at Harvard University in 1995. He is the author of numerous essays on early Irish literature, mythology, and language in journals such as *Éigse*, *Ériú*, *Celtica*, and elsewhere. His book *The Heroic Biography of Cormac Mac Airt* (1977) was critically acclaimed, as was his 2003 Bergin lecture entitled *Táin Bó Cúailgne and Early Irish Law* (2005). Professor Ó Cathasaigh is the Director of Graduate Studies and Chair of the Department of Celtic Languages and Literatures at Harvard University.

BRIAN Ó CONCHUBHAIR is an assistant professor at the Department of Irish Language and Literature, University of Notre Dame and a fellow of the Keough-Naughton Institute for Irish Studies. He recently edited *Gearrscéalta Ár Linne* and has published articles on Pádraic Ó Conaire, Liam Ó Flaithearta, Cathal Ó Searcaigh, Louis de Paor and Michelle Smith. He was also curator of an exhibition of Free State Art at Boston College.

ÉAMON Ó CUÍV, T.D., was appointed Minister for Community, Rural and Gaeltacht Affairs in July 2002. He was first elected to *Dáil Éireann* in 1992, having served as a Senator (1989–1992) and a member of Galway County Council (1991–1997). He served as Minister of State (July 1997–February 2001) at the Department of Arts, Heritage, Gaeltacht and Islands, with special responsibility for the Gaeltacht areas, the Irish language, and island development. He was also a member of the Forum for Peace and Reconciliation. His grandfather, Éamon de Valera, former Taoiseach and President of Ireland, visited the University of Notre Dame in 1919.

PHILIP O'LEARY received his Ph.D. from the Department of Celtic Languages and Literatures, Harvard University. He has published on various aspects of early Irish sagas and the literature of the Irish cultural revival. Acknowledged as the world's leading expert on twentieth-century Irish prose and the discourse of political and cultural debate in Ireland, his most recent monograph, *Gaelic Prose in the Irish Free State 1922–1939*, received the Michael Durkan Prize in 2004. This study continued the literary and cultural history of the Irish revival begun in *Prose Literature of the Gaelic Revival 1881–1921* which also won the Donald Murphy Prize at the Irish Studies American Conference in 1994. In collaboration with Margaret Kelleher, he co-edited the two volume, dual-language *Cambridge History of Irish Literature*. He is currently a full professor at Boston College.

CALVERT WATKINS is now Professor-in-Residence, Department of Classics and Program in Indo-European Studies, UCLA. His most recent book, *How to Kill a Dragon: Aspects of Indo-European Poetics* (1995, 2000), received the Goodwin Prize, APA, in 1998. Other books include: *Indo-European Origins of the Celtic Verb I. The Sigmatic Aorist* (1962), *Indogermanische Grammatik III/1. Geschichte der Indogermanische Verbalflexion* (1969) and *The American Heritage Dictionary of Indo-European Roots* (1985, 2000). He has also written over 150 articles and reviews, fifty-three of which are reprinted in the two volumes of his *Selected Writings*, edited by Lisi Oliver (1994). He served as President of the Linguistic Society of America in 1988 and as Chair of Harvard's Department of Linguistics for eleven years, most recently 1985–1991. He is an Honorary Member of the Royal Irish Academy (1968), a Fellow of the American Academy of Arts and Sciences (1973), a Corresponding Fellow of the British Academy (1987), and of the Acadèmie des Inscriptions et Belles-Lettres, Correspondant Etranger (1990), Associè Etranger, member de l'Instituit (1999). He has served as a scholar (1957–58), a Visiting Assistant Professor (1961–62) and most recently as a Visiting Professor (1981) at the Dublin Institute for Advanced Studies. He was recently honoured by the presentation of *Mír Curad, Studies in Honor of Calvert Watkins*, edited by J. Jasanoff, H.C. Melchert, and L. Oliver (1988), with some sixty-three contributions. He gave the Gaisford Lecture by invitation of the Faculty of Classics, University of Oxford in May 2000.

About the Artist

SEÁN Ó FLAITHEARTA, one of Ireland's leading emerging artists, was born on Oileán Árainn where he still lives. He studied at the National College of Art and Design, Dublin, the Pennsylvania School of Arts and the Ecole Nationale Superieure des Arts de la Cambre, Brussels. His latest exhibition 'Duch Yesenin' was held at the Wexford Arts Centre, September 2007. Seán can be contacted at seanoflaithearta@eircom.net

INNÉACS ¦ INDEX

READER'S NOTES

READER'S NOTES

READER'S NOTES

READER'S NOTES

READER'S NOTES

READER'S NOTES

READER'S NOTES